Grammar Builder

A grammar guidebook for students of English

5

A. Amin

R. Eravelly

F.J. Ibrahim

CAMBRIDGE
UNIVERSITY PRESS

CAMBRIDGE UNIVERSITY PRESS
Cambridge, New York, Melbourne, Madrid, Cape Town, Singapore, São Paulo

Cambridge University Press
10 Hoe Chiang Road, #08-01/02 Keppel Towers, Singapore 089315

www.cambridge.org
Information on this title: www.cambridge.org/9780521548632

© Cambridge University Press and Pan Asia Publications Sdn Bhd 2004

First published 2004
Fourth printing 2006

Printed in Singapore by Kyodo Printing Pte Ltd

Typeface Utopia. *System* QuarkXPress®

ISBN 0 521 54859 4 Grammar Builder Book 1
ISBN 0 521 54860 8 Grammar Builder Book 2
ISBN 0 521 54861 6 Grammar Builder Book 3
ISBN 0 521 54862 4 Grammar Builder Book 4
ISBN 0 521 54863 2 Grammar Builder Book 5

• • • • • • • INTRODUCTION • • • • • • •

To the student

This book is designed to help you master key concepts in English grammar easily and quickly. Students who need to take written exams as well as those who wish to write well will find the *Grammar Builder* series helpful.

You may use this book for self-study and practice. An Answers section is located at the back of the book.

To the teacher

The *Grammar Builder* series is a useful supplement to any main English language course and is suitable for both classroom teaching and self-study. The series focuses on written grammar and the key grammar concepts that students need to know for written exercises.

How the book is organised

The *Grammar Builder* series comprises five books for beginner to upper-intermediate level learners of British English. Books 1 and 2 are intended for learners who need to acquire the basics of grammar. Books 3 to 5 are for learners who need to strengthen their proficiency in grammar and improve their written English.

Each book is made up of 42 to 56 units, and units dealing with related topics (e.g. prepositions) are grouped together for ease of use.

A unit covers three to five grammar concepts and includes four to six different types of exercises. Key grammar concepts (e.g. tenses) taught in the lower level books are re-visited and expanded upon in the other books of this series. For a list of units, refer to the *Contents* at the beginning of each book.

The books use a simple but effective three-step approach (error identification, correction, and practice) to help learners master English grammar.

There are four pages per unit, and each unit is divided into three sections: *Checkpoint*, *Grammar Points*, and *Practice*.

All units begin with a *Checkpoint* section containing several pairs of numbered examples that show common grammatical errors and then their corrected forms. These examples of correct and incorrect usage demonstrate to the student how slight differences in expression can result in grammatical errors.

The students can then refer to the corresponding *Grammar Points* in the next section which explain the grammar concepts highlighted under *Checkpoint*, show how to apply the grammar concepts correctly, and provide more examples.

In the third section, *Practice*, students revise the grammar concepts they have learned by completing a group of exercises. (The answers can be found at the back of the book.) This enables quick revision of each concept, and allows students to see if there are any aspects that they do not fully comprehend. Students may review what they have learned by going through the *Grammar Points* again after completing each exercise. The *Grammar Points* can also be used for quick reference purposes.

There are six revision and evaluation tests towards the back of every book. These tests deal with most of the *Grammar Points* covered in each book.

CONTENTS

CONTENTS

UNIT 1.1 VERBS

base form

Look at the **A** and **B** sentences below. Find out why **B** is correct and **A** is wrong in the **Grammar Points** section.

GRAMMAR POINTS

1A	The employees **likes** the new layout of their office.	✗	
1B	The employees **like** the new layout of their office.	✓	1
2A	Where **does** Miriam **wants** the sofa?	✗	
2B	Where **does** Miriam **want** the sofa?	✓	2
3A	All of them **to see** the doctor today.	✗	
3B	All of them **have to see** the doctor today.	✓	3
4A	She **won't tells** us where she is going.	✗	
4B	She **won't tell** us where she is going.	✓	4

GRAMMAR POINTS

1 The base form is the simplest form of a verb. It does not have the 's', 'ed' or 'ing' ending. We use the base form for the present tense with plural noun subjects and the pronoun subjects **I**, **you**, **we** and **they**.

EXAMPLES: Those two supermarkets **stock** a variety of imported goods.
I **have** a lot to be thankful for.
You **need** to change your method of work.
We **buy** our office supplies from the shop across the road.
They **think** you are the best person for the post of chairman.

REMEMBER!

- The verb 'to be', 'to do' and 'to have' can be used as main verbs as well as auxiliary verbs.
  EXAMPLES: They **are** the engineers for the project.   (**are** as main verb)
  They **are repairing** the old bridge.   (**are** as auxiliary verb)

- The base form of a verb is also used to give instructions, warnings, advice or commands to the listener or to make requests.
  EXAMPLES: **Check** the expiry date on the cans.   *(instruction)*
  Don't **enter** that room.   *(warning)*
  Eat in moderation.   *(advice)*
  Put down your weapons!   *(command)*
  Help me carry these parcels, please.   *(request)*

Take note that **you** (the listener) is the subject in each of the above sentences.

---

2   We use the base form of a verb in all positive and negative questions containing the verb 'to do':

(a)   verb 'to do' + noun/pronoun + base form

   EXAMPLES: **Does/Doesn't** David **use** contact lenses?
   Do/Don't those people **know** the club's rules and regulations?

(b)   wh-word + verb 'to do' +noun/pronoun + base form

   EXAMPLES: **When does** Janelle **present** her paper at the conference?
   What didn't they **discuss** at the meeting?

3   We call the base form of a verb together with **to** 'an infinitive' or 'a non-finite verb'.
A sentence with an infinitive is not complete unless it contains a finite verb
as well.

   EXAMPLE: Ronald has **to finalise** the report this afternoon.   ☑

   finite verb   infinitive

   Ronald **to finalise** the report this afternoon.   ✗

   infinitive

> **REMEMBER!**
> - A verb is either finite or non-finite. A finite verb changes its form according to the tense and subject of the sentence. A non-finite verb does not change its form.
>
>   EXAMPLES: finite verb: like   non-finite verb: to go
>
>   Present tense   :   Grandma likes to go for short walks in the evening.
>   Past tense   :   Grandma liked to go for long walks when she was much younger.
>   Singular subject :   She likes to go for short walks in the evening.
>   Plural subject   :   They like to go for short walks in the evening.

4   We use the base form of a verb with all positive and negative modals.
(Examples of modals: **can**, **could**, **may**, **might**, **shall**, **should**, **must**)

   EXAMPLES: I **could** **revise** the timetable for you.   ☑

   modal   base form of verb

   I **could** **revised** the timetable for you.   ✗

   modal   base form + 'ed' ending

   Jay **mustn't** **disturb** the baby.   ☑

   negative form of modal   base form of verb

   Jay **mustn't** **disturbs** the baby.   ✗

   negative form of modal   base form + 's' ending

PRACTICE **A**   Circle the numbers of the sentences that use the base form of verbs correctly.

1   These houses are designed to suit the needs of the elderly.

2   He doesn't to let problems ruin his day.

3   When are you join us in a game of tennis?

4   Every residential area should have its own recycling centre.

5   Paul mustn't cycles fast on a wet road.

6   They wishes the trip to the mountains had been less strenuous.

7   Don't use your mobile phone while you are driving!

8   Why do you stay up very late every night?

9   Please to contribute items for our jumble sale on Saturday.

10 Did Mary get an autographed poster from her favourite singer?

YOUR SCORE
/10

PRACTICE *B*   Ten of the underlined verbs are incorrect. Write the correct
verbs in the boxes.

1 Don't <u>get</u> annoyed because I <u>didn't phoned</u> you yesterday.

2 The girls <u>asked</u> the actress <u>to posing</u> for a picture with them.

3 I <u>has</u> to <u>buy</u> two AA batteries for my torch today.

4 What <u>did</u> you <u>saw</u> when you walked up our driveway?

5 We <u>can gives</u> you a refund or you <u>can choose</u> another jacket.

6 Please <u>informs</u> the members that our chairman <u>has resigned</u>.

7 We <u>should remember</u> that both cars <u>needs</u> new tyres.

8 The tourists <u>didn't expect</u> the island <u>to being</u> so beautiful.

9 <u>Doesn't</u> Annie <u>know</u> it is time <u>go</u> to work?

10 <u>Made</u> sure no one tries <u>to enter</u> or leave this building.

YOUR SCORE
/10

PRACTICE *C*   Fill in the blanks with the correct verbs in the brackets.

1 Which items did you _____ ? (want / wanted)

2 Vicky, _____ a reply accepting the invitation to take part in the inter-school debate.
   (write / writes)

3 He might _____ in town to see his parents. (be / to be)

4 The environment council _____ punish those who have fires in their gardens.
   (hopes / must)

5 Almost every family in that area runs a cafe or rents rooms _____ to visitors.
   (cater / to cater)

6 Don't _____ too near the car in front of you. (go / going)

7 Please _____ the cookies in a tightly sealed container. (store / to store)

8 This liquid may _____ the stains on your sofa. (remove / removes)

9 Why didn't Ken _____ for the role of Julius Caesar? (audition / auditioned)

10 _____ a little seasoning to bring out the flavour of the meat.
   (Sprinkle / Could sprinkle)

YOUR SCORE
/10

4

can call	check	didn't read	know	let	listen
to call	to check	to read	to know	to let	to listen
must see	perform	repeat	say	tell	
see	to perform	to repeat	to say	to tell	

Fiona : Hi, Steve. Fiona here. I called (1) _____ you Darren Clipton's going (2) _____ here next month.

Steve : What? How do you (3) _____ ?

Fiona : It's in today's paper.

Steve : Really? Oh, I (4) _____ his performance. I (5) _____ to his songs all the time. Does the paper (6) _____ who is selling the tickets for his show?

Fiona : I don't know. I (7) _____ the whole article, Steve.

Steve : Please (8) _____ for me, Fiona. I'll wait.

Fiona : Okay . . . Here it is. You (9) _____ the reservations hotline at 108 – 344 – 5678.

Steve : Please (10) _____ the number, Fiona.

Fiona : 108 – 344 – 5678.

Steve : I've got it. Thanks for letting me know.

Fiona : You're welcome.

YOUR SCORE

/10

PRACTICE $\boxed{E}$ Underline the sentences with mistakes in the use of verbs and rewrite them correctly.

One day, just after my exams, My sister said, "Henry, stopped watching TV all day. Don't you has anything else to do? I think you and your friends should do something useful while waiting for your exam results. Why don't you put your talents to work? Look around our neighbourhood. Offer some sort of service. You could earns some money for yourselves."

Well, I took her advice and rounded up five friends. After three hours of brainstorming, we decided to sets up 'Youth at Work'. The next morning, we sent out flyers listing the things we could do, such as getting groceries, mowing the lawn, babysitting, washing cars, painting houses, etc.

That afternoon, our phones didn't stopped ringing. Today, six months later, 'Youth at Work' has 100 members. We serves not just our neighbourhood but other areas as well.

1 *Henry, stop watching TV all day.*

2 _____

3 _____

4 _____

5 _____

6 _____

YOUR SCORE

/10

UNIT 1.2 VERBS

with 's' and 'ing' endings

Look at the **A** and **B** sentences below. Find out why **B** is correct and **A** is wrong in the **Grammar Points** section.

			GRAMMAR POINTS
1A	Fatigue **make** us do strange things.	✗	
1B	Fatigue **makes** us do strange things.	✓	1
2A	Ross **replacing** the washer of the kitchen tap.	✗	
2B	Ross **is replacing** the washer of the kitchen tap.	✓	2
3A	The men **rush** across the road are medical workers.	✗	
3B	The men **rushing** across the road are medical workers.	✓	3

GRAMMAR POINTS

1 We use the base form of a verb with the 's' ending for the present tense in these ways:

(a) with singular noun subjects and the pronoun subjects **he**, **she** and **it**
> EXAMPLES: **He/She scrutinises** every document that is to be given to a client.
> **The painting/It enhances** the beauty of the room.

(b) with uncountable or collective noun subjects
> EXAMPLES:
>
> uncountable noun
> Music **soothes** me when I am stressed.
>
> collective noun
> The jury **needs** more time to reach a verdict.

REMEMBER!

- An **uncountable noun** refers to things that cannot be counted. It always takes a singular verb form, even if it ends in 's'.
  EXAMPLE: News **travels** quickly in the IT age.

- A **collective noun** refers to a group of people or things. It can take **both** a singular or plural verb. A singular verb is used to refer to the group as a unit. A plural verb is used to show that the focus is on the members that make up the group.
  EXAMPLES: **The community expects** better facilities for the handicapped. (**community** as a unit)
  The community meet once a month at the school hall to   (**community** as members
  discuss issues.   of the group)

- When the subject is a **noun phrase**, we decide whether to use a singular or a plural verb by looking at the **head word**. (A head word is usually the noun that is the most important part of a noun phrase.)
  EXAMPLE:
  noun phrase subject

  The soldiers' loyalty towards their officers **amazes** me.

  (head word)

2 We use the base form with the 'ing' ending together with the verb 'to be' in continuous tenses.

(a) present continuous tense : verb 'to be' (**am / is / are**) + base form with 'ing' ending
EXAMPLE: An insect **is creeping** up my arm.

(b) past continuous tense : verb 'to be' (**was / were**) + base form with 'ing' ending
EXAMPLE: They **were dyeing** the fabric an hour ago.

(c) future continuous tense : verb 'to be' (**will be**) + base form with 'ing' ending
EXAMPLE: The airplane **will be making** a brief stop at Dubai in 20 minutes.

3 The base form with the 'ing' ending is also called the present participle. (It is a non-finite verb.) We use it after a noun to describe or identify the noun. This type of 'ing' clause functions like a relative clause.

EXAMPLES:
'ing' clause
The men **standing** in the doorway look suspicious.
noun — present participle — finite verb

relative clause
The men who **are standing** in the doorway look suspicious.

'ing' clause
The boy **addressing** the group of visitors is one of our friends.
noun — present participle — finite verb

'ing' clause
We know the boy **addressing** the group of visitors .
finite verb — noun — present participle

PRACTICE *A* Cross out the incorrect verb forms to complete the sentences.

1 That cartoonist | create | creates | wonderful characters with just a few strokes of his pen.

2 Sandra | correct | corrects | her children whenever they make a mistake.

3 The lawyer | handles | handling | my case is out of town.

4 The ship's sail | is slacken | is slackening | now that the wind has dropped.

5 Mary and Lily | want | wants | to go for a drive in my new car.

6 She ordered food from a caterer | specialises | specialising | in Chinese food.

7 Mr Wearnes | lavish | lavishes | his wife with gifts on their wedding anniversary.

8 Peter | mutter | was muttering | to himself when I walked in.

9 Mr Kim and his wife | operating | are operating | a laundrette.

10 This cream | protect | protects | your skin from the harsh rays of the sun.

YOUR SCORE
10

PRACTICE *B* Fill in the blanks with the correct words in the boxes.

1 (a) Bob _____ his opponent during debates.

(b) Don't _____ your sister by taking her things without her permission.

| antagonise |
| antagonises |

2 (a) The girls _____ paper flowers are going to decorate the hall.

are making
making

(b) They _____ arrangements to fetch you from the bus station.

3 (a) The lady _____ her son's letter looks sad.

reads
reading

(b) My sister _____ poetry whenever she feels sad.

4 (a) He _____ the newspaper daily in search of a job.

scrutinises
scrutinising

(b) The editor _____ the report noticed it had a number of errors.

5 (a) The band _____ at the hotel lounge is from the Philippines.

entertaining
is entertaining

(b) She _____ her guests with stories of her travels.

YOUR SCORE

10

PRACTICE $\boxed{C}$ The verb in the box should be at one of the two places marked $\wedge$. Circle the correct $\wedge$.

1 Kathy $\wedge$ voluntary work at the hospital $\wedge$ once a fortnight.

2 The player $\wedge$ with the referee is $\wedge$ Alan.

3 Larry $\wedge$ the overhead bridge $\wedge$ to get to his office.

4 The athletes $\wedge$ impatiently $\wedge$ for the games to begin.

5 The expedition team $\wedge$ out earlier than the others wants to reach the village before $\wedge$ nightfall.

6 George $\wedge$ what you have done $\wedge$ for his family.

7 The government $\wedge$ a great deal of importance $\wedge$ on self-reliance.

8 The inhabitants $\wedge$ against $\wedge$ the logging activities in their area.

9 She $\wedge$ that Liz is the one who $\wedge$ deserves the praise.

10 The woman $\wedge$ to Samuel is $\wedge$ a TV reporter.

does
arguing
uses
are waiting
setting
appreciates
places
are protesting
insists
speaking

YOUR SCORE

10

PRACTICE $\boxed{D}$ The mistakes in the use of verbs have been underlined. Write the correct verb forms in the boxes.

Ellen Hunter running her own business. She

manage events such as annual dinners, talks

and birthdays. Those use her services include

banks, fashion houses and government agencies.

At the moment, Ellen is manage the

promotion of a new product for a cosmetic house.

1	
2	
3	
4	

She and her team of five assistants <u>having</u> many
things to do before the special occasion. For instance,
her assistants have <u>send</u> out invitation cards and
<u>packages</u> door gifts for the guests. Ellen
<u>need</u> to finalise the programme and plan what
she has to say as the Master of Ceremonies.

Ellen <u>demand</u> the best not only from
her assistants but also from herself. She sets the
standard and they have to follow it. Because her
work is highly professional, Ellen's clients often
<u>recommends</u> her to their friends and associates.

5 [ ]

6 [ ]
7 [ ]
8 [ ]

9 [ ]

YOUR SCORE
10

10 [ ]

PRACTICE **E** Underline the sentences with mistakes and rewrite them correctly using verbs with the 's' or 'ing' ending, or the 'ing' clause.

Tina : David, <u>looks at that sign!</u> The road leads to Dolphin's Bay is under repair.
David : That's all right. We can use the other road to Dolphin's Bay.
Tina : That road have a lot of potholes. I think we should go somewhere else today.
David : Okay. Take my mobile phone from the glove compartment and phone Martin. He lives about 20 minutes away. We'll visit him if he's free today.
Tina : His phone is ring . . . I don't think he's in.
David : Oh, I forgot. On Saturdays he goes riding or he play a game of tennis at his club.
Tina : Let's check where he is. I'll call him on his handphone . . . Hi, Martin. Tina here. Where are you?
Martin : Hi, I was just about to call you. I'm in front of your house. I wanted surprise the two of you.

1 *David, look at that sign!* _____

2 _____

_____

3 _____

_____

4 _____

_____

5 _____

_____

6 _____

YOUR SCORE
10

_____

UNIT 1.3 VERBS

with 'ed' ending

Look at the **A** and **B** sentences below. Find out why **B** is correct and **A** is wrong in the **Grammar Points** section.

GRAMMAR POINTS

1A	John **was accompany** his grandfather to the park.	✗	
1B	John **accompanied** his grandfather to the park.	✓	1
2A	The cat **abandoned** by its owner.	✗	
2B	The cat **was abandoned** by its owner.	✓	2
3A	I witnessed the accident **was caused** by that truck.	✗	
3B	I witnessed the accident **caused** by that truck.	✓	3

GRAMMAR POINTS

1

We use the base form of a verb with the 'ed' ending for the past tense.

EXAMPLES: Mary **encouraged** her daughter to study music.
The device **measured** her blood pressure accurately.
Tom's illness **caused** us a lot of anxiety.
The association **called** for a press conference on Saturday.

REMEMBER!

- The following are some ways of forming the past tense of regular verbs:

base form of verb + 'ed'
EXAMPLES: earn → earn**ed**
reign → reign**ed**

base form of verb ending in 'e' + 'd'
EXAMPLES: argu**e** → argu**ed**
refus**e** → refus**ed**

base form of verb ending in 'y̶' 'i' + 'ed'
EXAMPLES: bur**y** → bur**ied**
worr**y** → worr**ied**

base form of verb ending in a consonant
+ the same consonant + 'ed'
EXAMPLES: cram + **m** + ed → cram**m**ed
refer + **r** + ed → refer**r**ed

Note that the doubling of consonants does not apply to 'w', 'x' and 'y'.

- The past tense of an irregular verb does not consist of the base form of the verb with 'ed' ending.

EXAMPLES: bend → **bent**   catch → **caught**   go → **went**
set → **set**   rise → **rose**   w**ea**ve → w**o**ve

2

We use the past participle in perfect tenses with the verb 'to have' and passive sentences with the verb 'to be'.

EXAMPLES: They **have decided** to do the job.   (present perfect tense)
Ian **had called** for an ambulance.   (past perfect tense)
Your suggestions **are accepted**.   (passive sentence)
The widow **was comforted** by her friends.   (passive sentence)

■ The past participle is the base form of the verb with the 'ed' ending for a regular verb. It is formed in other ways for irregular verbs.

	Base form	**Past form**	**Past participle form**
Regular verbs	finish	finished	finished
	wipe	wiped	wiped
Irregular verbs (Two forms the same)	hear	heard	heard
	leave	left	left
Irregular verbs (Three forms different)	eat	ate	eaten
	take	took	taken
Irregular verbs (Three forms the same)	cost	cost	cost
	put	put	put

3 The past participle on its own is a non-finite verb. We use it after a noun to describe what happened to the noun. This type of 'ed' clause functions like a relative clause.

EXAMPLES:

'ed' clause

The skier **trapped** in the snowstorm is an American.

noun — past participle — finite verb

relative clause

The skier who **is trapped** in the snowstorm is an American.

'ed' clause

The car **abandoned** by the robbers had a false number plate.

noun — past participle — finite verb

'ed' clause

The police examined the car **abandoned** by the robbers.

finite verb — noun — past participle

■ Present participles are active in meaning while past participles are passive in meaning.

EXAMPLE:

'ing' clause

The pedestrian **suing** the motorist is very upset.   (**The pedestrian** is doing the action.)

present participle

'ed' clause

The pedestrian **sued** by the motorist is very upset.   (**The pedestrian** is receiving the action.)

past participle

11

PRACTICE *A* Cross out the incorrect verb forms to complete the sentences.

1 The policeman | issued | was issued | the motorist a ticket for speeding.

2 Gifts | exchanged | were exchanged | between the representatives of the two countries.

3 He | suffered | was suffered | a lot of bruises when he fell from a tree.

4 The building | designed | was designed | by Mr Shaw is remarkable.

5 His tenant | has decided | was decided | to move out of the apartment in September.

6 The tired old man accepted the seat | offered | was offered | by Mrs Evans.

7 Tours | arranged | have arranged | by that travel agency are hectic.

8 The information | provided | was provided | by the media was inaccurate.

9 The navy | have noticed | were noticed | some strange activities along the coastline.

10 We | served | were served | chocolate pudding by our hostess.

YOUR SCORE

10

PRACTICE *B* Fill in the blanks with either the present or past participle form of the verbs in the brackets.

1 This is the first stadium _____ (design) by local architects.

2 The buses _____ (provide) sports fans with transport were very comfortable.

3 The contingent _____ (march) into the stadium right now is from Canada.

4 The people _____ (seat) in the open stands were drenched during the heavy rain.

5 The spectators _____ (behave) in a rowdy manner were ordered to leave the stadium.

6 The athlete _____ (sprint) far ahead of the rest is from Ghana.

7 The trophy _____ (donate) by the sports media was a silver figure on a golden globe.

8 A doctor attended to the player _____ (injure) during the match between Italy and Korea.

9 The player _____ (honour) by the media for his skill and sense of fairplay was Vincent Mandela.

10 Police tried to control the large group of fans _____ (surround) Vincent Mandela.

YOUR SCORE

10

PRACTICE C Fill in the blanks with the correct words in the box.

arrived	covered	has cleared	huddled	loaded
was arrived	was covered	was cleared	were huddled	have loaded
have invested	made	recovered	rushed	suggested
were invested	were made	has recovered	was rushed	was suggested

1 The girls _____ around the fireplace are Emily's friends.

2 The food from the caterers _____ just before the first guest did.

3 The little boy _____ in mud from head to foot.

4 Mrs Booth suffered a stroke and _____ to hospital.

5 The land belonging to Farmer Hudson _____ for planting.

6 That soldier _____ from a gunshot wound.

7 They _____ a lot of time and money in that project.

8 We decided to take the route _____ by Sam.

9 The pancakes _____ by your mother are very light.

10 The boxes _____ onto the four lorries contained medical supplies.

YOUR SCORE
10

PRACTICE D Ten of the underlined verbs are incorrect. Write the correct verbs in the boxes provided.

A new TV programme <u>produce</u> by East-West Network — line 1 — *produced*

has <u>capture</u> the attention of millions of viewers throughout — 2

the world. The programme <u>called</u> *Cornerstones*. It is — 3

about people and values. The network crew <u>travelled</u> — 4

all over the world <u>to interviewed</u> individuals and — line 5

communities. They <u>were filmed</u> 10 episodes this year — 6

and <u>hope</u> to do another 10 next year. — 7

The first episode <u>screened</u> last night in both Germany — 8

and Holland. It <u>was featured</u> a tribe in Asia that — 9

<u>has retain</u> its old way of life despite an awareness — line 10

of modern science. The people <u>was interviewed</u> in the — 11

episode <u>lead</u> simple lives and illness is uncommon among them. — 12

"Your modern world <u>has brought</u> into existence — 13

more problems than solutions," <u>remarked</u> Koru Nokos, — 14

the tribal chief, to *Cornerstones*' Karen Ling. "<u>I was agree</u> — line 15

to this interview so that the outside world <u>can learnt</u> from us." — 16

YOUR SCORE
10

13

UNIT 2.1 SUBJECT-VERB AGREEMENT

the number of, a lot of, indefinite pronouns

Look at the **A** and **B** sentences below. Find out why **B** is correct and **A** is wrong in the **Grammar Points** section.

1A	The number of distinguished guests at the party **were** impressive.	✗	
1B	The number of distinguished guests at the party **was** impressive.	✓	1
2A	A lot of money **have been spent** on the new highway project.	✗	
2B	A lot of money **has been spent** on the new highway project.	✓	2
3A	Everybody in my office **hope** to get a bonus at the end of the month.	✗	
3B	Everybody in my office **hopes** to get a bonus at the end of the month.	✓	3

GRAMMAR POINTS

1   We use a singular verb with the phrase **the number of**. We use a plural verb with the phrase **a number of**.

EXAMPLES: **A number of** students **were** absent today.

           plural verb

       The number of club members **has increased** this year.

             singular verb

> **REMEMBER!**
> - The phrases **a number of** and **the number of** can only go with plural countable nouns.

2   We use singular verbs with the words **a lot of**, **all**, **all of**, **most of**, **some** and **some of** when they go with uncountable nouns. We use plural verbs with these words when they go with plural countable nouns.

EXAMPLES: **Most of** the stuff at the back of the storeroom **is** useless.

         singular noun   singular verb

       Most of our friends **are coming** to watch us perform tonight.

         plural noun   plural verb

 **A lot of** sympathy **needs** to be extended towards earthquake victims.

- singular noun
- singular verb

 **A lot of** drivers **need** extra practice before their driving test.

- plural noun
- plural verb

3 We use singular verbs with indefinite pronouns.

EXAMPLES: **Everybody is invited** to the wedding celebrations next week.

- pronoun
- singular verb

Nothing has been done to improve the drainage in our housing estate.

- pronoun
- singular verb

> **REMEMBER!**
> - Indefinite pronouns refer to people or things without pointing out exactly who or what they are. The following are indefinite pronouns:
>
> | anybody | anyone | anything | everybody | everyone | everything |
> |---------|--------|----------|-----------|----------|------------|
> | nobody | no one | nothing | somebody | someone | something |

PRACTICE *A*   Underline the correct verbs in the brackets.

1 A lot of concrete (was used / were used) to build this thick retaining wall.

2 Some geese (was splashing / were splashing) in the water.

3 The number of books written on the protection of wildlife (are / is) enormous.

4 Everything in the examination hall (look / looks) neat and orderly.

5 Anyone in that family (are / is) capable of cooking a good meal.

6 A number of tourists (was filming / were filming) the colourful pageant.

7 A lot of glue (has been used / have been used) to put up this giant poster.

8 No one (was able to see / were able to see) the signposts in the dark.

9 Most of the clothes on sale (don't / doesn't) appeal to me.

10 Something (are / is) wrong with my car. It just refuses to start.

YOUR SCORE

10

PRACTICE *B*   Fill in the blanks with the correct forms of the verbs in the brackets.

1 Everyone _____ (be) surprised when they heard the sounds of fireworks.

2 Nobody _____ (like) to be reminded of the mistakes he or she has made before.

3 We are pleased because the number of floats at the pageant _____ (have) doubled this year.

4 All the company's property _____ (be) sold last week to pay off its debts.

5 A number of members _____ (participate) in the club's new activities every day.

6 Something _____ (need) to be done about the litter in the shopping centre.

7 Most of the pollution in this city _____ (be) caused by cars and factories.

8 Anything that disturbs me while I'm reading _____ (annoy) me.

9 You don't have to call the police. Someone _____ (have) already reported the accident.

10 For hundreds of years, nothing _____ (have) changed the way of life of this unique community.

PRACTICE *C* Fill in the blanks with the words in the box. Each item may only be used once.

a lot of	a number of	anyone	anything	everybody
everything	nothing	somebody	something	the number of

1 _____ was busy at the hotel's reception counter, so we had to wait.

2 _____ rain has fallen and our driveway is completely flooded.

3 This room looks quite different from before. _____ in it has been rearranged.

4 _____ apartment blocks here have their own swimming pools.

5 _____ dented my car and just drove away.

6 _____ vehicles on the road today is relatively small because of the holiday.

7 Has _____ taken my notebook? I can't find it anywhere.

8 _____ about this place reminds me of my childhood home.

9 _____ except the wind disturbs the animals living in this arid desert.

10 _____ you offer is readily accepted by charity sale committees.

PRACTICE *D* Rewrite the sentences using correct verb forms.

1 A number of customers was queuing to pay for their purchases.

_____

_____

2 I can't contact Sarah. Someone have damaged the public phone in this booth.

_____

_____

3 A lot of freshly grated cheese are used for this pizza topping.

_____

_____

4 The number of students in the literature class have increased dramatically.

_____

_____

5 Everything been done to prevent the river from bursting its banks.

_____

_____

PRACTICE _E_   Underline the sentences that are incorrect and rewrite them using correct verb forms.

Betty shrieked with horror when she entered her bedroom. Everything was in a mess! Nothing were in its usual place anymore. Someone had ransacked her cupboards. A number of her clothes was strewn on the floor. Some of her shoes and handbags were on her bed. Her trinket box was wide open. All her jewellery were missing. She felt miserable because some of the pieces had been given to her by relatives and friends.

Everyone in the house was startled to hear Betty's cries. They rushed upstairs to find out what was wrong. The number of things stolen were not the only problem. Something inside Betty were deeply wounded. Somebody, a total stranger, had looked through all her personal things. Betty felt very upset.

1 _____

_____

2 _____

_____

3 _____

_____

4 _____

_____

5 _____

_____

UNIT 2.2 SUBJECT-VERB AGREEMENT

abstract nouns, **there** + verb 'to be'

Look at the **A** and **B** sentences below. Find out why **B** is correct and **A** is wrong in the **Grammar Points** section.

GRAMMAR POINTS

1A	His wealth **have not caused** him to forget the needs of others.	✗	
1B	His wealth **has not caused** him to forget the needs of others.	✓	1
2A	There **were** severe famine in some parts of Africa last year.	✗	
2B	There **was** severe famine in some parts of Africa last year.	✓	2

GRAMMAR POINTS

1   We use singular verbs with abstract nouns.

EXAMPLE: <u>Integrity</u> **is** an important quality in leadership.

(subject)   (singular verb)

REMEMBER!

■ An abstract noun refers to a feeling, an idea or a quality. It may be something that cannot be seen or touched.

EXAMPLES: excitement, freedom, intelligence, joy, wisdom, youth

■ Abstract nouns can be used:
(a) as subjects by themselves
(b) as head words in noun phrases

EXAMPLES: noun phrase – subject

Lots of **training** **is required** for a gymnast to gain international status.

(head word)   (singular verb)

noun phrase – subject

Her **skill** at designing clothes **has won** her several awards.

(head word)   (singular verb)

---

2   We can use the words **there** + verb 'to be' when we want to state that something exists or happens. When the subject that comes after the verb 'to be' is singular or uncountable, we use the singular form of 'to be'. When the subject is plural, we use the plural form.

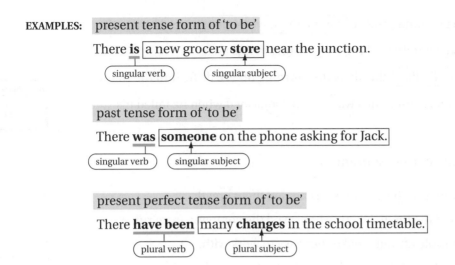

EXAMPLES: present tense form of 'to be'

There **is** a new grocery **store** near the junction.

(singular verb) (singular subject)

past tense form of 'to be'

There **was** **someone** on the phone asking for Jack.

(singular verb) (singular subject)

present perfect tense form of 'to be'

There **have been** many **changes** in the school timetable.

(plural verb) (plural subject)

PRACTICE *A* Underline the correct words in the brackets.

1 The truth about the situation in those two rival companies (is / are) going to be exposed.

2 His gentle manner of speaking (make / makes) everyone feel at ease.

3 There (was / were) public anger against the change in the tax laws.

4 There has been great (improvement / improvements) in that child's reading ability.

5 Bitterness between two departments often (cause / causes) problems in an organisation.

6 Gratitude (has / have) been conveyed to all those who donated to the charity.

7 The country's security (is / are) greatly threatened by foreign armies on the border.

8 There have been significant (change / changes) in the education system recently.

9 The tranquil surroundings of the 200-year-old palace (give / gives) us a glimpse into the past.

10 There (was / were) genuine loyalty among the troops who fought to protect the president.

YOUR SCORE

10

PRACTICE *B* Cross out the incorrect verb forms to complete the sentences.

1 There | was | were | a moment of silence to honour all those who had given their lives for the nation.

2 The speed at which the cheetah chases its prey | are | is | remarkable.

3 The power of the ruling party | was challenged | were challenged | by a popular uprising.

4 John's ability to read other people's minds | are | is | truly amazing.

5 There | has been | have been | great concern over the rise in the number of traffic accidents.

6 Bad weather on public holidays | discourage | discourages | people from going out.

7 Approval for the playground project | has been | have been | granted by the city council.

8 There | are | is | large numbers of pigeons nesting in this area.

9 The scent of roses | fill | fills | the air as the morning breeze drifts into the room.

10 Dave's wish to become a test pilot | was | were | squashed when he failed his eye test.

YOUR SCORE
10

PRACTICE *C* Tick the correct sentences.

1 His generous donations to the charities has helped them greatly.

2 Jack's management of the financial crisis has saved the company from ruin.

3 Kelly's calm and sensible attitude makes her easy to work with.

4 There were a crowd of spectators waiting for the motor car rally to begin.

5 The new waiter's efficiency was quickly noted by the manager.

6 The beautiful beaches of that island attract many visitors each year.

7 There were great relief among us when Mr Wellington arrived.

8 The majesty of the snow-covered peaks are unforgettable.

9 Temporary shelter was provided for all those who had lost their homes in the fire.

10 The stressful work environment have caused many people to leave the firm.

YOUR SCORE
10

PRACTICE *D* Circle the correct words in the boxes to complete the sentences.

1 There is some _____ that I bought for tonight's barbecue in the kitchen.
   chicken   chickens

2 That awful noise _____ all of us in the office.
   distract   distracts

3 Brian's theories of management _____ a lot of sense.
   make   makes

4 Low self-esteem _____ been discussed in many magazine articles.
   has   have

5 There _____ hundreds of passengers waiting in the departure lounge because of the sudden cancellation of flights.
   was   were

6 Fatigue sometimes _____ to a breakdown in the body's immune system.
   lead   leads

7 There _____ a number of details that have been deleted from this report.
   are   is

8 Several of the discounted items here actually _____ more than in the other outlets.
   cost   costs

9 There _____ interest among health-conscious people in aromatherapy oils.
   has been   have been

10 The renewal of one's youth _____ what the advertisement offers.
   are   is

YOUR SCORE
10

20

PRACTICE $\boxed{E}$ Fill in the blanks with the correct forms of the verbs in the brackets.

1 For many decades already, illiteracy _____ (be) an obstacle in the development of many countries.

2 Plenty of exercise _____ (contribute) to a person's health and vitality.

3 There _____ (be) extensive damage to the roof because of high winds this. morning.

4 Carelessness _____ (lead) to accidents on the road.

5 There _____ (be) so many types of fruits at the stall that it was difficult to make a choice.

6 The good attitude of this hotel staff always _____ (go) a long way towards making their guests feel welcome.

7 Rivalry among the villagers still persists. It _____ (prevent) them from cooperating for mutual benefit.

8 There _____ (be) a great deal of curiosity about Lisa's fiance. We only know that he comes from Cyprus.

9 Challenges in life _____ (help) to build character.

10 Anxiety _____ (grip) people before job interviews.

YOUR SCORE

10

PRACTICE $\boxed{F}$ Rewrite the sentences using correct verb forms.

1 There are something on the table. Does it belong to you?

_____

_____

2 The weather have been so hot in the last few days that many people have suffered sunburn.

_____

_____

3 Tolerance play an important role in making a happy community.

_____

_____

4 His obsession with house prices are often hard for his friends to bear.

_____

_____

5 The talents of the young musician was recognised by the music school.

_____

_____

YOUR SCORE

10

21

UNIT 2.3 SUBJECT-VERB AGREEMENT

adjectives as nouns, gerunds, units of measurement

Look at the **A** and **B** sentences below. Find out why **B** is correct and **A** is wrong in the **Grammar Points** section.

			GRAMMAR POINTS
1A	The elderly **requires** volunteers who can provide them with transport.	✗	
1B	The elderly **require** volunteers who can provide them with transport.	✓	1
2A	**Smoke** several cigarettes daily can damage a person's lungs.	✗	
2B	**Smoking** several cigarettes daily can damage a person's lungs.	✓	2
3A	Three hundred dollars **are** a lot of money to spend on a pair of shoes.	✗	
3B	Three hundred dollars **is** a lot of money to spend on a pair of shoes.	✓	3

GRAMMAR POINTS

1 We use plural verbs with some adjectives that behave as nouns.
EXAMPLES: **The young are** vulnerable to certain illnesses.

subject · plural verb

The homeless were helped by the Welfare Department.

subject · plural verb

These adjectives come with **the** in front of them and are used to refer to groups of people.
EXAMPLES: the old, the poor, the rich, the unemployed

The 's' or 'es' plural ending is not added to these words even though they always refer to more than one person.
EXAMPLE: The **injured** have been taken to the hospital. ✓

The **injureds** have been taken to the hospital. ✗

2 We use singular verbs with 'ing' verb forms that behave as nouns. Such verb forms are also known as gerunds.
EXAMPLES: **Cycling** up this slope **needs** a lot of stamina.

gerund · singular verb

Labelling of the tins **takes place** before they are packed for export.

gerund · singular verb

22

3   We use singular verbs with expressions of distance, money, time, weight, etc, if they refer to a single sum or quantity.

EXAMPLES: **Thirty million dollars has been spent** on the new train terminal.

subject   singular verb

Eight hours of good sleep enables us to be alert all day.

subject   singular verb

PRACTICE   *A*   Underline the correct words in the brackets.

1   The handicapped (don't often receive / doesn't often receive) enough consideration from the community.

2   (Ski / Skiing) down a mountain gives a sense of total freedom.

3   More than a million dollars (was donated / were donated) to help the earthquake victims in South America.

4   Forty minutes (was / were) the time suggested for baking the muffins.

5   (Worked / Working) during the school holidays has provided me with extra money.

6   During the French Revolution, the (oppressed / oppression) rose up against the government.

7   Ten miles (are / is) a long way to go to buy milk and eggs.

8   The (educated / education) have an important role to play in a nation's development.

9   Cooking (occupies / occupy) a great deal of my mother's time.

10   (Tailor / Tailoring) has earned Teresa sufficient money to support her family.

YOUR SCORE

10

PRACTICE   *B*   Tick the correct sentences.

1   Crossing this dangerous river require plenty of courage.

2   Five hundred thousand dollars was stolen from the bank vault this afternoon.

3   The guilty was detained by the police after yesterday's ambush.

4   Solving crossword puzzles takes up much of my free time.

5   More than two hours is needed to complete this assignment.

6   The wealthy has become richer because of the new tax cuts.

7   Bullying younger workers is a deplorable form of behaviour.

8 The sick in the refugee camps were attended to by a voluntary group of doctors.

9 Less than four hundred kilometres separate the city from the main port.

10 Polishing his model vintage cars keep my brother busy during weekends.

PRACTICE *C* Circle the correct words in the boxes to complete the sentences.

1 Climbing up steep mountain slopes _____ both endurance and stamina.

| require | requires |

2 After using the computer for a long time, looking into the distance for about five minutes _____ the eyes.

| relax | relaxes |

3 The disabled _____ easier access to public buildings.

| demand | demands |

4 The French _____ noted for their food and fashion.

| are | is |

5 Buying a life insurance policy _____ to ensure your children have some security.

| help | helps |

6 At least half an hour of exercise a day _____ wonders for one's health.

| do | does |

7 A thousand dollars _____ a lot of money to spend on a summer vacation.

| are | is |

8 The compassionate always _____ a helping hand to those in trouble.

| extend | extends |

9 Painting and listening to music _____ both excellent ways to relax.

| are | is |

10 Reading in poorly lit places _____ eyestrain.

| cause | causes |

PRACTICE *D* Fill in the blanks with the correct forms of the verbs in the brackets.

1 Kim's ability to sing both pop songs as well as jazz numbers _____ (make) her a sought-after entertainer these days.

2 The elderly _____ (have) special seats set aside for them at the concert tomorrow.

3 Our guide will take you to a section of the city where the rich and famous _____ (live).

4 Walking briskly up the slope daily _____ (help) me to keep slim.

5 Two hours _____ (be) a long time to wait for a taxi or a bus.

6 Almost fifteen thousand dollars _____ (be) handed over in compensation yesterday.

7 Mr Lee's talk on procrastination _____ (show) he has a sense of humour.

8 Diving into the sea from this high cliff _____ (be) only for the daring and adventurous.

8 The poor in every country _____ (deserve) to have an education.

10 Five kilometres _____ (be) quite a distance for her to walk every day to school.

PRACTICE *E*   Some of the sentences contain mistakes. Underline the mistakes and write the correct words in the boxes.

1 Harvesting takes place in late summer when the wheat grains are ripe.

2 Paying two million dollars for that grand old mansion are reasonable.

3 Discussing this problem is a waste of valuable time.

4 Roasted the lamb takes at least two-and-a-half hours.

5 The disabled was taken on a special conducted tour of the historic fort.

6 Weeding this large garden is an exhausting job.

7 Four hundred dollars is a large sum of money to pay for a minor repair.

8 The soldiers were awarded medals for their courage during the war.

9 Honest is an important virtue.

10 Famous have their photos printed in the society columns of the papers.

PRACTICE *F*   Rewrite the sentences using correct verb forms.

1 The selfish seldom notices the pain and suffering of others.

_____

_____

2 Teach children requires creativity and versatility.

_____

_____

3 More than a million dollars were spent by the government on improving the facilities in schools.

_____

_____

4 Working 48 hours without stopping have made him ill.

_____

_____

5 The underprivileged was treated to a special dinner last night.

_____

_____

UNIT 3.1 SIMPLE PRESENT AND PRESENT CONTINUOUS TENSES

Look at the **A** and **B** sentences below. Find out why **B** is correct and **A** is wrong in the **Grammar Points** section.

			GRAMMAR POINTS
1A	My father **is reading** the newspapers every morning before leaving for the office.	✗	
1B	My father **reads** the newspapers every morning before leaving for the office.	✓	1
2A	Grace **takes** night classes in business studies for eight months and hopes to obtain a diploma later.	✗	
2B	Grace **is taking** night classes in business studies for eight months and hopes to obtain a diploma later.	✓	2
3A	The conducted tour of the museum **is beginning** in half an hour.	✗	
3B	The conducted tour of the museum **begins** in half an hour.	✓	3
4A	In the play, Pete **is portraying** a young man who loses his heart to a beautiful but cold woman.	✗	
4B	In the play, Pete **portrays** a young man who loses his heart to a beautiful but cold woman.	✓	4

GRAMMAR POINTS

1

Simple present tense	Present continuous tense
We can use this to refer to regular actions (habits), current situations or facts in general.	We can use this to refer to new habits (or repeated actions) which happen around the time of speaking or writing.
EXAMPLE: David **complains** a lot about everything because he's an impatient person.	EXAMPLE: Andy **is complaining** a lot about his work lately. He used to be a happier person.

2

Simple present tense	Present continuous tense
We can use this to refer to more long-lasting or permanent situations.	We can use this to refer to situations which are temporary (lasting for a short time around the present).
EXAMPLE: Penny **works** in her father's construction company.	EXAMPLE: Terence **is running** his aunt's shop until she recovers from her illness.

3	Simple present tense	Present continuous tense
	We can use this to refer to actions which are going to happen very soon, or future actions which happen regularly according to a timetable or schedule.	We can use this to refer to planned future actions.
	EXAMPLE: The show **starts** in 15 minutes.	EXAMPLE: Some old friends **are visiting** us next week.

4	Simple present tense	Present continuous tense
	We can use this to refer to short actions happening at the time of speaking (e.g. during sports commentaries). We also use this in reviews of plays, films or books.	We can use this to refer to actions (especially longer actions) happening at the time of speaking or writing.
	EXAMPLE: The ball **goes** into the net and it's another point for the Reds in this exciting basketball final!	EXAMPLE: The lecturers **are holding** a meeting now to discuss the students' progress.

PRACTICE _A_   Underline the correct verb forms in the brackets.

1 Our neighbour (comes / is coming) over now for a game of chess with my father.

2 Eduardo (kick / kicks) the ball into the net. It's another goal for the Italians!

3 Adam (lectures / is lecturing) part-time in the college while he is pursuing his doctorate.

4 Tim (accuses / is accusing) us of causing his computer problem.

5 The game wardens (are patrolling / patrol) the reserve at intervals to ensure the animals are safe from poachers.

6 To appease the workers who are on strike, the management (is promising / promises) to improve conditions in the factory.

7 She (is seeing / sees) more of her family nowadays. She used to visit them only once a month.

8 Jason often (is keeping / keeps) very late hours. I am worried about his health.

9 Mr Hogan (is producing / produces) Shakespeare's *Romeo and Juliet* for the drama festival which opens in two months' time.

10 Mrs Lee (is resting / rests) at home after the surgery last week. She will be back at work by the end of the month.

PRACTICE **B** Fill in the blanks with the correct tense of the verbs in the box.

deny	design	object	permeate	play
set off	stay	train	vanish	worry

1 Water _____ the top layers of the soil and is taken in by the roots of plants.

2 The city _____ thousands of fireworks to celebrate this year's Arts Festival.

3 Paramedics _____ for long hours at the hospital before they are sent out to answer calls for help.

4 My aunt always _____ about her health and insists that she is very ill.

5 The art of making handcrafted furniture _____ these days because of the competition from low-cost factory products.

6 Tim Hawke _____ the role of a small-town lawyer who fights against corruption and injustice in this movie.

7 We _____ at a friend's place for a few months until our house is completed.

8 He _____ that he has been doing careless work.

9 She _____ the interior of both homes and offices .

10 He _____ to the inheritance laws in this country.

YOUR SCORE
10

PRACTICE **C** Cross out the incorrect verb forms in the boxes to complete the sentences.

1 The contractors | are guaranteeing | guarantee | that they will be able to refurbish the office to our satisfaction.

2 The team | is making | makes | some striking costumes for the international competition next month.

3 My father | does | is doing | the cooking while my mother is in hospital.

4 The management council | intend | is intending | to review its parking fee guidelines at the next meeting.

5 In this film, Julian Russell | is acting | acts | as a young nobleman who falls in love with a farmer's daughter.

6 Joan | is taking | takes | part in tomorrow's debate. She and her team members are debating the proposition that 'Capital punishment should be abolished'.

7 History always | is repeating | repeats | itself. This has been shown many times.

8 At the moment, the Rotarians | are mapping | map | the route for the treasure hunt.

9 Alice | is spending | spends | the next few days at my house before flying back to Melbourne.

10 Howard | brings | is bringing | home a lot of work from the office and this always upsets his wife.

YOUR SCORE
10

28

PRACTICE D Circle the correct words in the boxes to complete the sentences.

1 The government _____ on all able-bodied young men to sign up for the armed services.

| are calling | calls | is calling |

2 Sue can't come to the phone right now. She _____ for her house keys, which she seems to have misplaced.

| is looking | look | looks |

3 Tom and Julie _____ a cybercafe in their neighbourhood.

| are opening | open | opens |

4 When my father _____ home from work, it is usually well past 6.30 in the evening.

| arrive | arrives | is arriving |

5 The boys and I frequently _____ about whose turn it is to use the car.

| are fighting | fight | fights |

6 When the high-tech bubble _____ , economies all over the globe will suffer.

| burst | bursts | is bursting |

7 Kate _____ for courses in business and finance next term.

| enrol | enrols | is enrolling |

8 Jessie _____ beautiful window displays for this department store.

| create | creates | is creating |

9 The supermarket _____ part-time assistants to help out during the holiday season next month.

| hire | hires | is hiring |

10 Young people from all over the war-torn country _____ together to make a public appeal for peace.

| are coming | come | comes |

YOUR SCORE

10

PRACTICE E Some of the sentences below are incorrect. Rewrite them correctly.

1 We think of going to the flea market in the park this Sunday.

_____

_____

2 You always say that you need a holiday but you have not taken a day off for months.

_____

_____

3 For the whole of next week, the college organises career talks to give students an in-depth knowledge of the various professions.

_____

_____

4 Carol is lecturing in psychology at an institute of management. She has been there for five years.

_____

_____

5 Robin and his family move to an apartment in my area next month.

_____

_____

YOUR SCORE

10

29

UNIT 3.2 SIMPLE PAST TENSE

Look at the **A** and **B** sentences below. Find out why **B** is correct and **A** is wrong in the **Grammar Points** section.

GRAMMAR POINTS

1A	In 1974, my uncle and his family **are leaving** to settle in Sydney, Australia.	✗	
1B	In 1974, my uncle and his family **left** to settle in Sydney, Australia.	✓	1
2A	Throughout World War II, planes continually **bomb** enemy positions and installations.	✗	
2B	Throughout World War II, planes continually **bombed** enemy positions and installations.	✓	2
3A	Many years ago, the band **used to performed** at lunchtime in the square.	✗	
3B	Many years ago, the band **used to perform** at lunchtime in the square.	✓	3

GRAMMAR POINTS

1 We use the simple past tense for an action or an event that occurred in the past and is finished at the time of speaking. To indicate the past, we use adverbs or phrases of time such as the following:

at one time	many years ago	in 1990
last month	later	once

EXAMPLE:
Sometime last year, Anne **decided** to begin riding classes for children at her ranch to help pay for the cost of running the stables. *(Anne's making the decision is a past action which is over.)*

2 We use the simple past tense to refer to an action which took place over a period of time in the past and is finished, or to report certain past events or situations in newspapers, magazines or journals.

EXAMPLES: Andrew **served** as a test pilot with the air force for six years before he joined a commercial airline. *(past action lasting for a period of time)*

Hundreds of schoolchildren, cheering and waving flags, **greeted** the visiting heads of state. *(report on a past event)*

3 We use **used to** + base form of verb to refer to an action or an event which took place regularly in the past but which does not happen anymore.

EXAMPLE: We **used to swim** and **play tennis** every Sunday at the club when we were college students.

30

PRACTICE A Tick the correct sentences.

1 We pass by the office just now but we didn't see Angie.

2 The ministry deliberated for some years before introducing computers into schools.

3 Last night, I have a shock when I went to my car and found its tyres missing.

4 The years from 1975 to 1985 saw a boom in that country's construction industry.

5 We use to mix the cake batter with a wooden spoon before we bought a blender.

6 The chairman launch the new insurance scheme for the workers last year.

7 Later, the mayor congratulated the teams for putting on a splendid show.

8 As a boy of 16, I used to walk up this hill very often to find a quiet place to read.

9 The thick acrid smoke sting my eyes and I could not see where I was going.

10 Uncle Bill's tales of adventure thrilled us and we believed every word he said.

YOUR SCORE
10

PRACTICE B Underline the correct words in the brackets.

1 In the olden days, workers (treat / treated) their employers with great formality.

2 Not long ago, Brazil (set up / sets up) a conservation scheme to save the giant turtles of the Amazon from extinction.

3 In the 20th century, advances in medical science and communications (outstrips / outstripped) anything that man had imagined.

4 Sandra (is trying / tried) to persuade me to go on the expedition to the National Forest because she didn't want to go alone.

5 Peter's present job as a television reporter occasionally (placed / places) him in life-threatening situations.

6 Marriage counsellors normally (settle / settled) disputes by bringing both parties together to talk things over.

7 Paul's heroic act of rescuing the baby trapped inside the burning house (made / make) the headlines in the evening paper.

8 My aunt sometimes (overwhelms / overwhelmed) the family with her kindness.

9 Lucy and I (are living / live) in Perth where we run a successful catering business.

10 My brothers (use to sail / used to sail) together on this lake when we lived here years ago.

YOUR SCORE
10

PRACTICE C Fill in the blanks with the correct present tense or past tense forms of the verbs in the brackets.

1 The news of the military uprising _____ (shake) the stability of the nation.

31

2 The stiff formal fashions for women in the Victorian age _____ (be) cumbersome and uncomfortable.

3 The police department _____ (still investigate) the cause of the massive collision on the highway this morning.

4 The rain _____ (beat) against the window and kept us awake all night.

5 In the 1950's, the prices of most commodities _____ (be) so low that people today find them unbelievable.

6 He _____ (now think) of selling the shoe store because of high overheads and poor sales.

7 A half-century ago, many people _____ (scoff) at the idea that women would rise to positions of importance.

8 These days, Jeff _____ (begin) to be more aware of his responsibilities.

9 My father _____ (surprise) everyone in the family last week by organising a birthday party for his sister.

10 Her beautiful, traditional dress _____ (stun) the audience who gasped in admiration.

YOUR SCORE
10

PRACTICE $\boxed{D}$ Circle the correct words in the boxes to complete the sentences.

1 Last Sunday night, a car driven by a reckless young man _____ and fell into a canal near my house.

| overturn   overturned |

2 The nurses _____ with the hospital management to give them free time to revise for the exams.

| are pleading   plead |

3 Aunt Zelda _____ the times when the old house was full of people.

| use to recall   used to recall |

4 The boys of the seventh cavalry _____ out their duties diligently when they were sent to war.

| carried   carry |

5 Women in the tribe _____ their babies to their backs and work in the fields for hours.

| tie   tied |

6 A renewed interest in ethnic languages and customs _____ among many communities now.

| is spreading   spreads |

7 We _____ over all aspects of the problem last night and have come to a decision.

| think   thought |

8 All morning, the senate vigorously _____ the president's proposal to give medical benefits to the poor.

| debate   debated |

9 Doctors always _____ us to eat in moderation and exercise regularly.

| advise   advised |

10 Our parents _____ us when we were very young so that we would grow up to be respectful and well-mannered.

| use to   used to |
| discipline   discipline |

YOUR SCORE
10

PRACTICE $\boxed{E}$ Rewrite the sentences and correct them.

1 Sam threatening to quit his job three days ago because he was bored.

_____

_____

2 In the spring, we usually planted rose bushes all along the garden wall so we can enjoy the blooms in the summer.

_____

_____

3 Rescue teams dig tirelessly last night to pull out the trapped miners from the pit.

_____

_____

4 Last year we frequently meet at weekends and discuss common problems we faced.

_____

_____

5 Glen always take charge of the office while Miss Richards is away and he ensures that everything runs smoothly.

_____

_____

PRACTICE $\boxed{F}$ Rewrite the report below in the simple past tense.

As I watch, the club members take out card tables and set them up. Tuesday is their games evening and most of them like to play bridge or whist.

One woman plays a game of solitaire. She sometimes get up to walk around and observe the games at the other tables.

Halfway through the evening there is a break for refreshments. A waiter serves tea and coffee and everybody enjoys conversation with their friends. Some people go home after this, but the enthusiastic players stay until quite late.

As I watched, _____

_____

_____

_____

_____

_____

_____

_____

UNIT 3.3 PAST CONTINUOUS TENSE

Look at the **A** and **B** sentences below. Find out why **B** is correct and **A** is wrong in the **Grammar Points** section.

GRAMMAR POINTS

				GRAMMAR POINTS
1A	Lucy **struggle** to change her punctured car tyre for more than an hour on the highway yesterday.	✗	
1B	Lucy **was struggling** to change her punctured car tyre for more than an hour on the highway yesterday.	✓	1
2A	While Gloria was doing her laps at the pool, her coach **timed** her.	✗	
2B	While Gloria was doing her laps at the pool, her coach **was timing** her.	✓	2
3A	The elderly couple were crossing the road this morning when a motorcyclist **was knocking** them down.	✗	
3B	The elderly couple were crossing the road this morning when a motorcyclist **knocked** them down.	✓	3
4A	Whenever we visited grandfather last year, he **always reminding** us to work hard.	✗	
4B	Whenever we visited grandfather last year, he **was always reminding** us to work hard.	✓	4

GRAMMAR POINTS

1 We use the past continuous tense to show that an action was going on at a definite time in the past, or that an action or situation continued for a period of time in the past.

EXAMPLES: At 4.30 yesterday afternoon, I **was giving** a solo recital at the music academy. *(definite time in the past)*
Paul and his little son **were painting** with crayons and watercolours for hours before dinnertime. *(continuous action in the past)*

2 We use the past continuous tense or the simple past tense for two actions that were going on at the same time in the past.

EXAMPLES: Alex **was checking** the accounts while Cynthia **was reading** her report.

past continuous tense

Alex **checked** the accounts while Cynthia **read** her report.

simple past tense

3 To show that something happened while a longer action was going on in the past, we use the past continuous tense for the longer action and the simple past tense for the shorter action.

EXAMPLE:

Ted and I **were trying** to find our French dictionary when a friend **came** and **lent** us his.

⎣ past continuous tense ⎦   ⎣ simple past tense ⎦

4 We use the past continuous tense to refer to repeated actions in the past with adverbs of frequency such as **always** or **forever**, or for future action that was planned in the past but did not take place for some reason.

EXAMPLES: Aunt Flora **was forever telling** me to registering for driving lessons.
(repeated action)
Zack **was going to accept** the job offer in London but changed his mind later.
(future action planned in the past but which did not happen)

PRACTICE $\boxed{A}$ Circle the numbers of the correct sentences.

1   While I rearrange the bookshelves, I found some old photographs.

2   At this time yesterday, we going to visit our grandparents.

3   She was suffering from a toothache the whole afternoon.

4   While the president was speaking, his secretary Jackie was making short notes for reference.

5   As the cars were speeding around the racing circuit, we hear a loud explosion.

6   Amy was keeping score as the teams battled for first place in the science quiz.

7   Cathy wiping the tears from her eyes as Mr O'Neil was playing the beautiful music.

8   The supervisors at the factory were always pressing for better working conditions.

9   We were so exhausted that we slept the whole morning.

10   The plane was flying at such a low altitude that we were having a clear view of the Colorado River.

YOUR SCORE

10

PRACTICE $\boxed{B}$ Cross out the incorrect verb forms in the boxes.

1   Helen │ testify │ testified │ for more than 20 minutes this afternoon at the hearing in the High Court.

2   While Bob │ polished │ was polishing │ his car, his sons were cleaning the wheels.

3   Les │ complain │ complained │ of eyestrain for some weeks before he changed his glasses.

4   We │ were going to face │ are facing │ a surging crowd of demonstrators in the square so we turned back.

5   Throughout the night, the rescue boats │ are looking for │ were looking for │ survivors of the plane crash.

35

6 People | fought | were fighting | to save their homes as the fire spread quickly through the village.

7 While we sat chatting at the dining table, the waitress | brought | were bringing | in bowls of steaming hot soup.

8 John | navigated | was navigating | the speedboat when it crashed into the ramp.

9 The aroma of freshly-baked bread | fills | filled | the air when the baker opened the oven door.

10 While we | dig | were digging | for artifacts at the site, Dr Williams suddenly gave an excited shout.

PRACTICE *C* Fill in the blanks with the correct forms of the verbs in the brackets.

While Tom (1) _____*was taking*_____ (take) a sharp bend in the road, I shouted out to him to reduce the speed. He (2) _____ (ignore) me completely. He (3) _____ (enjoy) the music that (4) _____ (blare) over the speakers. Angrily I (5) _____ (reach) for the knob and switched off the radio. Tom glared at me and turned it on again. We (6) _____ (quarrel) about his reckless behaviour when I (7) _____ (see) a huge truck on the other side. It (8) _____ (puff) up the slope and occupied more than half the road. Tom (9) _____ (cut) to the left to avoid the truck. The car (10) _____ (fly) off the road and landed against a tree. As we (11) _____ (crawl) out of the window numb with shock, the music was still playing.

PRACTICE *D* Some of the verbs in the sentences are incorrect. Underline them and write the correct verbs in the boxes.

1 We cleared the undergrowth in the garden when we heard a hissing sound and saw the snake.

2 Katy holding on tightly to the ladder while Timmy climbed up to the roof to get the tennis balls.

3 Terry coughing so badly last night that she couldn't sleep.

4 I was going to visit my aunt last Friday but I didn't have the time.

5 The movie this afternoon is very entertaining. I didn't feel bored at all.

6 At about 11 last night, Tony was counting the money
   and putting it away in bags to be taken to the bank.

7 Sara was mentioning the times when we all slept
   in my tree house and we laughed at the memory.

8 At the showroom this afternoon, while the salesman
   was pointing out all the exciting features of a new
   car, we were admiring another model.

9 Joan was going to take up medicine but she
   decided to do pharmacy instead.

10 I was feeling ill so I excused myself from the
   meeting.

PRACTICE E Rewrite the sentences and correct them.

1 We were knowing that everything in the report was grossly exaggerated.

   _____

   _____

2 Alice is thinking of leaving the company when someone approached her with an
   attractive job offer.

   _____

   _____

3 James waiting for property prices to rise last month and he finally sold his house last
   week.

   _____

   _____

4 Peter and Lisa going to get married in June but the wedding has been postponed.

   _____

   _____

5 Yesterday, the developers trying to evict the squatters from the area but the people
   refused to move.

   _____

   _____

UNIT 3.4 PRESENT PERFECT TENSE

Look at the **A** and **B** sentences below. Find out why **B** is correct and **A** is wrong in the **Grammar Points** section.

1A	We **have reported** the robbery to the police yesterday.	✗	
1B	We **have reported** the robbery to the police. / We **reported** the robbery to the police yesterday.	✓	1
2A	Mrs Kelly **managed** the accounts section for more than 12 years. She is due to retire soon.	✗	
2B	Mrs Kelly **has managed** the accounts section for more than 12 years. She is due to retire soon.	✓	2
3A	I **didn't give** your message to Jackie yet. She was not at school today.	✗	
3B	I **haven't given** your message to Jackie yet. She was not at school today.	✓	3
4A	I **hadn't time** for lunch today. I'll get some tea and sandwiches later.	✗	
4B	I **haven't had time** for lunch today. I'll get some tea and sandwiches later.	✓	4

GRAMMAR POINTS

1 We use the present perfect tense, like the simple past tense, to talk about completed actions. However, unlike the simple past tense which is used with definite time phrases, we do not state the exact time of an action with the present perfect tense.

EXAMPLES:

SIMPLE PAST TENSE

Patrick **conducted** a workshop for young working adults last week . *(completed action at definite time)*

PRESENT PERFECT TENSE

Patrick **has conducted** a workshop for young working adults. *(completed action with no exact time given)*

2 We use the present perfect tense with words like **since** and **for** to refer to an action that began in the past and is still going on at the point of speaking.

EXAMPLES:

SIMPLE PAST TENSE

I **studied** at this college for five years. *(I am no longer there.)*

I **was** in this college in 1998. *(I am no longer there.)*

PRESENT PERFECT TENSE

I **have studied** in this college for five years. *(I am still there.)*

I **have been** in this college since 1998. *(I joined the college in 1998 and I am still there.)*

3 We use the present perfect tense and not the simple past tense with adverbs of indefinite time such as **already** and **just** to show completed actions, and **yet** to show that an action is expected to happen but has not taken place at the point of speaking.

We use **never** and **ever** with the present perfect tense to refer to a time frame that began in the indefinite past and continues up to the present. We do not use these words with the simple past tense.

EXAMPLES:
They **have already signed** the agreement with our firm. *(completed action)*
Have you **ever noticed** the squirrels in our park? *(Did you notice them in the past?*
Have you noticed them up to now?)

4 We use the present perfect tense to refer to a time frame that began in the recent past and is not over yet at the point of speaking.

EXAMPLES:
I **haven't seen** Linda this week. She **has been** so busy. *(This week is not over yet.)*
I **haven't had** time for breakfast. I **have** only **had** a cup of coffee this morning. *(This morning is not over yet.)*

PRACTICE A Circle the numbers of the correct sentences.

1 Lily served as a volunteer nurse since 1990. She is going to leave the service this year.

2 We have been in this school for six years. We will be moving on to college after our final exams.

3 Ann did not write to us yet. She is probably busy with her new job.

4 The club committee has just had a brainwave. It is going to have a musical extravaganza to raise funds.

5 Colin has met me at the bank this morning and we decided to have lunch together.

6 This has been a hectic week for Joan. She has been swamped with meetings and reports.

7 James has received a scholarship and intends to do a course in software engineering.

8 Malcolm remained a recluse most of his life. It is only now that he has decided to come out and make friends.

9 The electrician has already repaired the lights so they should be working now.

10 They have sold their house last Tuesday and moved to a small apartment in the city centre.

YOUR SCORE

10

PRACTICE B Tick the correct verb forms to complete the sentences.

1 In the last decade, there [ ] has been / [ ] was a significant breakthrough in the treatment of some terminal illnesses.

2 Since I changed jobs, I [ ] found / [ ] have found more time to relax and enjoy my hobbies.

3 Sue [ ] has inherited / [ ] inherited a house from her uncle who died last May.

39

4 Paul may lose his car because he [ ] didn't pay / hasn't paid [ ] the instalments on his loan for the past three months.

5 Poverty today [ ] forced / has forced [ ] some parents to leave their families in order to work overseas.

6 We [ ] were hanging / have hung [ ] out the carpets to dry because they are damp from the rain.

7 Bobby's writing [ ] became / has become [ ] neater and more legible nowadays, compared to what it was before.

8 In the last hundred years, man [ ] achieved / has achieved [ ] great advances in the fields of science and technology.

9 High levels of air pollution in some major cities [ ] are resulting / have resulted [ ] in breathing difficulties and lung problems among some residents.

10 I [ ] observed / have observed [ ] many changes in social customs when I last visited your country.

PRACTICE *C* Fill in the blanks with the correct forms of the verbs in the brackets.

Recently, there (1) _____ (be) several meetings at our local community hall and I expect to attend several more. Until now we (2) _____ (use) the hall for occasional events but now we (3) _____ (want) to organise regular meetings for different groups in our community.

When we asked, some doctors and teachers (4) _____ (recommend) a preschool playgroup. They said that children who (5) _____ (experience) a playgroup often settle more easily in regular school. Already several parents (6) _____ (ask) us to keep places for their children.

This week, I (7) _____ (talk) to my grandparents and some of their friends about a group for retired people. They said they (8) _____ (never think) about meeting at the hall, but I hope they will consider the idea.

My friends and I (9) _____ (discuss) holding a regular youth evening. We (10) _____ (always want) a place where we could play table tennis and practise our music.

PRACTICE $\boxed{D}$ Rearrange the words to form correct sentences.

1 a — across — and — beauty — has — health — in — interest — of — surge — swept — the — world.

_____

_____

2 cause — failure — found — haven't — of — of — security — system — the — the — the — we — yet.

_____

_____

3 Alice — everything — for — getting — has — meeting — ready — spent — the — the — week — whole.

_____

_____

4 cinema — gone — have — last — month — only — out — since — the — they — to — twice.

Since last month, _____

_____

5 already — figures — for — for — has — he — last — poor — reprimanded — sales — the — us — year.

_____

_____ for last year.

PRACTICE $\boxed{E}$ Rewrite the sentences below and correct them.

1 Five years ago, the two countries have promised to work together to establish peace in the region.

_____

_____

2 The two motorcyclists have just broke traffic regulations by going against the lights.

_____

_____

3 I haven't make up my mind yet about which courses to do in college.

_____

4 Didn't you ever gone bungee jumping before?

_____

5 We never learn where our former colleagues are working now.

_____

UNIT 3.5 PAST PERFECT TENSE

Look at the **A** and **B** sentences below. Find out why **B** is correct and **A** is wrong in the **Grammar Points** section.

			GRAMMAR POINTS
1A	She **forgot** her appointment with me and had gone out for lunch when I arrived at her office.	✗	
1B	She **had forgotten** her appointment with me and had gone out for lunch when I arrived at her office.	✓	1
2A	He **already passed** the message to Tom when we called him last night.	✗	
2B	He **had already passed** the message to Tom when we called him last night.	✓	2
3A	The stranded travellers **never felt** so relieved in their entire lives as when they saw the rescue vehicle.	✗	
3B	The stranded travellers **had never felt** so relieved in their entire lives as when they saw the rescue vehicle.	✓	3

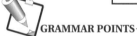GRAMMAR POINTS

1 When we refer to completed actions in the past, we can use different past tense forms to indicate what we mean.

EXAMPLES: SIMPLE PAST TENSE + SIMPLE PAST TENSE

As the U.S. stocks **rose**, the Asian market **rebounded**.

We use the past perfect tense for an action or situation that happened earlier, and the simple past tense for the action or situation that took place later.

EXAMPLES: PAST PERFECT TENSE + SIMPLE PAST TENSE

| The secretary **had prepared** all the reports | before the directors **arrived** for the meeting. |
| The situation **had** already **deteriorated** | when the two leaders **agreed** to peace talks. |

2 We use the past perfect tense with words like **already** and **just** to refer to actions which were completed before a specific time in the past.

EXAMPLES: Ann **had already walked** a hundred metres down the road when she **remembered** that she hadn't locked her front door. *(completed action before a specific time)*

We **had just had** our coffee break when we **met** some old friends outside the cafe.

3 We use the past perfect tense with time words and phrases such as **always** and **more than once** to refer to repeated actions in the past, **never** to refer to an action that had not taken place up to the point of speaking, and **yet** for an action that we expected to happen in the past but which had not taken place up to the point of speaking.

EXAMPLES: Our parents **had always coaxed** us to eat our vegetables when we were young.

The old janitor **had told** us **more than once** that the lifts were not functioning well but we had not paid attention.

The group **had never heard** of the famous scientists who Peter spoke about.

We **hadn't chosen** the venue for our weekend trip **yet** when a neighbour suggested the National Park.

PRACTICE *A* Tick the correct verb forms to complete the sentences.

1 At 8.00 p.m. last night, the residents in our housing estate | assembled / had assembled | to hear our parliamentary representative speak.

2 Joe and I | had sworn / have sworn | to keep this matter a secret from the rest of the group.

3 The suspects | already destroyed / had already destroyed | the files before the detectives arrived.

4 Paul | had just caught / has just caught | a glimpse of the distinguished visitor when the crowd pushed him aside.

5 We | have never said / never say | that the story you heard is untrue.

6 Angie | criticised / had criticised | the organisation for months before she saw any real change.

7 My brother is still on holiday. We | didn't hear / haven't heard | any details of the trip yet.

8 The television crew decided to hold a blood donation drive after they | have seen / had seen | the number of injured at the hospital.

9 Rescue helicopters | had searched / have searched | the whole area for the missing hikers for five hours before they finally found them huddled on the clifftop.

10 The children | asked / have asked | questions about the animals since their visit to the wildlife conservation centre.

YOUR SCORE

10

Fill in the blanks with the correct forms of the verbs in the brackets.

1 Everyone thought that James _____ (capture) the glorious colours of the sunset in his painting.

2 She _____ (not check) her e-mail yet to see if there are any messages for her.

3 Before the jury retired, the judge _____ (ask) them if they understood their duties.

4 The crowd _____ (grow) tired and restless after waiting all morning to see the mayor who appeared to be too busy to entertain them.

5 Ever since she was in high school, Betty _____ (always crave) to visit the Antarctic.

6 The slow economy _____ (force) many companies in the past few months to cut back on the numbers in their workforce.

7 Sarah _____ (never beg) for help from anyone before but last summer she needed everybody's assistance.

8 He _____ (type) his report when there was a sudden power failure.

9 The authorities _____ (not see) the damage illegal loggers have caused to the environment yet.

10 We _____ (just persuade) Dad to take us out for a meal when my mother announced that she preferred to eat at home.

YOUR SCORE

10

PRACTICE **C** Some of the verbs in the sentences are incorrect. Underline them and write the correct verbs in the boxes.

1 Alice just finished drawing cartoons on the blackboard when the teacher walked into the class.

2 Michael took my reference book by mistake this morning but he returned it to me just now.

3 The crowd outside the court protested loudly when the judge and the counsels walked out.

4 The little saplings that I had planted grew into tall trees by the time I came back to the old house many years later.

5 Mr Lim suffered from a serious illness for many years and was nursed by his daughter.

44

6 Political upheavals recently give rise to thousands of people fleeing to the safety of nations nearby.

7 I lose interest in reading this novel because it lacked depth so I returned it to the library.

8 Ann has always enjoyed travelling abroad since the time she was a little girl, but now she finds it stressful.

9 For years she had trusted Mr Cane to handle her estate until she discovered that he had swindled her.

10 Property values have fallen in this country because of a lack of investment capital.

YOUR SCORE
10

PRACTICE *D* Circle the letters of the sentences which are correct.

1 **A** I hadn't seen Jack for more than a month until I met him recently.
  B I didn't see Jack for more than a month until I met him recently.
  C I haven't seen Jack for more than a month.

2 **A** When Ted walked in, he looked different. He had grown a beard.
  B Ted looks different. He has grown a beard.
  C When Ted walked in, he looked different. He grew a beard.

3 **A** The boys never grumble about the long hours of practice before.
  B The boys have never grumbled about the long hours of practice before.
  C The boys had never grumbled about the long hours of practice before but now they want to see the coach.

4 **A** Shaz was just having her lunch when her friends came by for a visit.
  B Shaz had just had her lunch when her friends came by for a visit.
  C Shaz has just had her lunch when her friends came by for a visit.

5 **A** John had already driven to the intersection when he suddenly remembered that his briefcase was at home.
  B John already drove to the intersection when he suddenly remembered that his briefcase was at home.
  C John was already driving to the intersection when he suddenly remembered that his briefcase was at home.

YOUR SCORE
10

UNIT 3.6 PRESENT AND PAST PERFECT CONTINUOUS TENSES

Look at the **A** and **B** sentences below. Find out why **B** is correct and **A** is wrong in the **Grammar Points** section.

GRAMMAR POINTS

1A	We are thoroughly exhausted. We **are driving** all day and we need to rest.	✗	
1B	We are thoroughly exhausted. We **have been driving** all day and we need to rest.	✓	1
2A	Kelly **had been coughing** badly these past few days. She should go to the doctor's for a checkup.	✗	
2B	Kelly **has been coughing** badly these past few days. She should go to the doctor's for a checkup.	✓	2
3A	The department **had studied** the problem of flooding in the city for two months and has made its recommendations.	✗	
3B	The department **has been studying** the problem of flooding in the city for two months and has made its recommendations.	✓	3
4A	Laura **has been preparing** for her audition for weeks before they asked her to go for a screen test.	✗	
4B	Laura **had been preparing** for her audition for weeks before they asked her to go for a screen test.	✓	4

GRAMMAR POINTS

1 We use the present perfect continuous tense for an action or situation which began in the past and continues up to the point of speaking. The action may not be finished at this point.

We use the present perfect tense to refer to an action which began in the past and continues to the present. The action is finished at the point of speaking.

EXAMPLE: I **have been trying** to solve this physics problem for the past couple of hours. *(action is not finished)*

I **have tried** to solve this physics problem but I don't know how to do it. *(action of trying is over)*

2 We use the present perfect continuous tense to refer to a series of repeated actions or situations that began in the past and has continued to the present.

EXAMPLE: For the past three weeks, Sylvia and I **have been discussing** the final arrangements for the graduation dinner. *(certain times in the past three weeks, and action may or may not be finished)*

Sylvia and I **have already discussed** the final arrangements for the graduation dinner. *(action is finished)*

46

3 We use the present perfect continuous tense to refer to an action that is temporary in nature and that lasts for a short duration of time. We use the present perfect tense to refer to an action that is more permanent in nature and that lasts for a longer duration of time

EXAMPLE: I **have been practising** tennis every evening since the school holidays began.
(temporary action – shorter period of time)

I **have practised** tennis twice a week for the past two years.
(permanent action – longer duration of time)

4 We use the past perfect continuous tense to refer to an action which had been going on continuously up to that time in the past that we are talking about.

EXAMPLE: Mr Lee **had been managing** his factory for 25 years before he retired last year.

(continuous earlier action)

REMEMBER!

- The present perfect continuous tense is formed in this way:

  has / have + been + base form of verb + 'ing'

  EXAMPLES: has been giving
  have been criticising

- The past perfect continuous tense is formed in this way:

  had + been + base form of verb + 'ing'

  EXAMPLES: had been debating
  had been creating

PRACTICE *A* Underline the correct verb forms in the brackets.

1 Our clients (have been showing / have shown) great interest in the new product which we introduced just now.

2 The factory workers (had been requesting / had requested) a change in the work schedule since last year but the manager hasn't agreed to it.

3 My clothes look dirty and grimy. I (have been polishing / have polished) the car all afternoon.

4 Sandra was surprised to see her parents-in-law. She (hadn't expected / hasn't expected) them to visit.

5 The chairman's casual mention of reorganisation (had angered / have angered) the entire club because the members had already rejected the idea.

6 All the members (have been going / have gone) to a great deal of trouble to make the campaign a success and there has been a tremendous response from the public.

7 The landlord evicted two of the tenants last week. They (had been flouting / have been flouting) the house regulations for several months.

8 All motorists who (had violated / have violated) the traffic laws have to settle their fines as soon as possible.

9 Emma has just been informed about her new posting to Singapore. She (had been asking / has been asking) for a transfer for several months but there had been no reply until yesterday.

10 The residents in our housing area (had been appealing / have been appealing) for better lighting along our roads but the authorities haven't responded yet.

YOUR SCORE

10

1 The child has been crying for such a long time. The mother doesn't know what to do.

2 The government closed down some video arcades because they found that the owners had been breaking regulations.

3 We have been signing up for the basic computer course today.

4 Claire hasn't been sleeping well these last few weeks. She has been worried about the future.

5 He had been coming to see me about the house before I left for the office.

6 The report of the prince's marriage has been publishing in all the newspapers.

7 Mr Kim has been blaming himself for the accident which wrecked his car.

8 Flood waters inundated the coastal villages because it had been raining continuously for two days.

9 The customs officials have been inspecting our baggage. We are free to go now.

10 We had been expecting Mary to come but she had insisted on staying at home.

YOUR SCORE

/ 10

PRACTICE $\boxed{C}$ Fill in the blanks with the correct forms of the verbs in the brackets.

1 Lucy has misplaced her mobile phone. She _____ (look) for it all evening.

2 Rescue teams _____ (dive) underwater for the last two days in search of the car which was blown off the cliff on Monday morning.

3 We take this opportunity to thank everyone who _____ (put) in so much effort to make this excursion a success.

4 The kitchen was in a mess. The girls _____ (demonstrate) their new recipes to a large group of friends.

5 Chris _____ (already confirm) our hotel reservations long before we arrived in Osaka for our meeting.

6 Bad weather _____ (affect) all the flight schedules throughout this week and caused many passengers to be stranded.

7 Jennifer _____ (spend) long hours with children in the cancer unit of the hospital before she decided to take up medicine.

8 Our bags _____ (not arrive yet) when we disembarked and made our way to the immigration counter.

9 Concerned parents _____ (hold) meetings this month to discuss youth clubs in the area.

10 Keith _____ (plan) to come and see us before he left for his trip but he didn't have the time.

YOUR SCORE

/ 10

PRACTICE D Some of the verbs in the passage are incorrect. Underline them and write the correct verbs in the spaces.

No one knew exactly what (1) happened. There had been a deafening roar and the entire apartment block (2) had totter like a drunken sailor before it collapsed.

Rescue operations (3) have been underway since last night. Army engineers (4) have been using excavators to clear the rubble. Police (5) have bring in trained dogs to sniff out and locate people trapped under the debris. Paramedics (6) have been carrying survivors out on stretchers. Officials (7) had questioned witnesses the whole day to uncover the reasons behind the sudden collapse of the building. The government (8) has announced that an official enquiry will be set up immediately to investigate the disaster.

Meanwhile, family members and friends (9) have been gathering around the area and waiting anxiously. Some left after they (10) have received good or bad news.

_____   _____
_____   _____
_____   _____

PRACTICE E Rearrange the words to form correct sentences.

1 been — David — has — heavily — past — smoking — these — two — weeks.

David _____

2 bazaar — been — charity — for — for — has — months — preparing — the — the — committee.

The committee_____

_____

3 been — both — counsels — had — issuing — judge — strict — the — the — to — throughout — trial — warnings.

The judge _____

_____

4 all — been — but — couldn't — crowd — find — for — had — her — in — looking — morning — Sheila — the — we.

_____

_____ couldn't find her in the crowd.

5 all — and — baking — because — been — for — had — I — morning — Mariko — pies — sale — the — tired — we — were.

Mariko and I _____

_____

UNIT 3.7 SIMPLE FUTURE AND FUTURE CONTINUOUS TENSES

Look at the **A** and **B** sentences below. Find out why **B** is correct and **A** is wrong in the **Grammar Points** section.

GRAMMAR POINTS

				GRAMMAR POINTS
1A	At dawn tomorrow, the hurricane **will struck** the coast with winds of 100 miles per hour.	✗		
1B	At dawn tomorrow, the hurricane **will strike** the coast with winds of 100 miles per hour.	✓	1	
2A	Max **was going to organised** the dinner for this week but he couldn't get the venue he wanted.	✗		
2B	Max **was going to organise** the dinner for this week but he couldn't get the venue he wanted.	✓	2	
3A	Aaron **will be give** a speech before he proposes the toast at the wedding tonight.	✗		
3B	Aaron **will be giving** a speech before he proposes the toast at the wedding tonight.	✓	3	
4A	Janet **be joining** us for lunch as usual at the club this Friday.	✗		
4B	Janet **will be joining** us for lunch as usual at the club this Friday.	✓	4	

GRAMMAR POINTS

1   We use the future tense for actions or events that will happen in the future. We use the future tense with **will** to make predictions, to talk about actions which we cannot control or to refer to something which we decide to do at the time of speaking.

    EXAMPLES: John **will retire** as a senior engineer with the firm at the end of the year. *(future action)*

            Asha **will** certainly **win** the beauty contest this year. She is not only beautiful but has a dynamic personality as well. *(prediction)*

            I **will explain** it to you, Joan. *(intention to do something at the time of speaking)*

2   We use the verb 'to be' + **going to** + base form of verb for actions which we have already planned to do in the future and for events in the future.

     For actions which we had planned to do in the past but which did not occur, we use **was / were** + **going to** + base form of verb .

EXAMPLES: The prime minister **is going to open** the Asia Pacific Women Entrepreneur's conference this Thursday.   *(event planned for the future)*

Many industrial workers **are going to lose** their jobs unless the economic situation improves.   *(event which is likely to happen)*

Hilda **was going to come** shopping with me this morning but she felt ill and decided to stay at home.   *(planned action which did not happen)*

3   We use the future continuous tense to refer to actions or situations which will be going on at a certain time in the future.

EXAMPLE: They **will be announcing** the results of the elections just after 6 a.m. tomorrow.

4   We use the future continuous tense to refer to actions or situations in the future which have already been planned or which take place regularly.

EXAMPLES: The models **will be displaying** the summer collection at the international show in Paris this week.   *(planned action for the future)*

My whole family **will be participating** in the cross-country run as we do every year. *(regular action)*

REMEMBER!

- The future continuous tense is formed in this way:

  will be + base form of verb + 'ing'

  EXAMPLE: The Andersons **will be leaving** for the United Kingdom this Saturday.

- The future and future continuous tense can be formed using **shall** for **I** and **we** although it is more common to use **will** for both nouns and pronouns.

  EXAMPLE: I **shall** / **will be waiting** for you outside the café so don't be late.

PRACTICE *A*   Underline the correct verb forms in the brackets.

1   This birthday card (is assuring / will assure) Mary that I haven't forgotten about her.

2   We have to make our flight reservations early as hundreds of people (going to be leaving / will be leaving) for their holidays during the festive period.

3   The news of his promotion to a managerial position (is going to be / will being) a pleasant surprise for Bill.

4   This story set in the days of World War II (has captured / will capture) the imagination of all those who have read it.

5   Christine (is participated / will be participating) in the national judo championships as the youngest competitor.

6   Ann (had realised / realised) that she had made a mistake in going to the town centre when she saw that the shops were very expensive.

7   The committee (is going to choose / will be chosen) the team which will climb Mount Kinabalu next May.

8   The people (are awaiting / will awaiting) news of what really happened at the nuclear plant.

9   Time (had passed / will pass) so quickly that before you know it, we will see you again.

10   Tom (is going to coming / will be coming) to the sports complex this evening for a game of tennis with me.

YOUR SCORE
10

PRACTICE **B** Circle the numbers of the sentences which are correct.

1 The manager has reorganised the marketing department in an effort to cut losses.

2 The fighter jets are going to using a different route to fly into enemy territory.

3 I will be joining Steven tonight as I often do, to work on our term papers together.

4 Sue will excel in the business world. She is focused and determined to achieve her ambition.

5 Mrs Sim be so pleased to know that her proposals to improve the library facilities have been accepted by the council.

6 Laila is going to taking up a beauty course while waiting for her final exam results.

7 I've told Joe many times to tidy up his room but he tells me every time that he will do it after he has completed his reports.

8 Motorists will lined up to fill their tanks before the rise in petrol prices next week.

9 Angie and Tony are going to bought an old-fashioned farmhouse in the countryside.

YOUR SCORE

10

10 Property values in the city will spiral upwards as land becomes more scarce.

PRACTICE **C** Fill in the blanks with suitable words in the box.

had loved	hadn't realised	haven't yet decided	
was going to take up	will give	will have	will leave
will be reaching	won't be facing	will be studying	

I (1) _____ a major milestone in my life soon. I (2) _____ school to move on to the next phase — higher education.

With so many choices offered to school leavers, I (3) _____ what I would really like to do. My parents suggested that I go on to college. I think I (4) _____ it some serious thought. Earlier, when I was in the lower class, I (5) _____ designing. I believed that I (6) _____ architecture or graphic design. However, since then, my interests have been drawn towards business and e-commerce. I (7) _____ how difficult it is to make a decision. Fortunately, I (8) _____ the necessity of selecting a career right now. I (9) _____ a range of subjects when I enter college. In two years' time, I (10) _____ a clearer picture of the course of study I need to pursue the career I want.

YOUR SCORE

10

PRACTICE **D** Rewrite the sentences below correctly.

1 A few years back, my uncle is going to set up his own business but he didn't have sufficient capital.

_____

_____

2 In a worldwide recession, developing countries be hit the hardest because of falling demand for their exports.

_____

_____

3 I return the money I owe you as soon as I receive my salary at the end of the month.

_____

_____

4 Jasmine be expecting us to help her run the games stall at the funfair this Saturday.

_____

_____

5 I know it going to rain this afternoon. The sky is overcast and gloomy.

_____

YOUR SCORE
10

_____

PRACTICE _E_   Rearrange the words to form correct sentences.

1 be — cost — council — expected — expressway — far — more — new — of — than — the — the — the — will.

The cost _____

_____

2 by — company — going — implementing — increase — is — methods — modern — productivity — the — to — training.

_____

_____ modern training methods.

3 at — but — dinner — fell — going — ill — last — Maria — night — perform — she — suddenly — the — to — was.

Maria _____

_____

4 are — as — children — don't — have — I — make — safe — sure — the — to — will — worry — you.

You _____

_____

5 be — charge —during — games — hockey — in — in—Manila — Ranjit — team — the — the — of — will.

Ranjit _____

YOUR SCORE
10

_____

UNIT 3.8 FUTURE PERFECT AND FUTURE PERFECT CONTINUOUS TENSES

Look at the **A** and **B** sentences below. Find out why **B** is correct and **A** is wrong in the **Grammar Points** section.

			GRAMMAR POINTS
1A	By the end of August, the estate owners **will be settled** their labour problems.	✗	
1B	By the end of August, the estate owners **will have settled** their labour problems.	✓	1
2A	The new batch of trainees **will have just join** the course in two weeks' time.	✗	
2B	The new batch of trainees **will have just joined** the course in two weeks' time.	✓	2
3A	Mrs O' Brien **has been working** here for five years by the end of this month.	✗	
3B	Mrs O' Brien **will have been working** here for five years by the end of this month.	✓	3

GRAMMAR POINTS

1 We use the future perfect tense to refer to actions or situations which will be completed by a definite time in the future.

EXAMPLE: The mechanic **will have serviced** my car by Wednesday.

2 We use the words **already** and **just** with the future perfect tense to refer to actions or situations which will be finished by an approximate time in the future.

EXAMPLES:

By next week, Carl **will have already negotiated** the price of the house with the estate agent.

I **will have just entered** the university next April when my sister graduates.

> **REMEMBER!**
> ■ The future perfect tense is formed in this way:
> **will have** + past participle of verb
> EXAMPLES: will have gone
> will have calculated

3 We use the future perfect continuous tense when we want to refer to the duration of an action or an event at a definite time in the future. We usually use adverbs of duration and time to state how long the action will last and when it will take place.

EXAMPLE:

She **will have been studying** in Glasgow for three years by next September.

adverb of duration   adverb of time

> **REMEMBER!**
> ■ The future perfect continuous tense is formed in this way:
> **will have** + **been** + past participle of verb + 'ing'
> EXAMPLES: will have been raining
> will have been driving

Underline the correct verb forms in the brackets.

1 They (have broken / will have broken) the hostel rules by not informing the manager about the damage to the windows just now.

2 By three o'clock, we (were waiting / will have been waiting) for more than an hour for our school bus.

3 The young men whose names are on the memorial stone (sacrificed / will have sacrificed) their lives in World War II.

4 Sally (had already received / will have already received) the note we sent her by this afternoon.

5 By next Monday, Tim (has been staying / will have been staying) with us for four months.

6 Dad (was shocked / will have been shocked) to hear about the train crash and rushed home to find out whether we were safe.

7 By December, our grandparents (are managing / will have been managing) their grocery store for 25 years.

8 Vicki is not at home. She (had just gone / has just gone) to the salon to have a manicure.

9 Kay (has been helping / will have been helping) Dr Smith in the clinic for five years by next March.

10 We (have submitted / will be submitting) our recommendations regarding the public transport system to the authorities this Friday.

YOUR SCORE

10

Tick the sentences that are correct.

1 The price of eggs will have risen sharply by next week because of a supply problem.

2 The management committee has review the tenant's suggestions concerning security in the apartment building.

3 After a two-year delay, the government will have finally reorganized the public library system by September.

4 Samuel will represent the country as part of the junior bowling team at the Asian Games.

5 Helen will have been running the kindergarten for more than 10 years by the time she retires in January.

6 Everyone in the audience have been expecting the play to end on a dramatic note but they were disappointed.

7 Joe will have taken up his new appointment in Frankfurt by the end of the month.

8 Jerry and I will been working as journalists with the National Daily for five years by the end of next week.

9 We had already make the hotel reservations for our stay in Bangalore when we learnt that our trip was postponed.

10 Aunt Lily will have bake an apple pie for tea so let's not be late.

YOUR SCORE

10

PRACTICE **C** Fill in the blanks with suitable words in the box.

will have agreed	have already visited	have been constructing
will have been lecturing	had not heard	will have occupied ordered
will have played	will have reached	will have spoken

1 I _____ from Debra for more than a year when suddenly she called me today.

2 The convoy of military vehicles _____ the border crossing by this afternoon so we have to move quickly to avoid them.

3 At the end of this term, Shane _____ at our college for just under two years.

4 We won't get a good vantage point to watch the parade. The early birds _____ _____ the best seats by now.

5 Hundreds of people _____ the computer fair at the Trade Centre this morning.

6 The airlines probably _____ to an amicable settlement with the striking pilots by tomorrow.

7 The mayor just now _____ the mass evacuation of the villages closest to the active volcano.

8 By the end of the competition tonight, the teams _____ on the topic of equality of the sexes for the third time.

9 They _____ the suspension bridge over the delta for the last three years.

10 At the end of this season, our university _____ host to the inter-varsity games for the second time in four years.

YOUR SCORE
10

PRACTICE **D** Rearrange the words to form correct sentences.

1 been — for — have — in — November — our — school — she — teaching — this — twenty — will — years.

She _____

_____

2 already — Angela — bank — become — by — have — June — manager — of — senior — the — the — will.

Angela _____

_____

56

3 and — brought — flooding — have — Indian — monsoons — rain — subcontinent — the — the — to — torrential.

The monsoons _____

_____

4 by — cabin — cold — faces — frozen — have — in — our — reach — the — this — time — we — will.

Our faces _____

_____

5 after — already — bed — everyone — get — gone — have — home — movie — the — to — we — will — when.

When we get home _____

_____

PRACTICE *E* Rewrite the sentences below correctly.

1 Miss Cole been working as the executive secretary to the director for five years by this March.

_____

_____

2 The salaries commission will meet next week. We will be gather more information about the expected pay rise by then.

_____

_____

3 The accounts department will already check the figures before submitting the reports next Monday.

_____

_____

4 The defence lawyers have request for a postponement of the trial until they get an expert medical opinion.

_____

_____

5 The anti-vice squad had waiting all night for their man to give the signal before arresting the drugs syndicate.

_____

_____

UNIT 3.9 CONDITIONALS – THE PRESENT TENSE

Look at the **A** and **B** sentences below. Find out why **B** is correct and **A** is wrong in the **Grammar Points** section.

GRAMMAR POINTS

CHECKPOINT

1A	If there **will be** a sudden downpour which lasts for hours, it causes flash floods in low-lying areas.	✗	
1B	If there **is** a sudden downpour which lasts for hours, it causes flash floods in low-lying areas.	✓	1
2A	Linda **is often taking** her children swimming in the afternoon if she has free time.	✗	
2B	Linda **often takes** her children swimming in the afternoon if she has free time.	✓	2
3A	If you insist on breaking hostel regulations, I **send** you to the warden.	✗	
3B	If you insist on breaking hostel regulations, I **will send** you to the warden.	✓	3
4A	Unless they **don't meet** the management to talk things over, they will not solve the dispute.	✗	
4B	Unless they **meet** the management to talk things over, they will not solve the dispute.	✓	4

GRAMMAR POINTS

1 When we refer to general truths or facts, we can use the simple present tense both in the **if** clause and in the main clause.

EXAMPLES:

PRESENT TENSE	+	PRESENT TENSE
If we **dip** a piece of litmus paper in acid,	+	it **turns** blue. *(general truth)*
Water **boils**	+	if we **heat** it to a temperature of 100°C. *(fact)*

2 We can use the simple present tense in the **if** clause and also in the main clause when we refer to actions that take place regularly.

EXAMPLE:

PRESENT TENSE	+	PRESENT TENSE
Dad always **reads** the papers before leaving for the office	+	if he **wakes** up early.

3 When we refer to an action or an event which will probably happen in the future, make a promise, or give a warning, we can use the simple present tense in the **if** clause and the simple future tense in the main clause.

PRESENT TENSE   +   FUTURE TENSE

If Claire **maintains** her efficient performance,	+	she **will get** a promotion soon. *(possible action)*
If I **finish** my classes before five this evening,	+	I **will join** you for dinner. *(promise)*
If you **don't give** me a good reason for not doing the work,	+	I **will complain** to the manager. *(to give a warning)*

Note that it is the simple present tense and not the future tense that is most often used in the **if** clause.

4 We use the word **unless** (meaning 'if not') with a positive present tense verb, and the simple future tense with **will** in the main clause when we issue a warning or state a condition before an action can take place.

EXAMPLES: Unless + POSITIVE PRESENT TENSE   +   SIMPLE FUTURE TENSE

Unless you **agree** to these terms,	+	we **will** not **let** you go. *(threat or warning)*
Unless we **leave** now,	+	we **will miss** our train. *(stating a condition before an action can happen)*

> **REMEMBER!**
> ■ **Even if** is used in conditional sentences to mean 'it doesn't matter if'.
> EXAMPLE: I **will go** on a tour of Europe next year even if none of you want to come with me.

PRACTICE *A*   Circle the letters of the correct sentences.

1 **A**   If I will not catch the seven o'clock bus every morning, I will be late for school.
   B   If I don't catch the seven o'clock bus every morning, I will be late for school.
   C   If I catch the seven o'clock bus every morning, I won't be late for school.

2 **A**   I'll come for your birthday party if Dad gives me a lift.
   B   I come for your birthday party if Dad gives me a lift.
   C   I will coming for your birthday party if Dad gives me a lift.

3 **A**   If you will continue to practise, I think you will become a good pianist.
   B   If you continue to practise, I think you will become a good pianist.
   C   I think you will become a good pianist if you are continue to practise.

4 **A**   More people went for walks in the evenings if the weather is good.
   B   More people will go for walks in the evenings if the weather is good.
   C   If the weather is good, more people will go for walks in the evenings.

5 **A**   If our water supply is contaminated, it leads to serious health problems.
   B   If our water supply is contaminated, it will be leading to serious health problems.
   C   If our water supply will be contaminated, it will lead to serious health problems.

6 A We won't vote in this election unless our candidate listens to what we say.

   B We not vote in this election unless the candidate listens to what we say.

   C We will vote in this election if the candidate listens to what we say.

7 A If my father is free, he will usually takes us out for dinner on Sundays.

   B If my father is free, he will usually take us out for dinner on Sundays.

   C If my father is free, he take us out for dinner on Sundays.

PRACTICE *B*   Underline the correct verb forms in the brackets.

1 If rainwater (seeps / will seep) through limestone cliffs, it dissolves the limestone to form stalactites and stalagmites.

2 Our visitor (laughs / will laugh) if she sees the funny posters at the station.

3 If a ferry is overloaded, it (capsize / will capsize) on rough seas.

4 Unless the town council implements water conservation measures, city dwellers (experience / will experience) a severe water shortage.

5 Jessie will go there with her father if he (takes / will take) a day's holiday.

6 You should be more tactful. Otherwise, you (hurt / will hurt) someone's feelings.

7 Kelly has to slow down and relax. If she (persist / persists) in working all the time, it will affect her health.

8 If Dave (don't / won't) drive more carefully, he will probably cause an accident.

9 The president will declare a state of emergency in the country unless the rioting and bloodshed (ends / will end) .

10 There is a huge crowd of people watching the grand prix. If there (is / will be) any kind of accident, many spectators will be injured.

PRACTICE *C*   Complete the sentences with suitable words in the box.

if she comes home before her mother	the manager will be furious
if there is any sign of an enemy attack	unless we improve the entertainment facilities in the town
if the dog is disobedient	
if you listen attentively	unless they give us some money
it will usually stalk a weak and helpless member of the herd	you know that winter is approaching
	you will expose them to danger

1 Unless you keep matches and lighters out of reach of children, _____

_____

2 If a lioness is out on a hunt, _____

_____

3 Sandra often cooks dinner for the family _____

_____

4 The army will be on full alert _____

_____

5 People will stay at home _____

_____

6 _____

_____ he will be sent to his kennel.

7 _____

_____ if you interrupt the meeting at this point.

8 At dawn, you will hear the singing of birds and the hum of cicadas _____

_____

9 If the trees start to lose their leaves and it is cold in the mornings, _____

_____

10 _____

_____ , we won't be able to buy any of the items on sale.

YOUR SCORE

10

PRACTICE **D** Rewrite the sentences below correctly.

1 That tree is leaning precariously to one side. If there is a strong wind, it is falling on our rooftop.

_____

_____

2 The organisers of the charity game afternoon are wondering what happened to us unless we phone them to explain.

_____

_____

3 If you will wish to continue with this discussion ,you have to listen to our point of view.

_____

4 If deforestation proceeds at the present rate, it have an adverse effect on the environment.

_____

_____

5 If we listen to the village elders, we are inherit a wealth of knowledge from them.

_____

_____

YOUR SCORE

10

61

Look at the **A** and **B** sentences below. Find out why **B** is correct and **A** is wrong in the **Grammar Points** section.

				GRAMMAR POINTS
1A	If I had enough money, I **travel** to places I have always dreamed of seeing.	✗		
1B	If I had enough money, I **would travel** to places I have always dreamed of seeing.	✓		1
2A	If they **giving** you the chance to work in Geneva, you should accept it.	✗		
2B	If they **gave** you the chance to work in Geneva, you should accept it.	✓		2
3A	Tom **would never get** into such trouble with the directors if you had explained the situation.	✗		
3B	Tom **would never have got** into such trouble with the directors if you had explained the situation.	✓		3
4A	Mrs Heng wishes she **can afford** a new car to replace the old model she drives.	✗		
4B	Mrs Heng wishes she **could afford** a new car to replace the old model she drives.	✓		4

GRAMMAR POINTS

1   We use the simple past tense or the past continuous tense in the **if** clause, and **would** with the base form of the verb in the main clause to refer to actions or situations which are imaginary or for situations which are impossible.

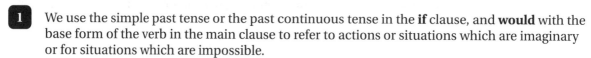

EXAMPLES: Simple Past Tense   + **would** + base form of verb

If I **owned** this beautiful mansion,   + I **would have** a large pool on the top floor to relax in and enjoy the view. *(imaginary)*

If I **were** the president,   + I **would allocate** more money to help the poor and needy. *(impossible situation)*

Note: We can also use other modal verbs like **could**, **might** and **should** in place of **would**.

2   We use the simple past tense in the **if** clause and **would** with the base form of the verb in the main clause when we give or ask for advice.

EXAMPLES: Simple Past Tense   + **would** (or other modal) + base form of verb

If the buyers **offered** you a good price for the house,   + you **should sell** it. *(offer advice)*

If you **were** in my position,   + what **would** you **do**? *(ask for advice)*

3 We use the past perfect tense in the **if** clause and the perfect conditional **would have** with the past participle of the verb in the main clause to refer to actions which never took place or results which would have been achieved if the actions had taken place.

EXAMPLES: Past Perfect Tense   + **would have** + past participle of verb

If we **hadn't been** so busy at the office,   + we **would have come** to see you in hospital. *(action never took place)*

If our business partners **had been** honest,   + our company **would** not **have lost** so much money. *(what the result might have been if the action had taken place)*

4 We use **wish + simple past tense** to refer to an imaginary situation or event which we would like to happen now.

EXAMPLE: I **wish** I **was** tall and slim so I could wear those elegant suits.

(wish + simple past tense)

When we want to refer to an event in the past which we think should have turned out differently, we use **wish + past perfect tense** .

EXAMPLE: We **wish** we **had remembered** to buy a birthday gift for Anne last week.
                          (we didn't buy a gift because we forgot)

(wish + past perfect tense)

PRACTICE **A**   Circle the numbers of the sentences which are correct.

1 If he had sufficient funds, he would set up a home for abused children.

2 If I am you, I would postpone the wedding until Dad recovers from his illness.

3 The second team could have won the match if they had had more stamina.

4 Developing countries will progress rapidly if they had effective economic planning.

5 I wish we reported to the personnel manager about the problems last week.

6 Jason would have been surprised if he had seen the letter the income tax authorities had sent him.

7 We would have gladly helped with you if you had asked for our support.

8 The logs would have fell from the lorry if an alert motorist hadn't informed the driver of the danger.

9 If Joan were more thrifty, she will put aside enough money to buy a car.

10 If James had spent more time with his family, his children might have heard more about about their family's history.

YOUR SCORE

10

PRACTICE **B**   Underline the correct verb forms in the brackets.

1 If there had been a jam on the highway, we (would be / would have been) late for the reception.

2 If people of different backgrounds (had learned / learned) to live in harmony, we would have a happier society.

3 Mark (would tell / would have told) Sarah of his admiration for her tennis skills if he had not been so shy.

4 If I were Janet I (fought / would fight) for freedom of expression in my newspaper column.

5 I wish I (am / were) more organised and meticulous in my work.

6 Julie (would come / would have come) to the party if she had the free time.

7 He (will become / would become) the first athlete to win all the track and field events if he won the 200-metre hurdles.

8 If you (woke / had woken) me up earlier, we would not have missed the train.

9 The doctors (would not postpone / would not have postponed) the operation if there had been three compatible blood donors.

10 The crowd would have been terribly disappointed if their favourite stars (hadn't appeared / wouldn't appear) for the concert.

YOUR SCORE
/ 10

PRACTICE *C* Fill in the blanks with the correct forms of the verbs in the brackets.

1 If the workmen had waited for instructions from the supervisor, they _____ (do) a better job.

2 Tessa would protest if she _____ (know) that she was almost chosen to represent our group at a public debate.

3 The world would _____ (be) a much more interesting place if animals talked.

4 If the mechanic _____ (work) on my car all day yesterday, it would have been ready by now.

5 If I _____ (be) the education minister, I would propose that schools commence with lessons at nine in the morning.

6 If man respected the environment, we _____ (not suffer) the effects of pollution.

7 I wish we _____ (buy) more food for our trip last night. Somehow the quantity doesn't seem enough for our four-day stay.

8 We _____ (reach) the island resort by now if we had taken the coastal road instead of the busy expressway.

9 If the board _____ (grant) her the scholarship, Barbara would do her best to achieve all that was expected of her.

10 Kate wishes she _____ (have) a more adventurous spirit like her sister Megan.

YOUR SCORE
/ 10

PRACTICE *D* Some of the sentences below contain incorrect verb forms. Underline them and write the correct verbs in the boxes provided.

1 Those people would win their independence by now if they had taken a united stand against their rulers.

2 I wish I had the patience my mother has to sew beautiful quilts.

3 The women of our great-grandmothers' time would be utterly amazed if they see the fashions of today.

4 I would have forgot this unfortunate incident if I were you.

5 If that heavy crane fell , it would do a great deal of damage.

6 If Sally bought this rare antique vase, she would have made a wise investment.

7 Household chores would be so much lighter if we had robots to do the work.

8 We wish we notice that the lady in the stationary car had required medical attention.

9 The air control tower should have advised the pilot to delay take-off if the weather had been so bad.

10 Jane would be pleasantly surprised if we took her out for dinner on her birthday.

YOUR SCORE
10

PRACTICE *E* Rewrite the sentences below without changing the meaning. Use the given words and make changes to the tense of the verbs where necessary.

1 If Tom were here, he would know what was wrong with the car.

If Tom had been here _____

2 The distinguished visitors would have been delighted if they had watched the tribal dances.

The distinguished visitors would be delighted _____

_____

3 I wish I had understood this problem. Then I would have been able to help you.

_____

_____ . Then I would be able to help you.

4 Sue might remember the password if you reminded her earlier.

Sue might have remembered _____

5 If the prosecution lawyers agreed, we would call the children to be witnesses.

If the prosecution lawyers had agreed _____

YOUR SCORE
10

_____

65

UNIT 4.1 ACTIVE AND PASSIVE VOICE

> tense and agreement, verbs with two objects, the use of **it**

Look at the **A** and **B** sentences below. Find out why **B** is correct and **A** is wrong in the **Grammar Points** section.

GRAMMAR POINTS

				GRAMMAR POINTS
1A	Active voice :	Simon teaches some of the club members watercolour painting.		
	Passive voice :	Some of the club members **is taught** watercolour painting by Simon.	✗	
1B	Active voice :	Simon teaches some of the club members watercolour painting.		
	Passive voice :	Some of the club members **are taught** watercolour painting by Simon.	✓	1
2A	Active voice :	The company gave us a variety of books for the library.		
	Passive voice :	We **were giving** a variety of books for the library by the company.	✗	
		A variety of books **were given** to us for the library by the company.	✗	
2B	Active voice :	The company gave us a variety of books for the library.		
	Passive voice :	We **were given** a variety of books for the library by the company.	✓	2
		A variety of books **was given** to us for the library by the company.	✓	
3A	Active voice :	People say that James is a brilliant lawyer.		
	Passive voice :	It **is say** that James is a brilliant lawyer.	✗	
		That James is a brilliant lawyer **say by people**.	✗	
3B	Active voice :	People say that James is a brilliant lawyer.		
	Passive voice :	It **is said** that James is a brilliant lawyer.	✓	3

GRAMMAR POINTS

1   When we change a sentence from the active voice to the passive voice, the tense of the verb has to remain the same and the verb has to agree with the subject in number.

EXAMPLE: The coach always **encourages** the children to practise different swimming strokes.

     (subject)   (active voice, present tense verb)

      The children **are encouraged** to practise different swimming strokes by the coach.

     (subject)   (passive voice, present tense verb)

2 When a verb in the active voice takes a direct and an indirect object, we can have two sentences with two different subjects in the passive voice.

EXAMPLE: My parents **sent** me food parcels regularly when I was studying overseas.

(active voice, past tense verb) (indirect object) (direct object)

I **was sent** food parcels regularly by my parents when I was studying overseas.

(passive voice, past tense verb)

Food parcels **were sent** to me regularly by my parents when I was studying overseas.

(passive voice, past tense verb)

Note: It is more common to begin with the person rather than the thing in the passive voice.

3 We use **it + the passive verb** when we refer to what people in general believe, feel or think about someone or something.

EXAMPLE: Everyone **predicts** that there will be a downturn in the economic situation.

(active voice, present tense verb)

It **is predicted** that there will be a downturn in the economic situation.

(passive voice, present tense verb)

PRACTICE *A* Fill in the blanks with the active or passive form of the verbs in the brackets.

1 It _____ (believe) that the prices of precious metals will fall soon.

2 We _____ (show) how to make batik prints with the materials we were given.

3 Brian _____ (select) as the new chairman by the committee.

4 Many people _____ (think) that the present system of education needs to be modified.

5 Tasha _____ (welcome) by close friends and relatives at the airport.

6 Paul _____ (diagnose) as suffering from arthritis after his knee began to hurt.

7 In my country, landslides often _____ (cause) the destruction of homes and crops.

8 It _____ (suggest) last week that a special fund be set up to give financial help to the needy in this city.

9 We _____ (provide) with accommodation when we go on our overseas assignment next Friday.

10 A children's home _____ (set up) in our area last month.

YOUR SCORE

10

PRACTICE $\boxed{B}$ Circle the letters of the correct sentences. There may be more than one answer for each question.

1 A The houses in the low-lying areas affected by the flood.
   B The flood affected the houses in the low-lying areas.
   C The houses in the low-lying areas were affected by the flood.

2 A Most of our old furniture will be sold at the garage sale on Sunday.
   B Most of our old furniture will be selling at the garage sale on Sunday.
   C We will sell most of our old furniture at the garage sale on Sunday.

3 A The landlord warned the tenants about their noisy behaviour.
   B The tenants was warned about their noisy behaviour by the landlord.
   C The tenants were warned about their noisy behaviour by the landlord.

4 A We will see a lower rate of growth in the next few years say by people.
   B People say that we will see a lower rate of growth in the next few years.
   C It was say that we will see a lower rate of growth in the next few years.

5 A Mike offered the top post in the personnel department.
   B They offered Mike the top post in the personnel department.
   C Mike was offered the top post in the personnel department.

6 A The telephone company sent us a reminder that we had not paid the bill.
   B We sent a reminder by the telephone company that we had not paid the bill.
   C We were send a reminder by the telephone company that we had not paid the bill.

YOUR SCORE / 10

PRACTICE $\boxed{C}$ Some of the verb forms underlined are incorrect. Write the correct verbs in the boxes.

1 Several houses <u>shaken</u> when tremors hit the mountain resort.

2 A high wall <u>was built</u> around the compound to keep out intruders.

3 Pearl S. Buck <u>wrote</u> books based on her experiences in China.

4 It <u>is believe</u> that peace between the two nations is possible.

5 All fears <u>were forgotten</u> when the children saw the toys in a corner of the clinic.

6 These richly beaded costumes <u>are worn</u> by the dancers when they perform.

7 Angela <u>born</u> in London but raised in Japan.

8 People <u>saying</u> that the company will be taken over by a foreign group.

9 The news of her transfer <u>shock</u> Jill very much.

10 Farmers in this region <u>grow</u> a variety of grapes both for the local wine industry as well as for export.

YOUR SCORE / 10

68

PRACTICE `D`   Rearrange the words to form correct sentences in the active or passive voice.

1 be — curb — drink-driving — expected — is — it — laws — new — passed — that — to — will.

It _____

_____

2 a — as — car — didn't — have — home — I — lift — me — my — offered — Sarah.

Sarah _____

_____

3 be — discussed — extension — for — new — next — plans — the — week — will.

Plans _____

_____

4 accepted — by — for — hotel's — improving — manager — services — suggestions — the — the — were.

Suggestions _____

_____

5 lawyer — murder — questioned — regarding — the — the — the — two — witnesses.

The lawyer _____

_____

YOUR SCORE /10

PRACTICE `E`   Rewrite the following passage in the passive voice.

People generally think that Angie is extremely good at organisation and decision-making. She acquired these skills during her six years as a junior executive at the firm. Her bosses noted her sound decisions and her efficiency. They promoted her to office manager in her seventh year at the firm. She runs the office with clockwork precision. She solves problems quickly and firmly. The rest of the staff respect her because of her fairness, warmth and honesty.

It is _____

_____

_____

_____

_____

_____

_____

_____

YOUR SCORE /10

UNIT 4.2 ACTIVE AND PASSIVE VOICE

passive infinitive, passive + 'ing' form, adverbs

Look at the **A** and **B** sentences below. Find out why **B** is correct and **A** is wrong in the **Grammar Points** section.

GRAMMAR
POINTS

 **CH**ECKPOINT

1A	Elaine is going **to transferred** to the Bangkok branch of the company soon.	✗	
1B	Elaine is going **to be transferred** to the Bangkok branch of the company soon.	✓	1
2A	We **enjoy been taken** to visit all the popular attractions in this city.	✗	
2B	We **enjoy being taken** to visit all the popular attractions in this city.	✓	2
3A	That documentary **never has been shown** in this part of the world.	✗	
3B	That documentary **has never been shown** in this part of the world.	✓	3

GRAMMAR POINTS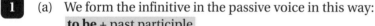

1   (a) We form the infinitive in the passive voice in this way:
    to be + past participle

    EXAMPLE: *active verb:* to offer
                   Victor wants **to offer** Tom a job in his studio.

                 passive verb: to be offered
                 Ming hopes **to be offered** a scholarship to study abroad.

    (b) We often use the passive infinitive after verbs such as **are to**, **have to**, **going to**, **hope to**, **need to**, **want to** and **would like to**. But we drop the **to** in front of the infinitive.
    EXAMPLES:
    Joanne **doesn't want to** ~~to~~ **be involved** in the musical presentation.
    They **have to** ~~to~~ **be reminded** that the closing date for the loan application is 1st June.

2   We form the passive voice of the 'ing' form by adding
    being + past participle after a finite verb.

    EXAMPLE:

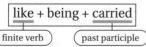

                The child **likes being carried** and cries when she is put in the pram.

> **REMEMBER!**
> - The following verbs are usually used with the passive 'ing' form:
>
> | | | |
> |----|----|----|
> | dislike | enjoy | hate |
> | like | love | prefer |
> | remember | | |

3 When we use adverbs of time, manner or frequency in the passive voice, we usually place them after the first word in a verb made up of two or more words.

EXAMPLES:

We | are **always** taught | to be kind and honest.
 └─ adverb ─┘

Sandra and Liz | have **seldom** been seen | at the gym.
 └─ adverb ─┘

The carpets | are **often** put out | to air in the sun.
 └─ adverb ─┘

I | was **gently** awakened | by my mother.
 └─ adverb ─┘

PRACTICE | *A* | Circle the letters of the correct sentences. There may be more than one answer for each question.

1 A He asked me to remind him of the appointment.
  B He asked me to be remind him of the appointment.
  C He asked to be reminded of the appointment.

2 A Dan would like to send to different part of the world to work.
  B Dan would like to be send to different parts of the world to work.
  C Dan would like to be sent to different parts of the world to work.

3 A The problem easily was solved when all the parties involved cooperated.
  B The problem was easily solved when all the parties involved cooperated.
  C The problem was solved when easily all the parties involved cooperated.

4 A The wealthy entrepreneur prefers to be remembered for his support of the underprivileged.
  B The wealthy entrepreneur prefers to remember for his support of the underprivileged
  C They prefer to remember the wealthy entrepreneur for his support of the underprivileged.

5 A Laura loves being given small gifts of bath oils and soaps.
  B They love to give Laura small gifts of bath oils and soaps.
  C Laura loves been given small gifts of bath oils and soaps.

6 A She wants everyone to recognise Bill's ability to manage the company.
  B She wants everyone to be recognise Bill's ability to manage the company.
  C She wants Bill's ability to manage the company to be recognised.

YOUR SCORE
10

Cross out the incorrect words in the boxes to complete the sentences.

1 He dislikes | being criticise | being criticised | regarding his work.

2 The entertainment for Sunday's dinner party | is carefully being arranged |
| carefully is being arranged | by Jason.

3 The women on the committee | are going to organising | are going to organise | a fashion
show.

4 The motorist wanted me | to be paid | to pay | for the damage to his car.

5 The little boys love | being treat | being treated | to ice-cream and cookies.

6 We | often have advised | have often advised | our neighbours to be more careful about fire
hazards in the home.

7 Jill appreciates | being tell | being told | about a possible promotion for her later in the year.

8 We | have to warned | have to warn | Charles about the dangers of bungee-jumping.

9 She would like | to penalise | to be penalised | for her mistakes rather than not being told about
them.

10 The university hopes | to award | to be awarded | scholarships to suitable students.

Fill in the blanks with the correct forms of the words in the brackets.

1 She would like _____ (reward) her employees with
a large bonus at the end of the year.

2 I prefer _____ (to post) to the audit department as I am an
accountant.

3 The government _____ (finally has agreed) to remove the road
barriers to ease traffic congestion.

4 Lots of things _____ (actually have been done) to alleviate
poverty during the last five years.

5 Yusof _____ (definitely will tell) his parents about his plans to
join the air force.

6 Mr Brody _____ (already has been informed) of the delay
in the shipment of the consignment.

7 He remembers _____ (take) to Disney World by his parents when
he was a little boy.

8 All items which _____ (be to recycle) should be placed in
separate disposal bags.

9 Sue loves _____ (invite) to parties by her friends as she likes
meeting people.

10 I hate _____ (disappoint) by the weather forecast.

PRACTICE **D** Rewrite the sentences correctly in the active or passive voice.

1 The hockey team wants to give due recognition for winning the inter-state trophy.

_____

_____

2 I would like to be apologised for my lateness last night.

_____

_____

3 These fine pieces of jewellery are to hand down to your children when they are older.

_____

_____

4 Most of us hate to humiliate in front of our friends.

_____

_____

5 Your parents have to tell about your decision to leave school and join a band.

_____

_____

PRACTICE **E** Rearrange the words to form correct sentences in the active or passive voice.

1 a — assembled — be — bookcase — form — parts — these — to — will.

_____

_____

2 a — being — dislikes — Henry — fool — like — treated.

_____

_____

3 car — completely — forgot — I — lock — morning — my — this — to.

_____

_____

4 a — be — firm — going — in — is — made — partner — Patrick — senior — the — to.

_____

_____

5 a — being — city — guests — guided — loved — of — on — our — taken — the — tour.

_____

_____

UNIT 4.3 ACTIVE AND PASSIVE VOICE

> to have something done, complement of verb, instructions

Look at the **A** and **B** sentences below. Find out why **B** is correct and **A** is wrong in the **Grammar Points** section.

GRAMMAR POINTS

1A	I am having my hair **style** in the salon at the moment.	✗	
1B	I am having my hair **styled** in the salon at the moment.	✓	1
2A	Active voice : She asked me to close the window because of the cold air. Passive voice : I **asked** to close the window because of the cold air.	✗	
2B	Active voice : She asked me to close the window because of the cold air. Passive voice : I **was asked** to close the window because of the cold air.	✓	2
3A	Active voice : They say that at least 10 people were injured in the accident. Passive voice : At least 10 people are said **to be injured** in the accident.	✗	
3B	Active voice : They say that at least 10 people were injured in the accident. Passive voice : At least 10 people are said **to have been injured** in the accident.	✓	3

 GRAMMAR POINTS

1 (a) When we want to say that we asked someone to do something for us and the person who performed the action is not important (and does not need to be mentioned), we use this structure:

had + object + past participle

EXAMPLES:

We **had** our house **redecorated** recently.   (= someone redecorated the house)

        ⌐object⌐   ⌐past participle⌐

We **redecorated** our house recently.   (= we did it ourselves)

Sandra **had** her car **serviced** last week.   (= someone serviced her car)

        ⌐object⌐   ⌐past participle⌐

Sandra **serviced** her car last week.   (= she serviced the car herself)

Notice that we leave out the preposition **by** and the noun after it.

EXAMPLES:

We **had** our house **redecorated** ~~by someone~~ recently.

Sandra **had** her car **serviced** ~~by someone~~ last week.

(b) When we speak of accidents or incidents that are caused by someone unknown to us, we may also use this structure:

had + object + past participle

EXAMPLES:

My mother **had** her handbag **snatched** in the market.   (= someone snatched her handbag)
Bill **had** his arm **fractured** in a rugby match.   (= someone broke Bill's arm)

2 When we change what someone instructs us to do into the passive voice, we use this structure:

subject + passive verb + infinitive

EXAMPLE:

Active voice   :   They **told** the nurses to take the childen back to the ward.
Passive voice :   The nurses **were told** to take the childen back to the ward.

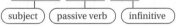

subject   passive verb   infinitive

If we want to identify the person who gave the instruction, we insert the preposition **by** and the instruction giver after the passive verb.

subject + passive verb + **by** + noun (instruction giver) + infinitive

EXAMPLE:

Active voice   :   The matron **told** the nurses to take the childen back to the ward.
Passive voice :   The nurses **were told** by the matron to take the childen back to the ward.

> **REMEMBER!**
> - The following verbs are often used in giving instructions:
>   - ask
>   - command
>   - order
>   - say
>   - tell

3 When we change an active voice verb which comes before a complement into the passive voice, we use this structure:

subject + passive verb + infinitive

EXAMPLES:

They **say** that Thomas is a millionaire because of his sharp business sense.
active verb   complement of the verb **say**

Thomas **is said** **to be** a millionaire because of his sharp business sense.
subject   passive verb   infinitive

They **believe** that the company failed because of ineffective management.
active verb   complement of the verb **believe**

The company **is believed** **to have failed** because of ineffective management.
subject   passive verb   infinitive

Note: We use the perfect infinitive **to have** + past participle to refer to an earlier action *(the company failed)*.

PRACTICE **A** Circle the letters of the correct sentences. There may be more than one answer for each question.

1 **A** We had an indoor swimming pool built in the basement last week.
   B We have an indoor swimming pool built in the basement last week.
   C We are having an indoor swimming pool built in the basement last week.

2 **A** The suspects asked to line up against the wall for an identification exercise.
   B The suspects were asked to line up against the wall for an identification exercise.
   C The detectives asked the suspects to line up against the wall for an identification exercise.

3 **A** We have had a new antenna fixed to improved our television reception.
   B We have had a new antenna fixed to improve our television reception.
   C The technician has fixed a new antenna to improve our television reception

4 **A** Many people say that Mr Morris is stern and lacks a sense of humour.
   B It is said that Mr Morris is stern and lacks a sense of humour.
   C Mr Morris is say by many people to be stern and lacks a sense of humour.

5 **A** They believe that the indigenous people have been treated unfairly by the civil authorities.
   B The indigenous people are believed to have been treated unfairly by the civil authorities.
   C The civil authorities are believed to have treated the indigenous people unfairly.

YOUR SCORE
10

PRACTICE **B** Underline the correct words in the brackets.

1 My sister (has the velvet cushion covers dry cleaned / have the velvet cushion covers dry cleaned) to maintain their colour and sheen.

2 The newly-opened café asked customers (to be written down/ to write down) their comments regarding its food and service.

3 It (is reported / is to be reported) that top fashion models keep to a carefully-controlled diet.

4 Vanessa and her husband (are said to begin/are said to have begun) a new line of hair-care products.

5 The cashier told everyone waiting (to be patient / to have been patient) because the computer system had crashed.

6 Residents in my area (have to be battle / have had to battle) sand and mud brought by flood waters.

7 We (have had to send / have to sent) our grandfather clock to the shop for repair.

8 Ryan (had his leg broken / had his leg break) while he was playing soccer.

9 Jennifer (is said to be / is said to being) the person organising the new help line.

10 Aunt Alice asked me (to pierce my ears / to have my ears pierced) so that I could wear the earrings she gave me.

YOUR SCORE
10

PRACTICE $\boxed{C}$ Rewrite the paragraph and correct the mistakes in the passive verb forms.

We had our porch and living room being renovated last month. Dad's architect friend, James, were invited to redesign the area. James is said is both innovative and bold in his ideas. He asked by Dad to create an informal setting for the living room. He did that by merging the porch and the living room using high French doors. These days, Dad often has been seen sitting inside the living room, enjoying the garden right at our doorstep.

_____

_____

_____

_____

_____

_____

_____

PRACTICE $\boxed{D}$ Rewrite the sentences in the passive voice.

1 Many people think that Bernard is capable of running his father's factory.

Bernard _____

_____

2 Sue asked the girls to help her get all the invitations ready.

The girls _____

_____

3 I will have the air-conditioners in the bedrooms cleaned as they are very dusty.

The air-conditioners_____

_____

4 The airline officials told us to wait for news of the flight from London.

We _____

_____

5 The director has had a new security system installed to protect the office from break-ins.

A new security system _____

_____

UNIT 5.1 DIRECT AND INDIRECT SPEECH

positive and negative statements

Look at the **A** and **B** sentences below. Find out why **B** is correct and **A** is wrong in the **Grammar Points** section.

GRAMMAR POINTS

1A	"**Afterwards, the mayor will**," said Miss Lee, "speak to the press."	✗	
1B	"**Afterwards**," said Miss Lee, "**the mayor will** speak to the press."	✓	1
2A	"Don't make so much noise," Judy said to us. Judy asked us **don't make** so much noise.	✗	
2B	"Don't make so much noise," Judy said to us. Judy asked us **not to make** so much noise.	✓	2
3A	"I haven't seen you for months," said Alice to Aunt Cora. Alice told Aunt Cora that she **hasn't** seen her for months.	✗	
3B	"I haven't seen you for months," said Alice to Aunt Cora. Alice told Aunt Cora that she **hadn't** seen her for months.	✓	3

GRAMMAR POINTS

1 In direct speech, we can place the reporting clause in these positions:
(a) before or after the quote

EXAMPLE: Miss Kanno said, "The girls might come later."
       (reporting clause)   (quote)

"The girls might come later," said Miss Kanno.
   (quote)   (reporting clause)

(b) between two parts of the quote

EXAMPLES: "Her hair," said Connie, "is long and lustrous."
  (noun group) (reporting clause) (second part of quote)

"Eventually," said Pat, "you will agree with me."
  (adverb) (reporting clause) (second part of quote)

"Dear Papa," she said, "I haven't heard from you in a while."
 (term of address) (reporting clause) (second part of quote)

78

"I came immediately," <u>said Dave</u>, "when I heard about the accident."

$\underbrace{\qquad}_{\text{clause}}$ $\underbrace{\qquad}_{\text{reporting clause}}$ $\underbrace{\qquad}_{\text{second part of quote}}$

2 In direct speech, when we make an order or a request, we use the base form of the verb. When we change from direct to indirect speech, we change the base form of the verb to the infinitive (**to** + base form) and place it after the reporting clause.

EXAMPLES:

Sally said to me, "Please **get** me a drink."

Sally asked me **to get** her a drink.

$\underbrace{\qquad}_{\text{reporting clause}}$ $\underbrace{\qquad}_{\text{infinitive}}$

"Don't be late," the teacher said to the class.

The teacher told the class **not to be** late.

$\underbrace{\qquad}_{\text{negative}}$ $\underbrace{\qquad}_{\text{infinitive}}$

3 In indirect speech, we report what someone has said using a **that**-clause. We usually make changes to the tense of the verb, pronouns, possessive adjectives and time expressions when we convert from direct speech to indirect speech.

EXAMPLE: "**I saw you** at the hotel **last week**," she said.

She said that **she had seen me** at the hotel **the previous week**.

> **REMEMBER!**
> ■ When a speaker makes two statements, the reporting verb **said** /**told** is used with the first statement.
> **EXAMPLE:** "There's someone outside," **Mark said**. "He has been there for some time."
>
> **Mark said** that there was someone outside. He had been there for some time.   ✓
>
> **Mark said** that there was someone outside. **Mark said** that he had been there   ✗
> for some time.
>
> ■ If a statement is true at the time of speaking (direct speech) and reporting (indirect speech), there is no need to change the tense of the verb.
> **EXAMPLE:** He said, "Thailand **is** part of the ASEAN group."
> He said that Thailand **is** part of the ASEAN group.

PRACTICE *A*   Circle the sentence number if the underlined reporting clause is in the correct position.

1 "This machine," <u>said the salesman</u>, "is one of our latest models."

2 "We have," <u>said Julie</u>, "been sitting in the car for such a long time."

3 <u>Mary said to the little boys</u>, "Don't play with the switches."

4 "Please get," <u>said Mrs Hong</u>, "me a cold drink."

5 "Lately," <u>said Mike</u>, "there have been a number of robberies in this neighbourhood."

6 "Betty, I managed," <u>said Rick</u>, "to get tickets for the concert."

7 "Mr William will see," <u>said the secretary</u>, "you after lunch."

8 "My dear Nita," <u>said Chris</u>, "I've a surprise for you."

9 "I met him," <u>said Ann</u>, "at Tony's house last week."

10 "I think she is," <u>said Connie</u>, "a charming person."

YOUR SCORE

10

Fill in the blanks with the correct verb forms, pronouns or possessive adjectives.

1 "We will do our best in the exams," my brothers promised.

   My brothers promised that they would do _____ best in the exams.

2 The sergeant said to us, "Walk in a single file to _____ barracks."

   The sergeant told us to walk in a single file to our barracks.

3 Stan said to us, "Be careful of pickpockets in the crowd."

   Stan warned us _____ careful of pickpockets in the crowd.

4 "Your shoes are very smart," said Sally.

   Sally told me that _____ shoes were very smart.

5 "Please wait in the car," said Roy, "while I buy parking coupons."

   Roy asked me to wait in the car while he _____ parking coupons.

6 The cook said to us, "Don't dirty the kitchen while you _____ ."

   The cook told us not to dirty the kitchen while we were baking.

7 "I have to tell Mandy about the incident," said Alex.

   Alex said that he _____ Mandy about the incident.

8 Mr Jones said to Jane, "Lock up the office before you _____ ."

   Mr Jones told Jane to lock up the office before she left.

9 "Please bring you own pillows," said Betty, "as I don't have enough."

   Betty asked us to bring _____ own pillows as she didn't have enough.

10 "Don't put any sugar in my tea," said Mrs Silva to me.

   Mrs Silva asked me _____ any sugar in her tea.

> **YOUR SCORE**
>
> 10

In the following pairs of sentences, one sentence is incorrect. Rewrite it correctly.

1 "Please call back later," said the nurse, "because Dr Sims is not in."
   The nurse told me please call back later because Dr Sims was not in.

   _____

   _____

2 Peter said to us, "Don't late for rehearsals tomorrow."
   Peter told us not to be late for rehearsals the following day.

   _____

   _____

3 The captain said, "My team intends to win the challenge trophy for our school."
   The captain said that his team intend to win the challenge trophy for their school.

   _____

   _____

4 "Pour the solution carefully into a beaker," my science lecturer said to me.

My science lecturer told me pour the solution carefully into a beaker.

_____

_____

5 "Pay attention while you're driving!" The instructor said to Louis.

The instructor told Louis to pay attention while he driving.

_____

_____

PRACTICE D Rewrite the sentences in direct speech.

1 Jenny said that those flowers were from Holland.

_____

2 The officer told Jill not to park in the no-parking zone.

_____

3 Ann asked the sales assistant to help her carry the purchases to her car.

_____

_____

4 Helen promised to bring my birthday cake later that evening.

_____

5 Mr Francis told his secretary that he didn't want any interruptions during the meeting.

_____

_____

PRACTICE E Rewrite the dialogue in indirect speech.

Jack   : "The weather is really bad."
Wendy : "It's raining very hard."
Jack   : "I am very worried about Lucy. She has to drive home in the rain."
Wendy : "Give Lucy a call, Jack, and tell her to wait until the rain subsides."

1 Jack said _____

2 Wendy said _____

3 Jack said _____

_____

4 Wendy asked Jack _____

_____

UNIT 5.2 DIRECT AND INDIRECT SPEECH

positive and negative questions

Look at the **A** and **B** sentences below. Find out why **B** is correct and **A** is wrong in the **Grammar Points** section.

			GRAMMAR POINTS
1A	Brian said, "Are you joining us for lunch?" Brian asked if **was I joining** them for lunch.	✗	
1B	Brian said, "Are you joining us for lunch?" Brian asked if **I was joining** them for lunch.	✓	1
2A	The man said to Sam, "Are you Mrs Cook's son?" The man asked Sam **is he** Mrs Cook's son.	✗	
2B	The man said to Sam, "Are you Mrs Cook's son?" The man asked Sam **whether he was** Mrs Cook's son.	✓	2
3A	They said to me, "Where did you meet Amy?" They asked me where **did I meet** Amy.	✗	
3B	They said to me, "Where did you meet Amy?" They asked me where **I had met** Amy.	✓	3
4A	Sheila said, "Why don't you like that story?" Sheila asked why **don't I like** that story.	✗	
4B	Sheila said, "Why don't you like that story?" Sheila asked why **I didn't like** that story.	✓	4

GRAMMAR POINTS

1 In an indirect question, we place the subject of the reported clause before the verb as in a statement. We usually change the tense of the verb as well as the pronouns, possessive adjectives and time expressions in the reported clause.

EXAMPLE: We said to Janet, "**Are you leaving** the company **next month**?"

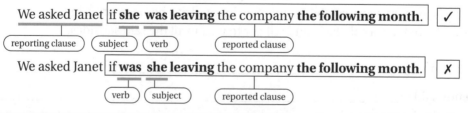

We asked Janet if **she was leaving** the company **the following month**. ✓

reporting clause — subject — verb — reported clause

We asked Janet if **was she leaving** the company **the following month**. ✗

verb — subject — reported clause

REMEMBER!

- In a direct question, the actual words of the speaker and the question mark are within quotation marks.

    EXAMPLE:

    "Does Penny come here often?" he said.

    quote — reporting clause — full stop to end sentence

- In an indirect question, the question mark and the quotation marks are not used.

- If the direct question is a wh-question, the wh-word is used to begin the reported clause.

2

When a direct question has a **yes** or **no** answer, we use **whether** or **if** to begin the reported clause.

EXAMPLE: Mum said, "**Are** the twins in their room?"

Mum asked me **if / whether** the twins **were** in their room.

3

When a direct question begins with the verb 'to do' or a wh-word with the verb 'to do', we leave out the verb 'to do' in the indirect question and change the tense of the main verb.

EXAMPLES:

Direct question	Indirect question
does ... want (present tense)	wanted (past tense)
did ... end (past tense)	**had** ended (past perfect tense)

Jeff said to us, "When **did** the match **end**?"

Jeff asked us when the match **had ended**.   ✓

Jeff asked us when **did** the match **had ended**.   ✗

.4

When a direct question begins with a wh-word and the negative form of the verb 'to do', we need to retain the verb 'to do' in the indirect question because it is the verb 'to do' which carries the tense.

EXAMPLES:

Direct question	Indirect question
doesn't understand (present tense)	**didn't** understand (past tense)
didn't understand (past tense)	**hadn't** understood (past perfect tense)

Susie said, "Who **doesn't want** milk in their tea?"
Susie asked who **didn't want** milk in their tea.

Tony said, "Sara, why **didn't** you **inform** me earlier?"
Tony asked Sara why she **hadn't informed** him earlier.

PRACTICE | **A** | Fill in the blanks with the correct verb forms, pronouns or time expressions.

1 Vicki said to me, "_____ you _____ to join my band?"
Vicki asked me whether I wanted to join her band.

2 "Are you going to leave for Paris next Monday?" Sybil said.

Sybil asked if I _____ to leave for Paris _____ Monday.

3 Sam said to Bill, "Why _____ you _____ your overcoat?"
Sam asked Bill why he didn't wear his overcoat.

4 "Is there enough food for me?" Dad said.

Dad asked if there _____ enough food for _____ .

5 Jane said to us, "_____ you _____ to go out earlier for dinner?"
Jane asked whether we preferred to go out earlier for dinner.

YOUR SCORE

10

1 "Does your dog usually go into your neighbour's garden?" Ben said to me.

Ben asked if _____ .

2 "Who doesn't want to go on the roller-coaster ride?" the tour guide said.

The tour guide asked _____ .

3 Fiona said, "Helen, are you interested in joining our sewing class?"

Fiona asked Helen _____ .

4 "How did you remove the grease marks from my shirt?" Jack said to his dry cleaner.

Jack asked his dry cleaner _____ .

5 Kellie said to me, "What don't you like about our plan?"

Kellie _____ .

YOUR SCORE
/10

PRACTICE $\boxed{C}$ Complete the direct questions in the sentences.

1 "Why _____" Sue asked.
Sue asked why they didn't want to go with us.

2 "Does _____" Joan said to me.
Joan asked me if my father always came home late.

3 David said to his grandfather, "_____"
David asked his grandfather if Grandma was going to take more golf lessons.

4 "_____" Miss Smith said.
Miss Smith asked if we were taking part in the contest.

5 Tom said, "_____"
Tom asked what subject she taught in college.

YOUR SCORE
/10

PRACTICE $\boxed{D}$ Rewrite the questions in direct speech or indirect speech.

1 Direct Speech   : "How far into the city does the commuter train go?" the lady said to Steve.
Indirect Speech : _____

_____

2 Direct Speech   : "Why did you take my bag?" Timmy said to me.
Indirect Speech : _____

_____

3 Direct Speech   : "Were the dogs well-behaved at the show?" the kennel owner said to Mr Gopal.
Indirect Speech : _____

_____

4 Direct Speech : _____

_____

  Indirect Speech : The doctor asked whether we were waiting to see him.

5 Direct Speech : _____

_____

  Indirect Speech : The interviewer asked me whether I had any experience of writing radio plays.

PRACTICE **E** Complete the dialogue in direct speech. Use the indirect questions in the brackets to guide you.

Officer : (1) _"Were you at a function at the club tonight?"_

  (The officer asked Stan whether he had been at a function at the club that night.)

Stan : "Yes."

Officer : (2) _____

_____

  (The officer asked Stan whether he had drunk any alcohol at the function.)

Stan : "No, officer. I just had orange juice."

Officer : (3) _____

_____

  (The officer asked Stan what time he had left the club.)

Stan : "I left the club at 11 p.m."

Officer : (4) _____

_____

  (He wanted to know if Stan had been speeding.)

Stan : "No, officer."

Officer : (5) _____

_____

  (He asked Stan whether he had seen the other car coming from the opposite direction.)

Stan : "Yes, I did."

Officer : (6) _____

_____

  (He wanted to know why Stan hadn't swerved to avoid the other car.)

Stan : "If I had swerved, I would have hit that fruit stall beside the road."

UNIT 6.1 MODALS

positive statements, passive structure

Look at the **A** and **B** sentences below. Find out why **B** is correct and **A** is wrong in the **Grammar Points** section.

			GRAMMAR POINTS
1A	You **better inform** Mrs Rama.	✗	
1B	You **had better / ought to / should inform** Mrs Rama.	✓	1
2A	It is 7 p.m. John's plane **will landing** now.	✗	
2B	It is 7 p.m. John's plane **will be landing** now.	✓	2
3A	Kitty's not here. She **may have went** to the neighbour's house.	✗	
3B	Kitty's not here. She **may have gone** to the neighbour's house.	✓	3
4A	My e-mail **would have received** by Emily yesterday.	✗	
4B	My e-mail **would have been received** by Emily yesterday.	✓	4

GRAMMAR POINTS

1 We can use **had better**, **ought to** or **should** when giving someone advice. However, when the advice given is about a past event or when it is a general comment about something, we can only use **ought to** or **should**.

EXAMPLES: The manager │ **had better / ought to / should** │ listen to his employees' complaints.

subject — modals — base form of main verb

Past event:

Farah **ought to / should** have kept our appointment but she didn't. ✓

Farah **had better** have kept our appointment but she didn't. ✗

General comment:

All schools **ought to / should** have library periods for the students. ✓

All schools **had better** have library periods for the students. ✗

REMEMBER!

■ Modals are usually used in statements to express the following:

ability – can, could	obligation – ought to, should
advice – had better, ought to, should	permission – can, may
certainty or intention – shall, will, would	possibility – could, may, might
necessity – must, need to	willingness – shall, will, would

2 We use a present participle with a modal to indicate something is possibly (**could**, **may**) or very likely to be (**must**, **should**) happening at the time of speaking, or will probably (**could**, **may**) or very likely (**shall**, **will**) be happening in the future. We use the base form of the verb 'to be' with the present participle in this way:

Subject + modal + **be** + present participle

EXAMPLES: The committee **could** be questioning the suspended player now.
subject — modal — base form — present participle — *(possible event now)*

The committee **must be** questioning the suspended player now.
(very likely event now)

The committee **could be** questioning the suspended player tomorrow.
(probable event in the future)

The committee **will be** questioning the suspended player tomorrow.
(very likely event in the future)

3 We use a past participle with a modal to indicate the speaker thinks it is possible (**could**, **might**) or very likely (**must**, **would**) that something happened in the past. It could also indicate that the speaker knows that something should have taken place in the past but didn't (**ought to**, **should**). We use it in this way:

Subject + modal + **have** + past participle

EXAMPLES: One of the witnesses **might** have noted down the number of the robbers' car.
subject — modal — base form — past participle — *(possible event in the past)*

The police **would** have arrested all the escaped prisoners by yesterday evening.
subject — modal — base form — past participle — *(likely event in the past)*

You **ought to** have accepted Mr Paulson's offer of a marketing job in his firm.
subject — modal — base form — past participle — *(something that did not occur)*

4 We can use passive verbs with modals in this way:

(a) Subject + modal + **be** + past participle

EXAMPLE: *Active voice:* Norman **could** oversee the project.
subject — modal — active verb

Passive voice: The project **could** be overseen by Norman.
subject — modal — passive verb

(b) Subject + modal + **have been** + past participle

EXAMPLE: *Active voice:* Richard **must** have sent that bouquet of roses.
subject — modal — active verb

Passive voice: That bouquet of roses **must** have been sent by Richard.
subject — modal — passive verb

PRACTICE $\boxed{A}$ Tick the correct sentences.

1 Lisa can teach us to make flowers out of ribbons and straw.

2 Our department will be undergoing a leadership training course this weekend.

3 Ian could sings well even as a little boy.

4 The procession must have began half an hour late.

5 These vouchers can be used at our café on the 10th floor.

6 That little girl's parents should have teaching her to read.

7 The motorcyclist ought to have slowed down when he saw the oncoming lorry.

8 He might calls in to see us this evening.

9 The cave must have been inhabited by hundreds of bats.

10 Jenny and Lara may be hold a garage sale this weekend.

YOUR SCORE

10

PRACTICE $\boxed{B}$ Complete the sentences with the correct words in the box.
Each word may be used more than once.

attend	attending	be	been	carry	carrying	cooperate	cooperated
has	have	make	made	send	sent	compete	competing

1 A copy of the agenda must be _____ to every committee member.

2 You should _____ printed the minutes of last year's annual general meeting by now.

3 The society's financial statement will _____ presented by the treasurer at the meeting.

4 Helen and Sam may _____ for the post of president.

5 Yasmin would _____ an excellent secretary because she is very organised and meticulous.

6 Mrs Haines, our adviser, will be _____ the meeting.

7 Last year's annual general meeting ought to have _____ attended by all members.

8 Voting of office bearers could _____ by a show of hands or by secret ballot.

9 Committee members must _____ out their responsibility to the best of their ability.

10 All committee members should _____ with one another to do what is best for the club.

YOUR SCORE

10

PRACTICE C Underline the correct words in the brackets.

1 You (might / **must**) submit your entry form by 30th September at the latest.

2 The train (**should** / should have) arrive any time now.

3 Irene (may leave / **may have left**) her shopping bag in the washroom.

4 These parcels (could fall / **could have fallen**) from that van.

5 The customers (**need to lodge** / need to be lodged) a complaint about the store's unreliable delivery service.

6 The information (should have passed on / **should have been passed on**) to the secretary yesterday.

7 One hundred athletes from 20 local clubs (will have undergone / **will be undergoing**) training at the National Sports Council next month.

8 Larry's car (might hit / **must have hit**) the lamp post as he was backing into the parking lot.

9 The students (**had better start** / better start) revising for their final exams soon.

10 The courier company (will be deliver / **will be delivering**) our package to your manager between 10 a.m. and noon tomorrow.

YOUR SCORE

10

PRACTICE D Rearrange the words to form correct sentences.

1 a — car — emergencies — first-aid — for — have — in — kit — should — you — your.
You should have a first-aid kit in your car for emergencies.

2 and — be — could — front — her — in — Maggie — row — sister — sitting — the.

3 a — been — by — dissatisfied — exposed — have — member — might — plot — the.

4 activity — join — morning — ought — team-building — the — they — to — tomorrow.

5 by — competition — have — magazine — now — of — selected — the — the — the — winners — would.

6 a — at — be — examination — given — medical — Mr Adams — once — should — thorough.

YOUR SCORE

10

89

UNIT 6.2 **MODALS**

negative statements, passive structure

Look at the **A** and **B** sentences below. Find out why **B** is correct and **A** is wrong in the **Grammar Points** section.

			GRAMMAR POINTS
1A	Ken **need not to** feel guilty because he forgot my birthday.	✗	
1B	Ken **need not / needn't** feel guilty because he forgot my birthday.	✓	1
2A	You **wouldn't crying** if you knew the end of the story.	✗	
2B	You **wouldn't cry** if you knew the end of the story. / You **wouldn't be crying** if you knew the end of the story.	✓	2
3A	Janet **should not ignored** the policeman's signal to stop just now.	✗	
3B	Janet **should not have ignored** the policeman's signal to stop just now.	✓	3
4A	My computer **couldn't hit** by a virus.	✗	
4B	My computer **couldn't have been hit** by a virus.	✓	4

GRAMMAR POINTS

1 We use **not** or its contraction **n't** to change a modal to its negative form. We drop **to** when we form the negative of **need to**. However, we keep **to** when we form the negative of **ought to**. The verb that follows has to be in its base form.

EXAMPLES:

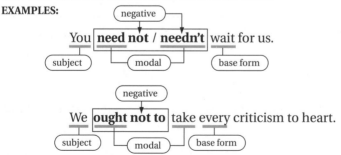

90

2 When we use a present participle with the negative form of a modal, we have to include the base form of the verb 'to be' in this way:

Subject + modal + **not** / **n't** + **be** + present participle

EXAMPLE:

negative modal

You **shouldn't** be doing all the work by yourself.

subject · base form · present participle

3 When we use a past participle with the negative form of a modal, we have to include the base form of the verb 'to have' in this way:

Subject + modal + **not** / **n't** + **have** + past participle

REMEMBER!

■ **Must not** and **shall not** cannot go with **have** + past participle.

EXAMPLE:

She **ought not to** have blamed me for our defeat in the finals. (We had lost in the finals.)

subject · negative modal · base form · past participle

4 We use passive verbs with the negative form of modals in this way:

(a) Subject + modal + **not** / **n't** + **be** + past participle

EXAMPLE:

negative modal

Active voice: They **couldn't** move the heavy artillery.

subject · active verb

negative modal

Passive voice: The heavy artillery **couldn't** be moved.

subject · passive verb

(b) Subject + modal + **not** / **n't** + **have been** + past participle

EXAMPLE:

negative modal

Active voice: A rainstorm **couldn't** **have shattered** the window.

subject · active verb

negative modal

Passive voice: The window **couldn't** **have been shattered** by a rainstorm.

subject · passive verb

1 You $\boxed{\text{can't}}$ $\boxed{\text{can not}}$ miss her. She's always the best-dressed among them.

2 They $\boxed{\text{shouldn't expected}}$ $\boxed{\text{shouldn't be expected}}$ to sell all the tickets within a fortnight.

3 Bill $\boxed{\text{might have not heard}}$ $\boxed{\text{might not have heard}}$ the wonderful news concerning Emma.

4 They $\boxed{\text{wouldn't be working}}$ $\boxed{\text{wouldn't working}}$ for you if they didn't respect you.

5 That lorry $\boxed{\text{ought not to parking}}$ $\boxed{\text{ought not to have been parked}}$ so close to our driveway.

6 I $\boxed{\text{shan't tell}}$ $\boxed{\text{shan't telling}}$ you the ending. Read the book and find out what happened.

7 This suitcase $\boxed{\text{may look}}$ $\boxed{\text{may not look}}$ small but it can actually hold a lot of things.

8 His complaints $\boxed{\text{mustn't be taken}}$ $\boxed{\text{mustn't have taken}}$ lightly.

9 Ivan $\boxed{\text{couldn't understood}}$ $\boxed{\text{couldn't have understood}}$ your message because he only speaks Russian.

10 We $\boxed{\text{needn't leave}}$ $\boxed{\text{needn't to leave}}$ now for the airport because there's not much traffic on the roads.

YOUR SCORE 10

PRACTICE $\boxed{B}$ Fill in the blanks with the correct modals in the boxes.

1 The accident _____ have taken place. Why wasn't there a signboard near the cliff to warn motorists of the danger?

| should | shouldn't |

2 Clare _____ listen to our advice and now she's lost a lot of money on the stock market.

| would | wouldn't |

3 The roof _____ be leaking! I had it repaired yesterday!

| can | can't |

4 We _____ get all the facts before we decide what to do next.

| need to | needn't |

5 You _____ protect your skin from the sun's UV rays.

| must | mustn't |

6 Jack _____ have spoken so harshly to the team when they were defeated.

| ought to | ought not to |

7 I _____ waste any more time trying to persuade Tom to change his mind.

| shall | shan't |

8 That excellent speech by the chairman _____ have been written by Paige. She has a way with words.

| could | couldn't |

9 We changed our minds about going to the beach. We _____ be spending the weekend in a cabin up on the mountain.

| will | won't |

10 The child who was sent to the hospital by ambulance _____ have been accompanied by a teacher.

| should | shouldn't |

YOUR SCORE 10

PRACTICE *C*   Rewrite the sentences in the passive voice.

1 They shouldn't have misplaced Mr Brown's folder.
   Mr Brown's folder shouldn't have been misplaced.

2 We cannot remove these reference books from the library.

3 The tourist guide ought not to have taken the tourists to that factory.

4 Our football club may not include David in the lineup against The Trojans.

5 The prosecution might not produce sufficient evidence against the murder suspect.

6 My workmen couldn't have damaged your staircase.

PRACTICE *D*   Underline the mistakes in verb forms in the conversation. Write the correct verbs in the blanks.

Sarinah : Kate <u>must take not</u> four teaspoons of sugar in her tea. She has a diabetic condition. I wouldn't surprised if her blood sugar level is high.

Mrs Tan : I've told her to take less but she won't listen to me. She began with two teaspoons of sugar, then she went on to three and now it's four!

Sarinah : You shouldn't had let her increase her sugar intake. You need to take her to a doctor and have him test her blood sugar level.

Mrs Tan : It's not just Kate. It's Jerry as well. I can't understand how both of them can eat chocolate, ice-cream, cake and biscuits all in the space of a day.

Sarinah : Your fridge needn't to be stocked with so many sweet snacks.

Mrs Tan : I let the children choose their own snacks when we go shopping for groceries.

Sarinah : You shouldn't have catering to their whims all the time. You could teach them to satisfy their hunger with fruit. It's got vitamins and fibre. You might not succeeded at first in getting them to enjoy fruit as a snack. They may grumble and complain but they will come to like fruit eventually.

1 *mustn't take / must not take*   4

2 _____   5

3 _____   6

UNIT 6.3 MODALS

positive and negative questions, passive structure

Look at the **A** and **B** sentences below. Find out why **B** is correct and **A** is wrong in the **Grammar Points** section.

			GRAMMAR POINTS
1A	**Do I must sign** every page of the document?	✗	
1B	**Must I sign** every page of the document?	✓	1
2A	**Could they hinting** that you are the winner?	✗	
2B	**Could they be hinting** that you are the winner?	✓	2
3A	Might James **have took** your jacket by mistake?	✗	
3B	Might James **have taken** your jacket by mistake?	✓	3
4A	Shouldn't the printer **switched off** after use?	✗	
4B	Shouldn't the printer **be switched off** after use?	✓	4

GRAMMAR POINTS

1 We can begin a question which has **yes** or **no** as the answer using a modal.
EXAMPLES:

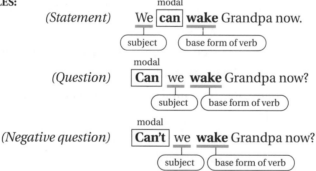

(Statement) We can wake Grandpa now.

(Question) Can we wake Grandpa now?

(Negative question) Can't we wake Grandpa now?

When we form a question with the modal, we do not normally make use of the verb 'to do'. Only the modal **need to** can be used with the verb 'to do'.
EXAMPLES:

(Question without modal) Do we wake Grandpa now?

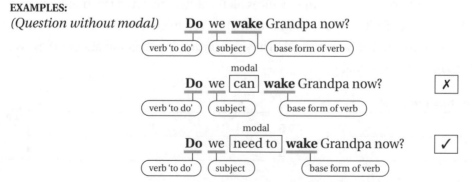

Do we can wake Grandpa now? ✗

Do we need to wake Grandpa now? ✓

94

2 We have to use the base form of the verb 'to be' when we use a **present participle** with a modal in a question.

EXAMPLE: **Shouldn't** you **be paying** attention to what the speaker is saying?   ✓

Shouldn't you **paying** attention to what the speaker is saying?   ✗

3 When we use the base form of the verb 'to have' in a question beginning with a modal, we must use a **past participle** after it.

EXAMPLES: **Would** Doreen **have sold** her apartment by now?   ✓
(past participle)

Would Doreen **have sells** her apartment by now?   ✗
finite verb (present tense)

Would Doreen **have selling** her apartment by now?   ✗
present participle

4 We have to use the base form of the verb 'to be' + past participle with a modal when the question is in the passive form.

EXAMPLES: **Can** these savouries **be eaten** with chilli sauce?   ✓

Can these savouries **eaten** with chilli sauce?   ✗

Can these savouries **eat** with chilli sauce?   ✗

Can these savouries **eating** with chilli sauce?   ✗

Can these savouries **ate** with chilli sauce?   ✗

1 Can Mr Stevens climbing these steep steps?

2 Did Joanna could catch the train after all?

3 Must you reject every suggestion I make?

4 Won't I be reimbursed for the goods damaged during transportation?

5 Shouldn't the park authorities be making sure no visitor feeds the animals?

6 Did the police stop the scuffle at the football stadium?

7 Might they teaching their parrot to talk?

8 Wouldn't she felt surprised if they had phoned from Brazil?

9 Couldn't he have told us earlier that he didn't like playing chess?

10 Should the club restricts members from bringing in too many guests?

YOUR SCORE
10

PRACTICE $\boxed{B}$ Circle the letters of the correct questions. There may be more than one answer for each question.

1 to ask for something
   A   May I borrow your setsquare, please?
   B   Might I have a little more of your delicious pie?
   C   Can Jane staying at my house this weekend?

2 to make a suggestion
   A   Will this bracelet matches your pearl earrings?
   B   Could Paul take charge of the students visiting the batik factory?
   C   Shall we remove the curry stain with some bleaching powder?

3 to inquire about possibilities
   A   Could Sue have taken Ariel's purse instead by mistake?
   B   Wouldn't it better to add honey?
   C   Might they have hidden the money below the floorboards?

4 to ask if something is necessary
   A   Must Henry and I raking the leaves in the garden now?
   B   Must you be blowing your trumpet so early in the morning?
   C   Doesn't he need to make amends for his bad behaviour yesterday?

5 to offer
   A   Would you like to read a magazine while waiting for the doctor?
   B   Shall I call for the bellboy to take Donna's luggage?
   C   Couldn't you have got our assistant manager to settle the customer's problem?

YOUR SCORE
10

PRACTICE $\boxed{C}$ Underline the correct words in the brackets.

1   May I (refer / to refer) to the letter you wrote on 17th September?

2   Could Maisie (download / downloaded) the environmental article you recommended?

3   Won't Lisa's plans to buy that house (delayed / be delayed) because she has so many expenses?

4   Shouldn't you (setting / be setting) a good example to the new staff?

5   Couldn't the others (assisted / have assisted) Mrs Joseph while I was away?

6   Would the manager (supporting / have supported) you if he had not been pleased with your work?

7   Might this (be / is) the answer to all your financial problems?

8   Can't the test (be postponed / postpone) since a number of the students are down with flu?

9   Should we (have bought / have buy) Lorna a bottle of perfume rather than this piece of silk?

10   Will you be (enjoy / enjoying) more fringe benefits in your new firm?

YOUR SCORE 10

PRACTICE $\boxed{D}$ Some of the questions are incorrect. Rewrite them correctly.

1   Shall I giving your sister some coaching in Maths?

Shall I give your sister some coaching in Maths?

2   Could Sue be photocopying the minutes of the meeting now?

_____

_____

3   Shouldn't the rally participants have drove slowly on the wet road?

_____

_____

4   Won't Sheila dismayed by the lack of response to her survey?

_____

_____

5   Couldn't Harry replaced Jim in the second half of the game?

_____

_____

6   Might I making a simple suggestion at this point?

_____

YOUR SCORE 10

_____

UNIT 7.1 **PREPOSITIONS**

Look at the **A** and **B** sentences below. Find out why **B** is correct and **A** is wrong in the **Grammar Points** section.

			GRAMMAR POINTS
1A	Kim was dressed **with** a navy blue suit for her office lunch.	✗	
1B	Kim was dressed **in** a navy blue suit for her office lunch.	✓	1
2A	The committee report **comprises of** 20 pages.	✗	
2B	The committee report **comprises** 20 pages. The committee report **consists of** 20 pages.	✓ ✓	2

GRAMMAR POINTS

1 When we use prepositions, we must know which ones go with certain verbs, adjectives or nouns. Sometimes, the word before a preposition controls our choice. Sometimes, the preposition must go together with the word that comes after it.

EXAMPLES: (a)  verb + preposition

I stopped **at** a bakery to buy some bread and cakes.
⎣verb⎦ ⎣preposition⎦

(b) adjective + preposition

Mary is **good with** person⎢children⎢.
⎣adjective⎦ ⎣preposition⎦

Mary is **good at** thing⎢Maths⎢.
⎣adjective⎦ ⎣preposition⎦

(c)  noun + preposition

The reason **for** the flight cancellation is still not known.
⎣noun⎦ ⎣preposition⎦

(d) verb + preposition + noun / pronoun

person
Raymond **agreed with** ⎢me⎢ that the meeting should be postponed.
⎣verb⎦ ⎣preposition⎦

thing
Raymond **agreed to** ⎢my suggestion⎢ to postpone the meeting.
⎣verb⎦ ⎣preposition⎦

- Prepositions are used to show how people or things relate to one another. The best way to remember which prepositions go with certain nouns, noun phrases, pronouns, adjectives or verbs is to check their use in a dictionary.

- Prepositions are used to help convey ideas like the following:

accompanying or in the same place – with	level – above, below
cause or purpose – because of, for	position – around, at, behind, in
condition or state of something – in, out of	showing support or opposition – against, for, with
content – about, in, of, with	similarity in manner – as, like
goal or target – at, to	source – from
having something – of, with, without	time – after, during, since
movement – into, over, through, towards	way of doing something – by, with

2 Some words do not require prepositions but other words which share the same meaning must have them.

(a) synonyms

EXAMPLES: I **arrived at** the town hall just before the show began. ✓

I **reached at** the town hall just before the show began. ✗

I **reached** the town hall just before the show began. ✓

admit – let in	accompany – go with	comprise, contain – consist of
exceed – go beyond	hit – strike at	request – ask for

(b) nouns derived from verbs

EXAMPLES:

verb

Mr Morgan and his secretary **discussed about** the company's annual report just now. ✗

preposition

Mr Morgan and his secretary **discussed** the company's annual report just now. ✓

noun

The **discussion about** the company's annual report took an hour. ✓

preposition

PRACTICE *A* Tick the correct sentences.

1 Jackie is fluent in Mandarin.

2 My boss intends to transfer me head office in September.

3 Emily tripped to her shoelaces while she was running.

4 I had an enjoyable outing with my cousins yesterday.

5 The millionaire knew he had to escape his kidnappers.

6 I think you should not boast your achievements.

7 We looked through the files but couldn't find the document I needed.

8 This sculpture is made of steel, rope and glass.

9 The tickets will be available the box office from 10 a.m. tomorrow.

10 Won't these chairs be ideal for our dining room?

YOUR SCORE

10

Fill in the blanks with the correct prepositions in the boxes.

1   The man _____ a limp is a war hero.

   The man _____ shorts and a Hawaiian shirt seems lost.

in
with

2   Did you hear _____ Billie's sister? She entered a contest and won a trip for two around the world.
   I've heard _____ that restaurant before. Isn't it the one with French windows and a lovely courtyard?

about
of

3   The bicycles at the hotel are available _____ hire at five dollars an hour.

   The express counter service at the bank is available _____ those above 55 years of age.

for
to

4   The evacuation _____ the flood victims was hampered by the shortage of boats.
   Their evacuation _____ the area was of the greatest urgency because a dam had burst.

from
of

5   Janet's mother was afraid _____ her because Janet often had to walk home alone in the dark.

   Marie is not afraid _____ failure. She sees it as a stepping-stone to further growth.

for
of

YOUR SCORE
10

Circle the letters of the correct answers. There may be more than one answer for each question.

1   **A**   The booming sound came from that room.
   B   She walked towards the booming sound.
   C   There is a booming sound at that room.

2   **A**   John spoke against beautification projects that ate into the budget.
   B   John was not in favour because of beautification projects that ate into the budget.
   C   John did not agree to beautification projects that ate into the budget.

3   **A**   I can't remember exactly where but there's an interesting café around here.
   B   That café is the ground floor of the Millennium Tower.
   C   I think the café is next to a shop selling sports goods.

4   **A**   I walked as Grandma when she wanted to visit her old neighbour.
   B   I accompanied Grandma when she wanted to visit her old neighbour.
   C   I walked with Grandma when she wanted to visit her old neighbour.

5   **A**   Our supporters were disappointed for our poor performance in the match.
   B   We were a disappointment to our supporters.
   C   We disappointed our supporters when the results were announced.

YOUR SCORE
10

PRACTICE D   Cross out the redundant prepositions in the dialogue.

Anna   :   Lee, what are you doing ~~at~~ here?
Rashid :   The same reason for why you're here, I think. Are you attending to the briefing for the youth expedition to Chile?
Anna   :   Yes. Oh, isn't it great because of that we're both on the same expedition! It'll be an adventure, don't you think? It'll be about fun to work with young people from different parts of the world who will be part of the expedition too.
Rashid :   It's a challenge I wouldn't want to miss out. We'd be working on with communities in the interior of Chile.
Anna   :   This weekend training will be very useful for us, I think.
Rashid :   The organisers are supposed to familiarise us with everything for we need to know about the expedition.
Anna   :   It says in the programme here that we'll be told on the rules we have to abide by during the whole expedition.
Rashid :   Oh! This should interest to all of us. According to the programme, the Chilean Ambassador is going to talk on the customs and traditions of his people.
Anna   :   Wow! I hope he wears his national costume or he sings with the national anthem of his country.
Rashid :   You do say the funniest things, Anna.

YOUR SCORE
10

PRACTICE E   Fill in the blanks with suitable prepositions.

Boredom! That was it! That was the cause (1) _____ my irrational behaviour these past two weeks. That was why I had been snapping (2) _____ the staff all the time. I slumped into my chair (3) _____ despair. I had worked for 15 years with the company. The realisation that I was bored made me anxious (4) _____ how I was going to work efficiently from now on. I sat quietly (5) _____ a while and then I switched on the computer and swiftly wrote my letter of resignation.

I walked purposefully (6) _____ Mr Brown's office, my letter in my hand. Outside his room, I stopped at the watercooler for a sip of water. My throat was parched. Beads of perspiration had begun to form on my forehead. It wasn't going to be easy, I knew, but I had to tell him. My life was such a drudgery. I didn't want to be (7) _____ administration anymore. I didn't want to have to ensure the office ran like clockwork every day.

Just then, Mr Brown opened his door and asked me to step (8) _____ his room. He said, "Lena, we're creating a new department that will deal solely (9) _____ our overseas partners. I want you to head that. It will mean doing quite a bit of travelling. Are you interested?"

My jaw dropped. My fingers trembled. Quietly, I crumpled my letter.

"What's that?" asked Mr Brown, pointing to the crushed paper in my hand.

"Oh, just one of my mistakes," I said. He must have known, for I heard him sigh (10) _____ relief.

YOUR SCORE
10

UNIT 7.2 **PREPOSITIONS**

Look at the **A** and **B** sentences below. Find out why **B** is correct and **A** is wrong in the **Grammar Points** section.

1A	Julia **dreamt about that she would meet** an old friend.	✗	
1B	Julia **dreamt about meeting** an old friend. Julia **dreamt that she would meet** an old friend.	✓ ✓	1
2A	I explained the career counsellor my problem.	✗	
2B	I explained my problem **to** the career counsellor.	✓	2
3A	He asked which places I went.	✗	
3B	He asked which places I went **to**. (informal) He asked **to** which places I went. (formal)	✓ ✓	3
4A	My brother was upset **to be** dropped from the team.	✗	
4B	My brother was upset **at being** dropped from the team.	✓	4

GRAMMAR POINTS

1 When we use a preposition after a verb, we cannot have a **that**-clause after it.
We can have a noun or a noun phrase after the preposition.

EXAMPLES:

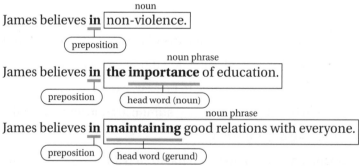

James believes in **that** everyone should be non-violent. ✗

James believes in **that** education is important. ✗

James believes in **that** he should maintain good relations with everyone. ✗

102

2 In some sentences, we place the object between the verb and the preposition that goes with it.
EXAMPLES:

(a) verb + object + preposition + noun / noun phrase

Mrs Parry **thanked** + Yusof + **for** + his helpfulness.

The media **informed** + the public + **about** + the total eclipse of the sun.

(b) verb + object + preposition + 'ing' form

Mrs Parry **thanked** + Yusof + **for** + helping her complete the office accounts.

3 We can use a preposition before a clause beginning with a wh-word. We can sometimes move the preposition to the end of the clause too.
EXAMPLES:

I wondered **in** which cupboard they had hidden our Christmas presents. *(formal)* ✓

I wondered which cupboard they had hidden our Christmas presents **in**. *(informal)* ✓

The customs officer asked me **from** where I had bought the carpet. *(formal)* ✓

The customs officer asked me where I had bought the carpet **from**. *(informal)* ✓

We were astounded **at** how the blind man had escaped from the burning building. ✓

We were astounded how the blind man had escaped from the burning building **at**. ✗

4 We can use the 'ing' form of a verb with a preposition in certain combinations.
EXAMPLES:

(a) verb + object + preposition + 'ing' form

Liza accused + her brother + **of** + **peeking** into the present cupboard.

(b) verb 'to be' + adjective + preposition + 'ing' form

Jimmy was + furious + **at** + **being** woken up at 6 a.m. to go for a morning walk.

(c) verb 'to be' + adjective + preposition + possessive pronoun + 'ing' form

Mr Woods was + amazed + **at** + his + **being** mistaken for his son.

PRACTICE *A* Circle the letters of the correct sentences.

1 **A** He is afraid that he will offend his friends.
  B He is afraid of offending his friends.
  C He is afraid of that he will offend his friends.

2 **A** Our manager insists that our work must be neat.
  B Our manager insists on our work be neat.
  C Our manager insists on our work being neat.

3 **A** I found out from where the parcel was sent from.
  B I found out from where the parcel was sent.
  C I found out where the parcel was sent from.

4 A Fiona asked me another chocolate cake recipe.

B Fiona asked me for another chocolate cake recipe.

C Fiona asked for another chocolate cake recipe from me.

5 A Mike was satisfied with coming out second in the competition.

B Mike was satisfied that he had come out second in the competition.

C Mike was satisfied about come out second in the competition.

PRACTICE *B* Match the expressions in **A** with those in **B**. Then join them using the prepositions in the box.

> (at) (by) (from) (of) (over) (with)

	A		B
1	He managed to get to the airport	2	their neighbours' lack of civic-consciousness.
2	They are horrified		who this written message is.
3	The ambassador expressed deep sorrow		reminding us to clear up the mess in the garage.
4	We disagreed		hitching a ride from a friend.
5	I don't know		the failure of the negotiations.
6	The landlord is tired		the proposal to increase our club's subscription fees.

1 *They are horrified at their neighbours' lack of civic-consciousness.*

2 _____

3 _____

4 _____

5 _____

6 _____

PRACTICE *C* Rewrite each sentence. Leave out the **that**-clause and use the words in the brackets.

1 I reminded John that the meeting would take place as scheduled on 28th May.

(of) *I reminded John of the meeting on 28th May.*

2 My sister grumbled that I received more pocket money than her.

(about — my) *My sister grumbled about my receiving more pocket money than her.*

3 I am annoyed that you take your good health for granted.

(at — your) _____

_____

4 Charles was upset that we had not enjoyed the film he recommended.

(about — our) _____

_____

5 The staff assured their new manager that they would give him their support and loyalty.

(of — their) _____

_____

6 The family was pleased that I had made attempts to find a job.

(with — my) _____

_____

7 The woman complained that her next-door neighbour had a difficult personality.

(of — neighbour's) _____

_____

PRACTICE D Some prepositions are missing in the conversation. Insert ⋏ where they should be and write the correct prepositions in the given boxes.

Interviewer :	I'd like to congratulate you ⋏ your winning the	line 1	*on*
	competition. Yours was a wonderful composition.	2	
John Doe :	Thanks. I never thought that I would win	3	
	because I faced stiff competition the others.	4	
Interviewer :	Well, all the judges felt your song had	line 5	
	that extra something lacking in the others.	6	
John Doe :	I took part in some competitions before, but	7	
	didn't even make it to the semi-finals.	8	
Interviewer :	Did you do something different this time?	9	
John Doe :	Well, when I think back what I wrote earlier,	line 10	
	they were rather sentimental numbers. I wrote about	11	
	missing a loved one, broken hearts . . . that sort of	12	
	thing. This latest song is never giving up hope.	13	
Interviewer :	Was it based on a personal story?	14	
John Doe :	Yes. I was on drugs once. I was conscious what	line 15	
	I was doing but I didn't care. I ended up with no	16	
	money, no hope. One day, a friend spotted me in the	17	
	alley which had become my home. He took me to see	18	
	a counsellor and stayed by my side till I recovered	19	
	from my addiction. He never gave up on me. That	line 20	
	was why when I held up my trophy, I said, "Francis,	21	
	I know you're watching this. This is you."	22	

UNIT 8 SUBJECT AND PREDICATE

Look at the **A** and **B** sentences below. Find out why **B** is correct and **A** is wrong in the **Grammar Points** section.

GRAMMAR POINTS

1A	Had a very hectic day today at the office. I need to rest for a while.	✗	
1B	**I** had a very hectic day today at the office. I need to rest for a while.	✓	1
2A	He lent the book **to me** that I had been wanting to read.	✗	
2B	He lent **me** the book that I had been wanting to read.	✓	2
3A	Don't **making** so much noise! You're disturbing the other groups.	✗	
3B	Don't **make** so much noise! You're disturbing the other groups.	✓	3

GRAMMAR POINTS

1   A sentence is usually made up of a subject and a predicate. The predicate must contain at least one verb. It can also have an object, a complement or an adverbial.

EXAMPLES:

Subject	Predicate		
	Verb	**Object**	**Adverbial**
A group of volunteers	cleaned up	the school field	after Sports Day.

Subject	**Verb**	**Complement**
These people	are	members of the chess club.

2   A sentence can contain two objects – a direct object and an indirect object. A direct object is something which receives the action from the subject. An indirect object is usually someone who benefits from the action on the direct object.

EXAMPLE: At the party, they   gave   the children   bags of sweets.
subject   verb   indirect object   direct object

The indirect object often comes before the direct object. We can put the indirect object after the direct object if it is in a prepositional phrase.

prepositional phrase

EXAMPLE: At the party, they   gave   bags of sweets   to the children.
subject   verb   direct object   preposition   indirect object

106

3 We usually use a sentence without a subject when we want to give an order, make an offer or suggestion, or give a warning. Such sentences are known as imperatives. We use the base form of verbs with imperatives and we form negative imperative sentences by adding 'do not'.

EXAMPLES:
Be quiet! *(order)*
Have a piece of pie. *(offer)*
Write neatly so people can read your work. *(suggestion)*
Do not leave the gate of the house unlocked. *(warning)*
Don't smoke in here. *(order)*

REMEMBER!
- A noun or pronoun can be used with the imperative to show precisely who you are speaking to.

EXAMPLES:
noun
James , show Mr Cole to my office, please. *(request)*
pronoun
You , stop bullying that child. *(order)*

PRACTICE *A* Fill in the blanks with the correct words in the boxes.

1 _____ too close to the main road. You might be knocked down by a car.
| Don't be playing | Don't play |

2 _____ can't see what all the fuss is about. After all, we think that going on a world tour is a common thing nowadays. | They | We |

3 _____ to the managing director, Sam. He wants to know how you feel about your new posting. | Must speak | Speak |

4 He helped _____ the stack of files to the car. | me carrying | me to carry |

5 _____ up that ladder, Bobby. You could fall and hurt yourself.
| Don't climbed | Don't climb |

6 Alex has bought _____ so we don't have to go out and buy lunch.
| for us some food | some food for us |

7 Sue handed _____ while she searched for the car keys. | to her husband the shopping | the shopping to her husband |

8 _____ on the alert! You don't know who's watching you. | Be | Have to be |

9 _____ going to be surprised to see all of us at the centenary celebrations.
| The director | The director is |

10 _____ some dessert, Fred. We have lots to choose from.
| Have | Want to have |

YOUR SCORE
10

PRACTICE *B* Circle the letters of the correct sentences.

1 **A** Don't know what they want us to do.
 B We don't know what they want us to do.
 C What they want us to do we don't know.

2 **A** Betty is a pastry chef at the institute of catering and hospitality.
 B A pastry chef at the institute of catering and hospitality is Betty.
 C Betty a pastry chef is at the institute of catering and hospitality.

3 A Throughout the night, people heard gunfire as explosions rocked the city.

  B People heard gunfire throughout the night as explosions rocked the city.

  C People heard gunfire as explosions rocked the city throughout the night.

4 A They served to all the participants at the seminar light refreshments.

  B To all the participants they served light refreshments at the seminar.

  C They served light refreshments to all the participants at the seminar.

5 A At the nature reserve, the animals waiting for the summer rains to fill the waterholes.

  B At the nature reserve, the animals waited for the summer rains to fill the waterholes.

  C For the summer rains to fill the waterholes, the animals waited at the nature reserve.

6 A Read as much as possible to improve your language.

  B Reading as much as possible to improve your language.

  C You must read as much as possible to improve your language.

7 A Don't being so fussy! You need to be a little less critical.

  B Don't be so fussy! You need to be a little less critical.

  C Don't so fussy! You need to be a little less critical.

YOUR SCORE

10

PRACTICE C Complete the sentences with the expressions in the box.

that you don't upset the whole tray of cakes.
me copies of the annual report.
a deep breath please, so that I can check your lungs.
because I can't hear what you're saying.
Joanne with a beautiful cashmere jacket.
late or we'll miss the opening number of the show.
are members of the state's basketball team.
cleaned their catch for the day and dried it in the sun.
we were helping out at the charity bazaar.
are part of the Alpine forests.

1 Don't be ⎯⎯⎯⎯⎯⎯⎯⎯⎯⎯⎯⎯⎯⎯⎯⎯⎯⎯⎯⎯⎯⎯⎯⎯⎯⎯⎯⎯⎯⎯⎯⎯⎯⎯⎯

2 Colin presented ⎯⎯⎯⎯⎯⎯⎯⎯⎯⎯⎯⎯⎯⎯⎯⎯⎯⎯⎯⎯⎯⎯⎯⎯⎯⎯⎯

3 Those magnificent pine trees ⎯⎯⎯⎯⎯⎯⎯⎯⎯⎯⎯⎯⎯⎯⎯⎯⎯⎯⎯⎯

4 She passed ⎯⎯⎯⎯⎯⎯⎯⎯⎯⎯⎯⎯⎯⎯⎯⎯⎯⎯⎯⎯⎯⎯⎯⎯⎯⎯⎯⎯⎯⎯

5 Speak louder ⎯⎯⎯⎯⎯⎯⎯⎯⎯⎯⎯⎯⎯⎯⎯⎯⎯⎯⎯⎯⎯⎯⎯⎯⎯⎯⎯⎯⎯

6 Make sure ⎯⎯⎯⎯⎯⎯⎯⎯⎯⎯⎯⎯⎯⎯⎯⎯⎯⎯⎯⎯⎯⎯⎯⎯⎯⎯⎯⎯⎯⎯⎯

7 Take ⎯⎯⎯⎯⎯⎯⎯⎯⎯⎯⎯⎯⎯⎯⎯⎯⎯⎯⎯⎯⎯⎯⎯⎯⎯⎯⎯⎯⎯⎯⎯⎯⎯⎯⎯

8 All afternoon, ⎯⎯⎯⎯⎯⎯⎯⎯⎯⎯⎯⎯⎯⎯⎯⎯⎯⎯⎯⎯⎯⎯⎯⎯⎯⎯⎯⎯

9 The fishermen _____

10 Those colourfully-dressed young men _____

PRACTICE $\boxed{D}$ Mark with $\wedge$ where a word is missing in the sentence. Then underline in the brackets the type of word that is missing.

1 Have to watch for pickpockets in this part of the city . (object   subject   verb)

2 I left the note in your letterbox . It must be still . (adverbial   complement   verb)

3 We gave the reply cards so she would know the numbers attending the wedding .
(direct object   indirect object   verb)

4 The girls looked for Katy in but there was no sign of her .
(adverbial   direct object   indirect object)

5 All night long , Bill to hear some news of his sons and their boat but the coastguard had no news for him . (direct object   indirect object   verb)

6 Post for me Karen . I'm in a terrible rush this morning . (adverbial   direct object   verb)

7 She very unreasonable. It's difficult to work with her . (indirect object   object   verb)

8 Have to get our scripts ready . The drama finals are just three months away .
(object   subject   verb)

9 This restaurant serves excellent food. Its Caesar's salad is .
(adverbial   complement   direct object)

10 Anna, go to the bank and get some cash for .
(complement   direct object   indirect object)

PRACTICE $\boxed{E}$ Some of the sentences are incorrect. Rewrite them correctly.

1 Following that car! We musn't lose sight of it.

_____

2 Several efforts Glen made to get in touch with us yesterday.

_____

3 Richard was the first member of his family to join the merchant navy.

_____

4 Have got to show more understanding towards Peter. You know he has to deal with many problems.

_____

_____

5 Don't be thanking us for these gifts. We think you deserve every one of them.

_____

_____

UNIT 9.1 RELATIVE CLAUSES

with **who**, **which** and **that**

Look at the **A** and **B** sentences below. Find out why **B** is correct and **A** is wrong in the **Grammar Points** section.

			GRAMMAR POINTS
1A She was one of the bird-watchers **which** camped here.	✗		
1B She was one of the bird-watchers **who** camped here.	✓	1
2A We are honouring the **patriots fought** for freedom.	✗		
2B We are honouring the **patriots who fought** for freedom.	✓	2
3A I gazed at **Mount Fuji which** looked mysterious at dusk.	✗		
3B I gazed at **Mount Fuji, which** looked mysterious at dusk.	✓	3

GRAMMAR POINTS

1 A relative clause describes a noun in the main clause. We use a relative clause beginning with **who** to describe people. We use a relative clause beginning with **which** to describe all nouns except people.

EXAMPLES: He is the playwright **who** / ~~which~~ won the prize.
      This is the play ~~who~~ / **which** won the prize.

> **REMEMBER!**
>
> ■ Most relative clauses begin with a relative pronoun (**that**, **which**, **who** or **whom**). The relative pronoun is usually the subject or object of the verb in the relative clause.
>
> ■ Traditionally, **who** is used as the subject while **whom** is used as the object of the relative clause. But nowadays, it is more common to use **who** as both the subject and object.
>
> **EXAMPLE:**
>
>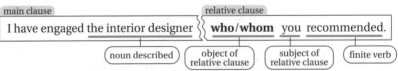
>
> ■ When **who** or **which** is the object of the relative clause, the subject of the relative clause comes after it.

2 Sometimes, **who** or **which** is the object of the finite verb in the relative clause. In these cases, we can drop **who** or **which**.

EXAMPLES:

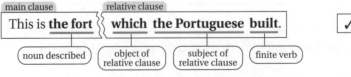

which = the fort = object of the verb **built**

This is the fort ~~which~~ the Portuguese built.   ✓

110

We cannot drop **who** or **which** when it is the subject of the relative clause.

EXAMPLE:

main clause | relative clause

This is **the fort** {{ **which** kept the town secure. ☑

noun described | subject | finite verb

which = the fort = object of the verb **kept**

This is the fort ~~which~~ kept the town secure. ☒

---

3 A relative clause can be defining or non-defining. A defining relative clause with **who** or **which** identifies the people or things, or tells others what sort of people or things we are referring to.

EXAMPLE:

main clause | defining relative clause

She likes **doctors** {{ **who** speak frankly. (identifies **what sort of doctors** she likes: the frank sort)

noun described

A non-defining relative clause with **who** or **which** does not identify the people or things we are referring to but gives more information only. We put a comma before a non-defining relative clause.

EXAMPLE:

main clause | non-defining relative clause

We visited Paris {{ , }} which both of us loved. (gives more information about Paris)

comma before non-defining clause

We cannot drop **who** or **which** from a non-defining relative clause.

EXAMPLE: We visited Paris, ~~which~~ both of us loved. ☒

REMEMBER!

■ A relative clause beginning with **that** can describe all nouns including people.

EXAMPLES: She is the designer **that**/**who** I admire. ☑

This is the pendant **that**/**which** I want. ☑

■ A non-defining relative clause cannot begin with **that**.

EXAMPLES: I saw Anna, **who**/~~that~~ seemed lonesome.

He borrowed my tape, **which**/~~that~~ he never returned.

PRACTICE *A* Cross out the incorrect items in the boxes to complete the sentences.

1 He is kind towards the youngsters | were | who were | placed in his care.

2 That was the decision | which | , which | I regret to this day.

3 Laura completed one course of antibiotics | that | , that | did not help her.

4 The authorities demolished the huts | had | that had | been built on state land.

5 The inspector questioned the man | that | which | Julie had identified.

6 This is the most puzzling incident | I | , that I | have ever come across.

111

7 Jake went to see his father | who | , who | was working in Beijing.

8 Jane is studying genetics | which | , which | she finds fascinating.

9 These records will tell us the things | we | , which we | need to know.

10 He is the most innovative teacher | that | which | we have come across.

PRACTICE **B** Circle the letters of the items in the boxes that go in the places marked with ⟨.

1 He sent his mother a bouquet, ⟨ cheered her.

2 I know of cockatoos ⟨ can converse fluently.

3 You are one of those people ⟨ always work too hard.

4 John is looking for a contractor ⟨ he can trust.

5 The children miss their grandmother, ⟨ doted on them.

6 It was a speech ⟨

7 He distrusts people ⟨

8 She often gets splendid marks ⟨

9 Mr Menon was the most effective chairman ⟨

10 I was the boy ⟨

A	that
B	which
A	which
B	who
A	which
B	who
A	that
B	, that
A	that
B	who
A	inspired us.
B	that inspired us.
A	who flatter him.
B	, who flatter him.
A	, which she never flaunts.
B	which she never flaunts.
A	, that we ever had.
B	we ever had.
A	which your sons befriended.
B	who your sons befriended.

PRACTICE **C** Circle the letters of the correct sentences.

1 A The Internet is an invention which must not misuse.
  B The Internet is an invention that we must not misuse.
  C The Internet is an invention which we must not misuse.

2 A Felix revisited the islands of the Hebrides, which had captivated him.
  B Felix revisited the islands of the Hebrides which had captivated him
  C Felix revisited the islands of the Hebrides that had captivated him.

3 A He no longer believes the stories which she tells him.
  B He no longer believes the stories that she tells him.
  C He no longer believes the stories she tells him.

4 A She worries about the people, who took a risk to save her.

   B She worries about the people who took a risk to save her.

   C She worries about the people that took a risk to save her.

5 A This is the marketing executive who secured the most deals this month.

   B This is the marketing executive secured the most deals this month.

   C This is the marketing executive that secured the most deals this month.

PRACTICE D Underline the correct items in the brackets.

Each year, universities in the West take in quite a number of students **1** (which / who) come from Asian countries. Such a student may initially feel lost in an environment **2** (which / , which) is unfamiliar. He experiences a reaction **3** (that / who) sociologists call 'culture shock'. The culture, or way of life, around him is vastly different from the one **4** (that / , that) he knew back home. He sees types of behaviour **5** (puzzle/ which puzzle) him. He longs to be back in his homeland with his own people **6** (who / , who) seem to him so much friendlier than those around him.

After some time, the Asian student may undergo experiences **7** (that / , that) change his outlook. He may even lose the beliefs **8** (he / , which he) once valued. However, this does not happen to a student **9** (which / who) is sure of his own cultural identity. He takes the best **10** (the / , which the) West can offer; but he does not lose his Asian roots.

PRACTICE E Rewrite the sentences correctly using relative clauses beginning with **who**, **which** or **that**.

1 This is the waterfall, which we visited last year.

   This is the waterfall which we visited last year.

2 The sports committee congratulated the athletes which had won gold and silver medals.

   _____

   _____

3 The doctor prescribed a new tranquiliser, that did not agree with me.

   _____

4 We must find a guide, who has been there many times.

   _____

5 Mr Thomas is a teacher can hold us spellbound with his stories.

   _____

6 She poured tea into little cups, were made of fine porcelain.

   _____

UNIT 9.2 **RELATIVE CLAUSES**

with **whose**

Look at the **A** and **B** sentences below. Find out why **B** is correct and **A** is wrong in the **Grammar Points** section.

			GRAMMAR POINTS
1A	Milan is a city **its** fashion houses are influential.	✗	
1B	Milan is a city **whose** fashion houses are influential.	✓	1
2A	We'll ask our new classmate **whose** father is a politician.	✗	
2B	We'll ask our new classmate**, whose** father is a politician.	✓	2

GRAMMAR POINTS ─────────────────

1 We use a relative clause beginning with **whose** to show that the noun after **whose** is connected to or belongs to the noun before it.

EXAMPLES:

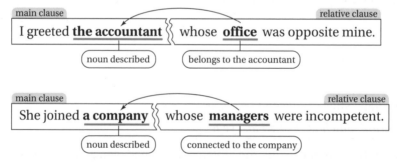

2 A relative clause with **whose** can be defining or non-defining. A defining relative clause with **whose** identifies the people or things, or tells others what sort of people or things we are referring to.

EXAMPLE:

main clause	defining relative clause (explains **which cave** we entered)
We explored the cave	whose limestone formations are a well-known tourist attraction.

A non-defining relative clause with **whose** does not identify the people or things we are referring to but gives more information only.

EXAMPLE:

(does not explain **which friend** or what sort of friend embarrassed me)

main clause		non-defining relative clause
I was embarrassed by my friend	**,**	whose mobile phone kept ringing during the concert.

comma before non-defining clause

PRACTICE *A*   Tick the correct sentences.

1 I know many women whose careers and family lives combine well.

2 She avoids colognes their fragrance is too strong.

3 They found Jake whose life they saved through first aid.

4 We'll support the candidates whose policies we like.

5 Kay beckoned to the child whose broken toy she had repaired.

6 He is defending a woman whose he knows her family.

7 Ken will join the college whose soccer team needs him.

8 The librarian found many books that the pages were torn.

9 Dan is teaching at his old school whose pupils are as naughty as he was.

10 We looked after Sally's pet monkey, whose antics we enjoyed.

YOUR SCORE

10

PRACTICE *B*   Circle the letters of the correct sentences.

1 A That is the old lady, whose memoirs amazed the nation.
   B That is the old lady whose memoirs amazed the nation.
   C That is the old lady whose daughter amazed the nation.

2 A We've seen her antiques, whose value she doesn't know.
   B We've seen her antiques, whose value is enormous.
   C We've seen her antiques whose value she doesn't know.

3 A They are proud of the country whose independence they helped to establish.
   B They are proud of the country independence they helped to establish.
   C They are proud of the country whose independence was established through their efforts.

4 A I stared at the man whose music had delighted my father.
   B I stared at the man whose name I was trying to recall.
   C I stared at the man whose twin was a famous footballer.

115

5 A The tourists visited the Grand Canyon, whose magnificence awed them.
   B The tourists visited the Grand Canyon whose magnificence awed them.
   C The tourists visited the Grand Canyon, magnificence awed them.

PRACTICE **C** Rearrange the words in the boxes to form relative clauses. Rewrite the sentences using the relative clauses at the end.

1 I envied my brother Alan. | achievements – could – I – match – not – whose |

I envied my brother Alan, whose achievements I could not match.

2 We have bungled the experiment. | future – is – our – success – to – vital – whose |

_____

3 Lisa entered the Horizon Hotel. | cameramen – crowded – lobby – was – whose – with |

_____

4 She talked to a reporter. | face – recognised – she – whose |

_____

5 He thanked the lawyer. | brilliance – had – his – case – saved – whose |

_____

6 They stood by the Red Sea. | history – knew – so – they – well – whose |

_____

PRACTICE **D** Tick the box if the A and B sentences have the same meaning.

1 A The clerk apologised to the woman whose file he had lost.
   B The clerk apologised to the woman. He had lost her file.

2 A They welcomed Miss Simpson, whose credentials were excellent.
   B They welcomed Miss Simpson. Her credentials were excellent.

3 A Dr Chan bumped into Dr Fong, whose student he had been.
   B Dr Chan bumped into Dr Fong. Dr Fong had been Dr Chan's student.

4 A He had a job whose pressures he could cope with.
   B He had a job. He could cope with the pressures of the job.

5 A She chose jewellery whose beauty would enhance hers.
   B She chose jewellery. Her beauty would enhance its beauty.

6 A My father was born in a coastal town whose alleys smelt of fish.
   B My father was born in a coastal town. His alleys smelt of fish.

7 A I have good friends, whose moral support I value.
   B I have good friends. I value their moral support.

8 A My boss sits behind a table whose size proclaims his status.
   B My boss sits behind a table. His size proclaims his status.

9 A Our museum has a new curator whose energy is boundless.

   B Our museum has a new curator. The curator's energy is boundless.

    ☐

10 A The children had a plan whose ingenuity stunned us.

    B The children had a plan. They were stunned by our ingenuity.

    ☐

YOUR SCORE / 10

PRACTICE *E* Rewrite the sentences in the passage correctly using relative clauses with **whose**.

(1) I am lucky to be a student parents have a realistic outlook on success at school. (2) They are people their expectations I can meet without stress. (3) I am also fortunate to be in my school whose policy is to help every student progress at his or her own pace. (4) Free from tension, I find myself discovering abilities their existence I never realised. (5) I hope to become a person, whose development is balanced. (6) This will enable me to face a world its challenges get harder each day.

1 *I am lucky to be a student whose parents have a realistic outlook on success at school.*

2 _____

3 _____

4 _____

5 _____

6 _____

YOUR SCORE / 10

PRACTICE *F* Underline the correct items in the brackets.

We had a delightful holiday in Bali **1** (whose / , whose) attractions we had long wanted to sample. We chose lodgings **2** (whose / , whose) simplicity appealed to us. We are people **3** (who / whose) need to escape occasionally from urban life. We also decided to avoid places **4** (that / whose) cultural shows were meant for tourists.

Through persistent enquiries, we found a group of Balinese dance students **5** (whose / who's) repertoire few tourists had seen. In our search for paintings, we came upon a ramshackle building **6** (that / whose) housed a fine gallery. It displayed works **7** (range / whose range) and power were incredible. We also discovered one of those beaches **8** (which / whose) purity is pristine. Most importantly, we got to know the Balinese people **9** (whose / , whose) warmth and hospitality touched our hearts. It was a visit **10** (which / whose) we will never forget.

YOUR SCORE / 10

UNIT 9.3 **RELATIVE CLAUSES**

after subjects of main clauses

Look at the **A** and **B** sentences below. Find out why **B** is correct and **A** is wrong in the **Grammar Points** section.

			GRAMMAR POINTS
1A	The plans **are not practical which have been made**.	✗	
1B	The plans **which have been made are not practical**.	✓	1
2A	The **scene moved** us was the parting of mother and child.	✗	
2B	The **scene that/which moved** us was the parting of mother and child.	✓	2
3A	**Diana whose** friendship I **valued suddenly** moved away.	✗	
3B	**Diana, whose** friendship I **valued, suddenly** moved away.	✓	3

GRAMMAR POINTS

1 When we use a relative clause to describe the subject of the main clause, we insert the relative clause after the subject and before the finite verb of the main clause.

EXAMPLE:

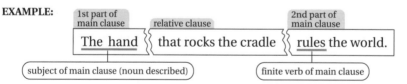

2 We can drop **who**, **which** or **that** when it is the object of the finite verb.

EXAMPLES:

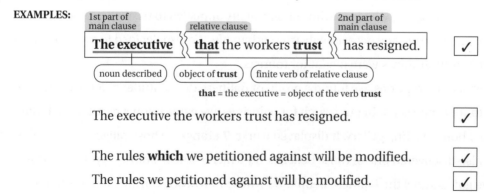

The executive the workers trust has resigned. ✓

The rules **which** we petitioned against will be modified. ✓

The rules we petitioned against will be modified. ✓

We cannot drop **who**, **which** or **that** when it is the subject of a relative clause.

EXAMPLE:

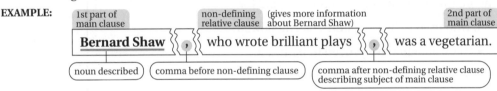

| 1st part of main clause | relative clause | | 2nd part of main clause |
| **The song** | **which** made Bing Crosby famous | | is still popular. | ✓ |

noun described · subject of relative clause

The song made Bing Crosby famous is still popular. ✗

3 A relative clause describing the subject of the main clause can be defining or non-defining. A defining relative clause identifies the people or things or tells others what sort of people or things we are referring to.

EXAMPLE:

| 1st part of main clause | defining relative clause (identifies the sort of person who is unkind) | 2nd part of main clause |
| A person | who enjoys housework | is a good roommate. |

4 A non-defining relative clause does not identify the people or things we are referring to but gives more information only. We always put a comma before and after such a non-defining relative clause.

EXAMPLE:

| 1st part of main clause | | non-defining relative clause (gives more information about Bernard Shaw) | | 2nd part of main clause |
| **Bernard Shaw** | , | who wrote brilliant plays | , | was a vegetarian. |

noun described · comma before non-defining clause · comma after non-defining relative clause describing subject of main clause

> **REMEMBER!**
> - A non-defining relative clause cannot begin with **that**.
>   EXAMPLE: Hitler, ~~that~~ /who was a dictator, committed many atrocities.

PRACTICE *A* Some of the sentences contain words which can be dropped. Put brackets around these words.

1 *The candidates (that) I invigilated behaved very well.*
2 The vacation which I took made me feel better.
3 The people who came this morning upset our schedule.
4 The fire drill which occurred at midnight surprised everyone.
5 The reporters who the principal briefed want more information.
6 The mosquitoes that torment me are also a health hazard.
7 The traders who lost their shops in the fire have put up temporary stalls by the roadside.
8 The principles which we hold help us make sensible decisions.
9 The discipline master, who can also be compassionate, punishes the monks.
10 Friends that you can trust fully are valuable.
11 The clown who the children love will perform again tonight.

YOUR SCORE

10

PRACTICE *B* Underline the correct words in the brackets.

1 The man (beat / that beat) you at chess has won the championship.
2 The meadows (look parched now which were once green / which were once green look parched now).

3 This city, which looks enchanting at night (is / , is) ugly in the daytime.

4 The people (who / , who) we are expecting have not called.

5 The plot (that they hatched / , that they hatched,) has been discovered.

6 The girl (who wanted / wanted) to be a doctor is now a cardiologist.

7 The bunch of keys (which / , which) I usually put here has vanished.

8 Venice, (that / which) I yearn to visit, is next on my itinerary.

9 The team (that / , that) we have been supporting is almost certain to win.

10 Children (who / who are) very bright need special handling.

YOUR SCORE
10

PRACTICE C Tick the correct sentences.

1 Mrs Cook lives next door who is a manicurist.

2 Our boat, which we've given a fresh coat of paint, looks almost new.

3 The window, that your son broke has to be paid for.

4 My father, who used to be very stern, has mellowed.

5 The stocks they bought have proved to be sound.

6 Your visit, that surprised everyone, was superbly timed.

7 One of the things annoyed him was my absence.

8 The voice whose purity I love belongs to a young soprano.

9 The chair belongs to our neighbour which is broken.

10 The best students of the engineering course this year have already been offered jobs.

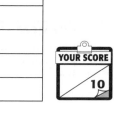
YOUR SCORE
10

PRACTICE D Rewrite the sentences correctly.

1 The argument convinced them was put forward by a child.
   The argument that / which convinced them was put forward by a child.

2 The Statuesque, that is a five-star hotel, offers special rates for senior citizens.

3 One of the parties has been arrested that signed the contract.

4 Their leader, that they all revere, is seriously ill.

5 Youngsters who feel neglected, are likely to get into trouble.

6 Your departure which nobody expected saddened us all.

YOUR SCORE
10

PRACTICE E Join the sentences under **A** to those under **B**. Change the sentences under **B** into relative clauses beginning with **who**, **which** or **whose**.

	A
1	The permit is for two years.
2	The article is about my grandmother.
3	You are merely talking about tolerance.
4	The baby looks increasingly like me.
5	Africa draws me irresistibly
6	Countries need this programme.

	B
	They will issue it to us.
	She spoke up for women's rights.
	You should practise it.
	My cousins have adopted him.
	I long to explore its mysteries.
	Their populations are multi-ethnic.

1   *The permit which they will issue to us is for two years.*

2   _____

3   _____

4   _____

5   _____

6   _____

YOUR SCORE

10

PRACTICE F Underline the incorrect sentences and rewrite them correctly.

A habit nearly ruined my school career was studying at the last minute. My mother put me on a study schedule from the first day of each year, who was a strict disciplinarian. The schedule, which was quite realistic, would have brought me painlessly through examinations. However, the promises, which I made to my mother, were undermined by my passion for fantasy novels. My favourite stories whose authors wove wonderful dreams enticed me away from my textbooks.

My mother, who was trusting though strict, did not suspect the true nature of the 'studying' in my room. The crazy cramming which I did just before examinations was somehow sufficient to get me through lower secondary school. The disaster cured me of 11th-hour marathons came at upper secondary level.

1   *A habit that/which nearly ruined my school career was studying at the last minute.*

2   _____
    _____

3   _____
    _____

4   _____
    _____

5   _____
    _____

6   _____
    _____

YOUR SCORE

10

UNIT 10.1 ADVERBIAL CLAUSES

with **because, as, since**

Look at the **A** and **B** sentences below. Find out why **B** is correct and **A** is wrong in the **Grammar Points** section.

CHECKPOINT

				GRAMMAR POINTS
1A	The war **had ended because** we rejoiced.	✗		
1B	We **rejoiced because** the war **had ended**.	✓	1
2A	Because he lacked sleep, **so** his reflexes were slow.	✗		
2B	Because he lacked sleep, his reflexes were slow.	✓	2

 GRAMMAR POINTS

1   We use an adverbial clause beginning with **because** to give the reason for what is happening or what is stated in the main clause.

EXAMPLES:

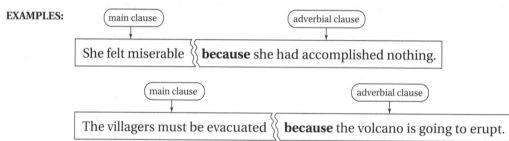

main clause   adverbial clause

She felt miserable 〉〉 **because** she had accomplished nothing.

main clause   adverbial clause

The villagers must be evacuated 〉〉 **because** the volcano is going to erupt.

2   We can place an adverbial clause beginning with **because** after or before the main clause.

EXAMPLES:

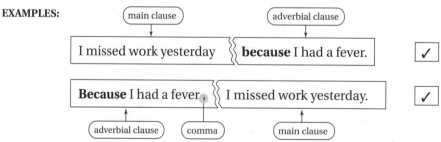

main clause   adverbial clause

I missed work yesterday 〉〉 **because** I had a fever.   ✓

Because I had a fever, 〉〉 I missed work yesterday.   ✓

adverbial clause   comma   main clause

When we place the adverbial clause before the main clause, we must put a comma after the adverbial clause. We must not add **so** between the two clauses.

EXAMPLE: **Because** I had a fever, **so** I missed work yesterday.   ✗

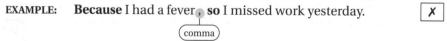

comma

PRACTICE *A* Underline the adverbial clauses in the sentences.

1 She looks confident <u>as her clothes suit her personality</u>.

2 Because he helped us once, we must support him now.

3 Since you are a good speaker, you should join the debating society.

4 Laughter is therapeutic because it helps us to relax.

5 As the instructions are clear, you shouldn't make a mistake.

6 They decided to sell their car since they needed the money.

7 Because the harvest was splendid, they held a special thanksgiving feast.

8 As Sally is rather extravagant, she does not have much money saved.

9 The captain was annoyed because a boy had stowed away on the ship.

10 Since exercise promotes health, everyone should do it regularly.

11 I can't join you as I've promised to babysit tonight.

YOUR SCORE

/10

PRACTICE *B* Cross out the incorrect words in the boxes to complete the sentences.

1 Since I sent the parcel by courier, | so you | you | should get it tomorrow.

2 He couldn't keep up | because | because of | the pace of the training was punishing.

3 Excessive exposure to sunlight is | beneficial | dangerous | as it can lead to skin cancer.

4 Because the gymnasium is close by, | I | so I | exercise there very often.

5 We love standing on that hilltop | because | it's because | the view is breathtaking.

6 Your name will be struck off the register since you | always | rarely | attend the classes.

7 As he wanted to learn Chinese, | he | so he | found a tutor.

8 She | did not enjoy | enjoyed | the cruise because she was sick most of the time.

9 Since the trains are fully booked, we | will | won't | have to go by plane.

10 He said to me, "As you | dislike | like | adventure, I've organised a hiking trip to the high mountains."

PRACTICE *C* Fill in the blanks with the correct words in the boxes.

1 We hurried back _____ a storm was brewing.

2 She didn't eat the meat as it was _____ .

3 Since I'm not needed, _____ leave now.

4 He could lift heavy weights _____ he was strong.

5 You are respected since you _____ forget a promise.

6 Because his investment strategy failed, _____ lost a lot of money.

7 As they are short-staffed, delays are _____ .

8 The dress looked _____ as it was well cut.

9 Her gifts _____ us because they are imaginative.

10 They _____ him since he spoke convincingly.

because	because of
tender	tough
I'll	so I'll
because	it's because
always	never
he	so he
common	uncommon
dowdy	smart
bore	delight
opposed	supported

PRACTICE *D* Rewrite the sentences correctly using the words in the brackets. Place the adverbial clauses after the main clauses.

1 The dessert was a disaster it's because I forgot the sugar. (because)

_____

2 Since she has a gruff manner of speaking, so she is often misunderstood. (since)

_____

3 As they praised me too highly, so I felt embarrassed. (because)

_____

4 You must act fast because of time is running out. (as)

_____

5 As the night is very cold, you will need your cardigan. (because)

_____

PRACTICE *E* Rewrite the sentences without changing the meaning. Use the words provided.

1 A As the music was nostalgic, I wept on hearing it.

  B I _wept on hearing the music_ because _it was nostalgic._

2 A They received a complaint. Their kitchen was dirty.

  B Since _____

3 A I daren't even touch those ornaments since they are fragile.

  B As those ornaments_____

4 A Smoking is harmful. It should be avoided.

  B Smoking _____ since _____

5 A She was protective of her father. He had delicate health.

  B Because her father_____

6 A Because the room was comfortable, she spent a lot of time in it.

  B _____ as _____

YOUR SCORE
10

PRACTICE *F* Join the sentences in the brackets using **since**, **as**, **because**, **as** and **since** in that order.

You say you'd love to live in my country. You'd be rid of chilly winters. (You haven't been to my 'sunny paradise'. You have no idea how boring it can be.) (The climate depresses me. The only change is from hot and dry to hot and wet.) (I prefer your temperate climate. The four seasons give variety to life.) (I've lived in both countries. I can make a fair comparison.) (I even enjoyed your worst winters. They made the prospect of spring doubly delightful.)

You say you'd love to live in my country because you'd be rid of chilly winters.

_____

_____

_____

_____

_____

_____

_____

YOUR SCORE
10

UNIT 10.2 ADVERBIAL CLAUSES

> ## with **although**, **though**, **even though**, **while**

Look at the **A** and **B** sentences below. Find out why **B** is correct and A is wrong in the **Grammar Points** section.

GRAMMAR POINTS

**CH**ECKPOINT

			GRAMMAR POINTS
1A	The players lost the football match **because** they tried their best.	✗	
1B	The players lost the football match **although** they tried their best.	✓	1
2A	Although this computer is expensive **but** it breaks down easily.	✗	
2B	Although this computer is expensive**,** it breaks down easily.	✓	2

GRAMMAR POINTS

1   We use an adverbial clause beginning with **although** to show that what is happening or stated in the main clause cannot be changed or prevented by what is happening or stated in the adverbial clause.

EXAMPLES:

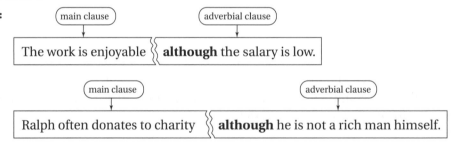

2   We can place an adverbial clause beginning with **although** after or before the main clause.

EXAMPLES:

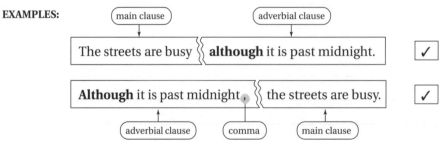

When we place the adverbial clause before the main clause, we must put a comma after the adverbial clause. We must not add **but** between the two clauses.

EXAMPLE: **Although** it is past midnight **,** **but** the streets are busy.   ✗

126

- Adverbial clauses beginning with **even though**, **though** and **while** have the same function as adverbial clauses beginning with **although**.

  EXAMPLE:

  (main clause)　　　　　　　　　　　　(adverbial clause)

  She has a lovely voice ⟩⟩ **although / even though / though** she is not beautiful.

- Rule 2 applies to adverbial clauses beginning with **even though**, **though** and **while**. But adverbial clauses beginning with **while** are more commonly used before the main clause.

  EXAMPLE:

  While she is not beautiful, ⟩⟩ she has a lovely voice.

  ↑ adverbial clause　　(comma)　　(main clause)

- An adverbial clause with **although**, **though**, **even though** or **while** has a subject and a finite verb. The finite verb must agree with the subject.

  EXAMPLES:

  Although / Though　} she is my classmate, ⟩⟩ I have never spoken to her before.
  Even though / While

  adverbial clause　　(subject)(finite verb)　　　　　　main clause

  Although / Though　} they are my classmates, ⟩⟩ I have never spoken to them before.
  Even though / While

  adverbial clause　　(subject)(finite verb)　　　　　　main clause

PRACTICE $\boxed{A}$　Underline the adverbial clauses in the sentences below.

1　Although Adam is only two, he enjoys spicy curries.

2　She enjoyed the movie though I found it boring.

3　He is still planting rubber even though other trees are more lucrative.

4　Though he turned 80 yesterday, he is still formidable at chess.

5　Even though our new car has power steering, I still have problems parking it.

6　I consider myself lucky although I've had a few setbacks during my life.

7　While this satin dress is too shiny for daytime, it is perfect for evenings.

8　Although ginseng can boost energy, too much of it has the opposite effect.

9　A firm bed is good for your back although a soft one feels more luxurious.

YOUR SCORE
10

10　While he is a good manager, he is sometimes overzealous in trying to improve the quality of work.

PRACTICE $\boxed{B}$　Cross out the incorrect words in the boxes to complete the sentences.

1　Even though Kay likes sweet things, | but she | she | does not eat too many.

2　You can't stop the ageing process although | can | you can | slow down the signs of ageing.

3　Although she has retired as a teacher, she | often | seldom | goes back to her old school to do some voluntary work.

4 The birds are now eating from my hand though they | shy | were shy | at first.

5 Though some tourists know of this beach, | is | it is | still unspoilt.

6 While we did have some problems in the beginning, | all | but all | is well now.

7 She managed to escape | even though | since | the security was tight.

8 I don't speak Spanish although I | have known | known | many Argentinians.

9 Though his books are all bestsellers, most of them are | realistic | unrealistic |.

10 She adjusts quickly to new ways while her sister | is less | less | flexible.

PRACTICE C Rearrange the words in the boxes to complete the sentences.

1 The bride looked radiant | her — light — make-up — though — very — was. |

The bride looked radiant though her make-up was very light.

2 | a — arts — expert — he — is — martial — while, | he has a scholarly air.

_____

3 | acts — even — she — though — well, | she prefers writing scripts.

_____

4 The necklace is exquisite | a — although — designed — hurry — in — it — was. |

_____

5 | although — glamourous — hair — long — looks, | this short cut is more practical.

_____

6 Many of us don't drink enough water | essential — even — for — health — is — it — though. |

_____

_____

PRACTICE D Circle the letters of the correct sentences.

1 A She likes pastel shades though bright colours suit her better.
   B Though bright colours suit her better, but she like pastel shades.
   C Though bright colours suit her better, she likes pastel shades.

2 A While the children's menu has variety, the dishes for adults are dull.
   B Although the children's menu has variety, the dishes for adults are dull.
   C Although the dishes for adults are dull but the children's menu has variety.

3 A A large park is close by though we living in the city centre.
   B Even though we live in the city centre, a large park is close by.
   C A large park is close by though we live in the city centre.

4 A Although the forgery was skilful, the handwriting specialist could detect it.

   B The handwriting specialist could detect the forgery even though it was skilful.

   C While the forgery was skilful, but the handwriting specialist could detect it.

5 A Though he does not have the necessary qualification, he has valuable experience.

   B He has valuable experience though he has the necessary qualification.

   C While he does not have the necessary qualification, he has valuable experience.

YOUR SCORE
10

PRACTICE *E* Join the sentences using the words in the boxes to form adverbial clauses. Place the adverbial clauses before the main clauses.

1 He went on driving. He felt dizzy. | even though |

Even though he felt dizzy, he went on driving.

2 It is a double room. It isn't bigger than the single rooms in other hotels. | while |

_____

3 She's walking steadily. She's wearing high-heeled shoes. | although |

_____

4 We went outdoors unprotected. The sun was scorching. | though |

_____

5 You must obey the rules. You are the president's son. | even though |

_____

6 I was very late. They accepted my apology. | although |

_____

YOUR SCORE
10

PRACTICE *F* Rewrite the passage and correct the adverbial clauses.

   Many women manage well, though they have to juggle career and family responsibilities. While some newspaper articles have attributed juvenile problems to working mothers this allegation is unfair. According to surveys, teenagers can be troubled even though their mothers are always at home. A close relationship can be maintained between a mother and her teenage children although she at work for part of the day. Though she can't be with them for hours on end, but she can give them quality time every day.

_____

_____

_____

_____

_____

_____

_____

YOUR SCORE
10

UNIT 10.3 ADVERBIAL CLAUSES

with **as**, **since**, **when**, **while**

Look at the **A** and **B** sentences below. Find out why **B** is correct and **A** is wrong in the **Grammar Points** section.

GRAMMAR POINTS

CHECKPOINT

1A	She **was crying** as she walked away.	✗	
1B	She **cried** as she walked away.	✓	1
2A	It **caused** trouble since we bought it.	✗	
2B	It **has caused** / **has been causing** trouble since we bought it.	✓	2

GRAMMAR POINTS

1 We use an adverbial clause beginning with **as** or **while** for an action which takes place at the same time as another action in the main clause.

(a) We usually use the same simple or continuous tense for both clauses if both actions start and end at about the same time.

EXAMPLES:

REMEMBER!
■ The simple tense is usually used to signal a short action, whereas the continuous tense is usually used to signal a longer action.

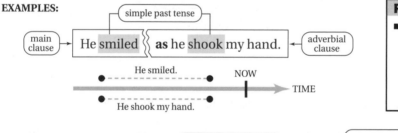

(b) We usually use the continuous tense for the adverbial clause if a longer action takes place before and continues throughout the action in the main clause. (The simple tense is usually used for the main clause.)

EXAMPLES:

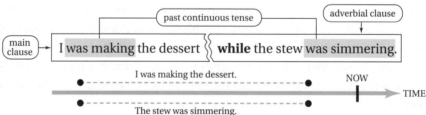

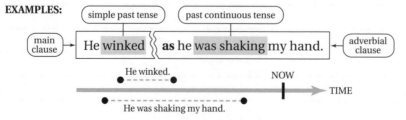

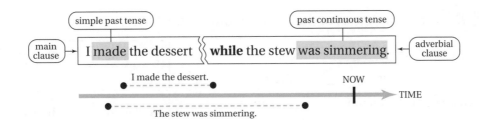

2 We use an adverbial clause beginning with **since** for an action or an event which began at a point in the past and continues to the present moment. We usually use the perfect tense in the main clause and the simple past tense in the adverbial clause.

EXAMPLE:

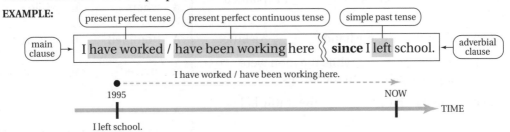

REMEMBER!

■ An adverbial clause beginning with **when** can be used for an action that takes place just before another action in the main clause. The simple tense is usually used in both clauses.

EXAMPLE:

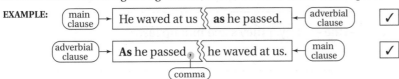

(I patted the bulldog's head. A moment later the bulldog growled.)

■ An adverbial clause beginning with **as**, **since**, **when** or **while** can be placed after or before the main clause.

EXAMPLE:

| main clause | → | He waved at us ⟩⟩ **as** he passed. | ← adverbial clause | ✓ |

| adverbial clause | → | **As** he passed **,** ⟩⟩ he waved at us. | ← main clause | ✓ |
comma

PRACTICE | A | Underline the adverbial clauses in the sentences.

1 Since he installed his new telephone, he has received many crank calls.

2 The boss glared at me when my mobile phone rang during the meeting.

3 The boy was fidgeting while his mother was gossiping with their neighbour.

4 As she hugged her brother, she pinched him playfully.

5 They have not been sleeping well since the accident occurred.

6 While the reporter interviewed us, the photographer took some pictures of our school.

7 He smiled at the little girl as she curtsied to him.

8 When the singer stepped out of the limousine, his fans mobbed him.

9 Since she arrived in Hollywood, she has been making a name for herself as a talented newcomer.

10 The boy chuckled when the pony nuzzled him.

YOUR SCORE

10

PRACTICE *B*   Circle the letters of the correct words in the boxes.

1	Since she was 15, she _____ a difficult life.	**A** has led	**B** led
2	He turned a somersault _____ he dived.	**A** as	**B** since
3	We saved up our extra income _____ others overspent.	**A** when	**B** while
4	The boy cleared his throat several times while he _____ his speech.	**A** deliver	**B** was delivering
5	They understood my difficulties _____ I explained the situation to them.	**A** when	**B** while
6	As I was giving her my card, my hand _____ a little.	**A** trembled	**B** was trembling
7	The customs officers _____ while the men were loading the smuggled goods onto the lorries.	**A** arrived	**B** were arriving
8	The vehicles came to a halt _____ the traffic lights turned red.	**A** since	**B** when
9	_____ the boat lurched, I grabbed my little sister.	**A** When	**B** While
10	Since the recession began, I _____ luxuries.	**A** cut out	**B** have cut out

YOUR SCORE
10

PRACTICE *C*   Rearrange the words in the boxes to complete the sentences.

1 The police tailed the fans film star — they — stalked — the — while.

_____

2 as — greeted — manager — new — the — they, they sized him up fast.

_____

3 The people have been assembling at the village square curfew — lifted — since — the — was.

_____

4 she — machine — the — bought — when, her life became easier.

_____

5 ancient — its — restored — since — splendour — was, tourists have flocked to the castle.

_____

YOUR SCORE
10

PRACTICE *D*   Tick the sentences that are correct.

1 The child howled when she saw the needle and syringe.

2 While you were away, your staff was having a wonderful time.

3 Since he returned from Paris, he behaved strangely.

4 The tyres screeched as the car turned a corner.

5 When the family needed cash, she was pawning a piece of jewellery.

6 Not a drop of rain has fallen since the year began.

7 Sheba was mewing piteously while I was scolding her.

8 As she clasped my hand, she was giving me an odd look.

9 The sound of the chimes is filling the air when the wind blows.

10 Since he underwent surgery, he has enjoyed excellent health.

PRACTICE E Rewrite the sentences using the correct verb forms.

1 They are close friends since they were in kindergarten.
They have been close friends since they were in kindergarten.

2 Anna was listening to music while she waited for her friends to arrive.

3 The two armed men were jumping off the train as it entered the railway station.

4 Since the stock market recovered, his financial situation improves.

5 The children rushed into the house when their mother was calling them to have dinner.

6 For a moment Jim was slipping as he was climbing up the ladder but he managed to steady himself.

PRACTICE F Rewrite the passage. Change the sentences in brackets into adverbial clauses using **since**, **while**, **while**, **as** and **when** in that order.

1 (Kate graduated.) , her friends have been urging her to dress better. Right through university, she wore baggy T-shirts and faded jeans 2 (Her fellow-students experimented with fashionable clothes.). Now, 3 (Kate is reading up for her first job interview.), her helpful friends are putting together an outfit to impress her interviewers. Kate thanks them 4 (She poses in the smart suit with matching accessories.). She quietly decides to wear a simple dress 5 (She goes for the interview.).

UNIT 10.4 ADVERBIAL CLAUSES

with **so that** and **so . . . that**

Look at the **A** and **B** sentences below. Find out why **B** is correct and **A** is wrong in the **Grammar Points** section.

GRAMMAR POINTS

CHECKPOINT

1A	She wanted them to study hard so that they **can** get good jobs.	✗	
1B	She wanted them to study hard so that they **could** get good jobs.	✓	1
2A	You did it **extremely** well that everyone was pleased.	✗	
2B	You did it **so** well **that** everyone was pleased.	✓	2

GRAMMAR POINTS

1 We use an adverbial clause beginning with **so that** to show the purpose of the action in the main clause. In the adverbial clause, we usually use a modal which is in the **same tense** (present or past) as the verb in the main clause.

EXAMPLE:

They elected Mr Samson **so that** he would voice their grievances.

> **REMEMBER!**
> - An adverbial clause beginning with **so that** can also show the result of an action in the main clause. A comma must be added between the clauses.
>   **EXAMPLE:**
>
>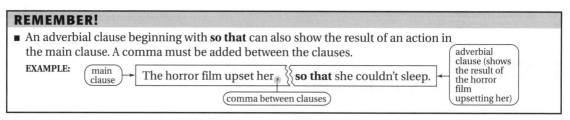
>
> The horror film upset her, **so that** she couldn't sleep.

2 We use **so . . . that** (**so** + adjective / adverb + **that**) to show that something happens because the subject in the main clause has an extreme quality or acts in an extreme way. We do it in this way:
so + adjective / adverb in main clause + adverbial clause beginning with **that**

EXAMPLES:

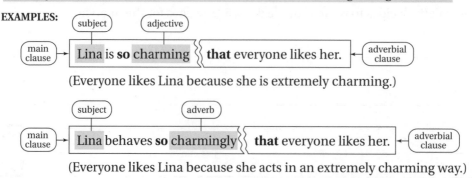

Lina is **so** charming **that** everyone likes her.

(Everyone likes Lina because she is extremely charming.)

Lina behaves **so** charmingly **that** everyone likes her.

(Everyone likes Lina because she acts in an extremely charming way.)

PRACTICE │ **A** │ Some of the sentences contain adverbial clauses that show purpose. Underline these adverbial clauses.

1 I quickly apologised <u>so that she would not be angry with me.</u>

2 He felt so nervous that he could not meet the interviewer's eye.

3 In order that Jim can find his way easily, we sent him a detailed map to our house.

4 Ken was badly treated as a child, so that now he is very timid.

5 Their land is so fertile that they have never experienced any food shortage.

6 I wish to see him alone so that I can speak frankly.

7 The movie stars issued a press statement in order that the rumours might stop.

8 Her car broke down on the highway, so that she was late for the appointment.

9 In order that they could meet more often, he moved to her city.

10 His personality is so cold that he is greatly disliked.

11 We are taking precautions so that the disease won't spread further.

YOUR SCORE

10

PRACTICE │ **B** │ Fill in the blanks with suitable words in the boxes.

1 We lodged a written complaint so _____ the authorities would take action.

as	that

2 In order that the weaker students _____ pass, he tutored them every day.

may	might

3 The boy _____ so careless that he keeps losing things.

is	was

4 She _____ her ears with cottonwool so that she would not be affected by the noise around her.

plug	plugged

5 He is groaning exaggeratedly so that we _____ pity him.

will	would

6 The meeting went so smoothly _____ our clients were full of praise.

in order that	that

135

7 They _____ so outrageously that everybody laughed.

8 She read the fine print again in order that she _____ not make any mistake before signing the document.

9 The food was so delicious _____ I forgot my diet.

10 I _____ sitting outside so that the pest control company can fumigate my house.

act	acted
will	would
so that	that
am	was

YOUR SCORE
/ 10

PRACTICE *C* Tick the correct sentences.

1 The firemen sprang into action, that soon the fire was under control.

2 I kept close to the wall so that the ferocious dog wouldn't notice me.

3 The ledge was narrow that I was terrified of falling.

4 She was so intrigued by the formations in the cave that she didn't mind the bats.

5 In order that the profit margin might increase, they reduced expenses.

6 We are cleaning the house thoroughly so that the owner was pleased.

7 The tornado was so powerful that it devastated the area.

8 The police surrounded the building, so that the robbers were trapped.

9 They attended the course in order that they may gain confidence.

10 That they can repair almost anything, they are so experienced.

YOUR SCORE
/ 10

PRACTICE *D* Underline the correct words in the brackets.

1 We need to be tactful so that we (will / would) not hurt other people's feelings.

2 I signed up for Maths tuition, (so that / that) I could get a better grade in my exam.

3 The tiger is (cunning / so cunning) that nobody can trap it.

4 Some people take supplements (in order that / in order to) they won't lack nutrients.

5 His toothache was (so / very) painful that he was awake all night.

6 In order that errors (can / could) be eliminated, they rechecked the programme.

7 The trial run is successful, so that we (can launch / launched) the product.

8 The facilities were improved so that the park (may / might) attract more tourists.

9 The cast of the musical acted superbly, (and so that / so that) the audience was delighted.

10 We arrived (extremely / so) late that the show was nearly over.

YOUR SCORE
/ 10

PRACTICE **E** Join the sentences using **so that**, **so . . . that** or **in order that**.

1 We accompanied him. He would not feel lonesome.

We accompanied him so that _he would not feel lonely._

2 The weather forecast was alarming. I postponed the trip.

_____ so _____ that

_____

3 You must build up her confidence. She won't be afraid to speak in public.

_____ so that _____

_____

4 They used special fertilisers. The plants might flourish.

In order that _____

_____

5 You have arranged the flowers expertly. Everyone is amazed.

_____ so _____ that

_____

6 He is seeing to every detail personally. Nothing may go wrong.

_____ in order that _____

_____

YOUR SCORE
10

PRACTICE **F** Rewrite the passage and correct the sentences.

Some people start to learn a foreign language in order they may experience something new. Others thought about learning another language so they can have a more interesting time when travelling abroad. They keep studying and listening to CDs, that they soon can communicate simple ideas. Often they become so interesting that they join a club where they can practice the language in a social setting. Order to become fluent, it is necessary to be with native speakers but all practice is useful.

Some people start to learn a foreign language in order that they may experience something new.

_____

_____

_____

_____

_____

_____

_____

YOUR SCORE
10

137

UNIT 10.5 ADVERBIAL CLAUSES

with **if** and **should**

Look at the **A** and **B** sentences below. Find out why **B** is correct and **A** is wrong in the **Grammar Points** section.

			GRAMMAR POINTS
1A	You can acquire competent language skills if you **persevered**.	✗	
1B	You can acquire competent language skills if you **persevere**.	✓	1a
2A	I believe she would relent if you **beg** her to join us.	✗	
2B	I believe she would relent if you **begged** her to join us.	✓	1b
3A	He might have helped her if she **confided** in him.	✗	
3B	He might have helped her if she **had confided** in him.	✓	2

GRAMMAR POINTS

1 (a) We use an adverbial clause beginning with **if** to show the condition for the action or event in the main clause. When the condition is fairly likely, we use the simple present tense or the present perfect tense in the adverbial clause beginning with **if**. We often use a modal + the base form of the verb in the main clause.

EXAMPLE:

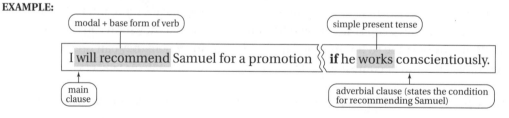

(b) When the condition is unlikely or impossible, we use the simple past tense in the adverbial clause beginning with **if**. We use **would**, **should**, **could** or **might** + the base form of the verb in the main clause.

EXAMPLE:

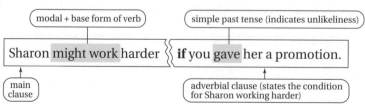

138

2 When the condition could have happened but did not happen, we use the past perfect tense in the adverbial clause beginning with **if**. We use **would have**, **should have**, **could have** or **might have** + the past participle in the main clause.

EXAMPLE:

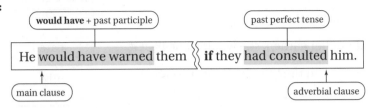

would have + past participle

past perfect tense

He would have warned them ⟨⟨ **if** they had consulted him.

main clause

adverbial clause

REMEMBER!

- To show a condition which is unlikely or impossible, **were** is used instead of **was** in an adverbial clause beginning with **if** when the subject is **I**.
  EXAMPLE: I would go on a trip around the world **if** I **were** a millionaire.

- An adverbial clause beginning with **if** can be placed **after** or **before** the main clause.
  EXAMPLES:

  main clause → You may borrow my sports car ⟨⟨ **if** you wish. ← adverbial clause   ✓

  adverbial clause → **If** you wish, ⟨⟨ you may borrow my sports car. ← main clause   ✓

  comma

- **Should** can be used instead of **if** to begin an adverbial clause which shows condition. The adverbial clause beginning with **should** is usually placed before the main clause. **Should** is followed by the subject and the base form of the verb.
  EXAMPLE: adverbial clause → **Should** you require any assistance, ⟨⟨ please feel free to call me. ← main clause

  subject   base form of verb

PRACTICE | **A** | Tick the correct sentences.

1 If I am James, I will resign from the company.

2 Fay would have fainted if she had seen you in this costume.

3 He'll be overjoyed if he'll get a chance to travel.

4 Should I bored you, I'd like you to tell me.

5 We'll take you round the campus if you like.

6 He would have swam farther if he had dared.

7 Should we lose in the finals, we must try to practise harder.

8 If I became wealthy overnight, I might decide to retire early.

9 They can take a break if they felt tired.

10 If she had flown in earlier, we could have met.

YOUR SCORE

10

139

Fill in the blanks with the correct words in the boxes.

1 _____ Maria join the army, I would join too.

if	should

2 I'll wake you up if your alarm _____ ring.

doesn't	won't

3 If she _____ about her garden, she wouldn't neglect it.

cared	cares

4 We _____ have been in time for the show if you had hurried.

may	might

5 You can enter if _____ got a pass.

you	you've

6 Should she _____ lonely, she could always call me.

feel	felt

7 If he _____ grandchildren, he would have doted on them.

had	had had

8 I _____ be fair to you if our positions were reversed.

will	would

9 If you had explained everything to him, he would _____ you a loan.

gave	have given

10 You may cite me as your referee _____ you like.

if	should

YOUR SCORE
10

PRACTICE *C* Cross out the incorrect words in the boxes to complete the sentences.

1 If this dog | is | were | mine, I'd train him properly.

2 They must be more enterprising | if | should | they wish to prosper.

3 You too might | be | have been | selected to represent the city if you had come for regular hockey practice.

4 He will be arrested if he | continues | will continue | disturbing the peace.

5 | If | Should | Jennifer contact you, please remind her to bring the dessert for the party.

6 If you had | give | given | me a clue, I could have decoded the message.

7 She couldn't finish it in two weeks if she | worked | works | non-stop.

8 Should it | rain | raining |, we could move the party into the house.

9 My roommate would have | cook | cooked | dinner if I had remembered to buy the groceries.

YOUR SCORE
10

10 If the packages | are | were | here, we'll start inspecting their contents.

PRACTICE *D* Rewrite correctly the adverbial clauses which show condition.

1 Everything will be explained should she investigates the matter.

Everything will be explained *if she investigates the matter.*

2 If you are committed to the idea, you would not behave in this way.

_____ you would not behave in this way.

3 We could have imported more cars if we anticipated the demand.

We could have imported more cars _____

4 Should she has any problem, I'd be happy to help.

_____ I'd be happy to help.

5 If he is put in charge, the venture would have failed.

_____ the venture would have failed.

6 You'll find the beach deserted if you'll go there tomorrow.

You'll find the beach deserted _____

PRACTICE *E* Underline the correct words in the brackets to complete the passage.

If I **1** (can / could) return to a certain time in my life, I would choose to be a teenager again. Some teenagers may laugh bitterly if I **2** (tell / told) them this. **3** (If / Should) they be asked their preferred age, they might **4** (said / say) 21 or one but not any of the teen years.

One teenager says that life would be bearable if she **5** (had / has) more freedom. Another claims that he will be happier if he **6** (is / were) entrusted with more responsibilities. Yet another confides that he **7** (will / would) give up anything he owned if he could exchange it for peace of mind.

If I **8** (had been / were) asked the same question as a teenager, I might have expressed similar feelings. Indeed, should my wish to turn back the clock **9** (are / be) granted, I would probably feel wretched. The turbulent teens can only retain their wonderful glow for me if they **10** (remain / remained) safely in the past.

PRACTICE *F* Fill in the blanks with suitable words to complete the sentences.

1 If they _____ listened, they wouldn't have made that mistake.

2 _____ she change her mind, we would welcome her back.

3 You may leave right now _____ you wish.

4 If I _____ his boss, I'd make him work hard.

5 He might _____ got himself into trouble if he had spoken up.

6 If their application _____ been approved, they can go ahead.

7 Should there _____ a flood, we'd have to be evacuated.

8 You _____ contact the airline staff if you have any difficulties.

9 We could _____ remained friends if I had not left the area.

10 I would help you if I _____ but I can't.

UNIT 10.6 ADVERBIAL CLAUSES

with **as**, **as if** and **as though**

Look at the **A** and **B** sentences below. Find out why **B** is correct and **A** is wrong in the **Grammar Points** section.

GRAMMAR POINTS

			GRAMMAR POINTS
1A	You must handle the matter **as how** you see fit.	✗	
1B	You must handle the matter **as** you see fit.	✓	1a
2A	He is reacting **as what** he always does to pollen.	✗	
2B	He is reacting **as** he always does to pollen.	✓	1b
3A	She is behaving as if she **owns** our community hall.	✗	
3B	She is behaving as if she **owned** our community hall.	✓	2

GRAMMAR POINTS

1 We use an adverbial clause beginning with **as** to describe how the subject in the main clause acts or feels.

(a) We do not add **how** after **as** in the adverbial clause.

EXAMPLE:

Ling doesn't care about fashion.

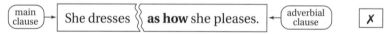

main clause → She dresses ⟩⟩ **as how** she pleases. ← adverbial clause   ✗

Ling doesn't care about fashion.

main clause → She dresses ⟩⟩ **as** she pleases. ← adverbial clause (describes how Ling dresses)   ✓

subject = Ling   verb = action

Meaning: How does Ling dress? She dresses in the way that she pleases.

(b) We do not add **what** after **as** at the beginning of an adverbial clause showing manner.

EXAMPLE:

The villagers plant rice **as what** their forefathers did.   ✗

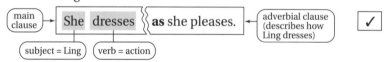

main clause → The villagers plant rice ⟩⟩ **as** their forefathers did.   ✓

subject = The villagers   verb = action   adverbial clause (describes how the villagers plant rice)

Meaning: How do the villagers plant rice? They plant rice in the way that their forefathers did.

2   We use an adverbial clause beginning with **as if** or **as though** to state how we think or imagine the subject in the main clause acts or feels.

An adverbial clause beginning with **as** (in Rule 1) refers to a real situation, whereas an adverbial clause beginning with **as if** or **as though** refers to an imagined situation.

To show that the situation we imagine is possible, we use the present tenses in the adverbial clause.

EXAMPLE:

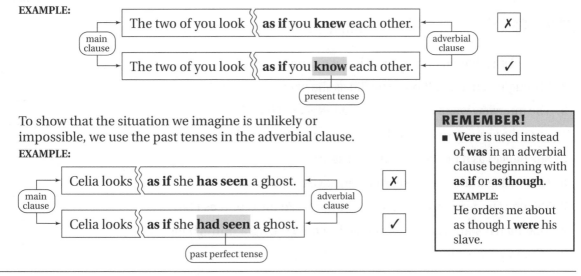

To show that the situation we imagine is unlikely or impossible, we use the past tenses in the adverbial clause.

EXAMPLE:

PRACTICE **A**   Fill in the blanks with the correct words in the boxes.

1 She is crying as if her heart _____ break.

will	would

2 You and your friends can do _____ you please.

as	as what

3 I'll fry the fish _____ you like it.

the way	as how

4 She speaks to her plants as though they _____ understand her.

can	could

5 We'll be together _____ we used to be.

like	like what

6 The bomb exploded at midnight _____ it had been timed to do.

as	as how

7 Julie felt _____ the world had ended.

8 I could not travel _____ I had dreamt of doing.

9 He treats his car as if it _____ a baby.

10 Some of my friends dress _____ pop singers do.

as	as though
like how	the way
is	were
as what	like

PRACTICE *B* Underline the correct words in the brackets.

1 This morning I went jogging (as / as what) I do every day.

2 Jim is sailing the boat as if he (had / has) done it since birth.

3 His play is a huge success (like how / the way) we knew it would be.

4 The warden hunts down latecomers as though lateness (is / were) a crime.

5 We should not hang around malls (like / like what) some people do.

6 Cynthia likes experimenting with hairstyles as many in her group (do / like).

7 After that grooming course, it seems (as / as if) he were a new person.

8 He is active again the way he (did / was) before his illness.

9 Since receiving that award, I feel as though I (can / could) conquer the world.

10 Even today, these songs delight my parents like they (did / do) long ago.

PRACTICE *C* Tick the correct sentences.

1 He looks as though he has never had a moment's anxiety.

2 Throughout her childhood, she did as she liked.

3 The interview was a disaster like I had expected it to do.

4 After the war our soldiers will never again be the way they were.

5 She dances as if her body were light as air.

6 I am taking things easy like what you advised me to do.

7 You don't understand because you haven't read the report as I have.

8 That man is staring at me as though he could see right through me.

9 Miss Tan doesn't teach us the way how Miss Lim did.

10 I maintain that I am right but they treat me as if I am quite mistaken.

PRACTICE *D* Rewrite the adverbial clauses correctly.

1 I will be frank with you as how I have always been.

I will be frank with you *as / like / the way I have always been.*

2 They are living thoughtlessly as if there is no tomorrow.

They are living thoughtlessly _____

3 She plays the violin like what her grandmother did.

She plays the violin _____

144

4 It is raining like it would never stop.

It is raining _____

5 We'll make this old building look splendid the way it used to be.

We'll make this old building look splendid _____

6 Dad treats strangers as though he has known them for year.

Dad treats strangers _____

PRACTICE *E* Cross out the incorrect words in the boxes to complete the passage.

The first day of my part-time job at a restaurant went smoothly as I had

1 | done | hoped | . I jotted down orders and table numbers like I had been told to **2** | be | do | .

I did not spill anything on anybody **3** | the way | the way how | I had seen new waiters do in movies.

I served the customers as though I **4** | had | have | been a waiter for years. I was a 'natural'

5 | as | as what | my fellow waiters admitted admiringly.

The next day, I strutted around as if the restaurant **6** | is | were | mine. I did not write down the

orders and table numbers **7** | like | like how | the other waiters did. Somehow, my memory let me

down **8** | like what | the way | memory sometimes does. I apologised to two bald customers for

having got them mixed up and they glared at me **9** | as though | the way | I had insulted them. Back

in the kitchen, the other waiters started laughing as they had never **10** | burst | done | before.

PRACTICE *F* Rewrite the sentences correctly.

1 He is unmoved by the tragedy as if he is made of stone.

He is unmoved by the tragedy as if he were made of stone.

2 The machine is not functioning as how it should be.

_____

3 Our top sprinter runs as though his feet have wings.

_____

4 They want to go on protecting her as they have always protected.

_____

5 I've learnt not to be thoughtless the way I did in my youth.

_____

6 You act as if you know the answers to all these political problems.

_____

UNIT 11.1 REPORTED CLAUSES

with **that**, **whether**, **if**

Look at the **A** and **B** sentences below. Find out why **B** is correct and **A** is wrong in the **Grammar Points** section.

				GRAMMAR POINTS
1A	I realised that excessive exercise **was** harmful.	✗		
1B	I realised that excessive exercise **is** harmful.	✓		1
2A	She proposed that we **stayed** at her uncle's farmhouse this weekend.	✗		
2B	She proposed that we **stay** at her uncle's farmhouse this weekend.	✓		2
3A	Roy's checking if / whether **is the chalet** free.	✗		
3B	Roy's checking whether or not **the chalet is** free. Roy's checking if / whether **the chalet is** free.	✓ ✓		3
4A	The air stewardess asked **if** I wanted coffee, tea or orange juice.	✗		
4B	The air stewardess asked **whether** I wanted coffee, tea or orange juice.	✓		4

GRAMMAR POINTS

1 We use a clause beginning with **that** to report a statement or someone's opinion. We often use the past tense for the main clause and the reported clause. But we can also use other tenses in the reported clause depending on the meaning we want to convey.

EXAMPLES:

                                          reported clause
The doctor's research revealed | **that** too much exercise **was** harmful. |
                  ⌒ past tense ⌒   ⌒ past tense ⌒

                                              reported clause
The survey showed | **that** most children **are** familiar with the Internet these days. |
        ⌒ past tense ⌒   ⌒ present tense ⌒

(The simple present tense in the reported clause emphasises that the statement is still true at the time of reporting.)

                              reported clause
My friends felt | **that** I **have neglected** them these past few days. |
        ⌒ past tense ⌒   ⌒ present tense ⌒

(The present perfect tense in the reported clause emphasises that the event happened in the recent past.)

                          reported clause
My friends felt | **that** I **had neglected** them last month. |
        ⌒ past tense ⌒   ⌒ past tense ⌒

(The past perfect tense in the reported clause emphasises that the event happened further back in the past.)

146

> **REMEMBER!**
> - The reported clause is very useful, especially in writing. It is often used to present information that we have read or heard about somewhere else.
> - These are some verbs that are commonly used with reported clauses beginning with **that**:
>   announce, claim, discover, explain, feel, hope, learn, mention, reveal, say, think
> - The word **that** can often be omitted from its reported clause.
>   EXAMPLE: I knew **that** you would come. ✓   I knew you would come. ✓

2 When a reported clause beginning with **that** is used with a verb like **advise**, **demand**, **insist**, **propose**, **recommend**, **request**, **suggest**, etc, we use the base form of the verb or modal + verb in the reported clause.

EXAMPLES:

reported clause

The committee suggested that the college move to the capital city.   ✓

(past tense)   (base form of verb)

reported clause

The committee suggested that the college should move to the capital city.   ✓

(past tense)   (modal + verb)

3 We use a clause beginning with **if** or **whether** to report someone's query or a question that has **yes** or **no** as its answer. But we use the word order for a statement, not a question, in the reported clause.

EXAMPLE:

reported clause

He wants to know if / whether I can give him a lift to work.   ✓

(subject + verb)

reported clause

He wants to know if / whether can I give him a lift to work.   ✗

(verb + subject)

In such cases, the word **whether** can be followed by **or not**.

EXAMPLE:

reported clause

He wants to know whether or not I can give him a lift to work.   ✓

(subject + verb)

> **REMEMBER!**
> - These are some verbs that are commonly used with reported clauses beginning with **if / whether**:
>   ask
>   enquire
>   wonder

4 We use a reported clause beginning with **whether** when the question offers a choice of two or more possibilities as the answer.

EXAMPLE:

reported clause

He wondered whether he was Chinese, Japanese or Korean.   ✓

reported clause

He wondered if he was Chinese, Japanese or Korean.   ✗

PRACTICE *A*   Circle the correct sentences.

1 **A**   They asked whether or not she intended to emigrate.

   B   They asked if she intended to emigrate.

   C   They asked that she inform them of her decision about emigrating.

2 **A**   We knew that the Earth was not at the centre of the universe.

   B   We knew that the Earth is not at the centre of the universe.

   C   We know the Earth is not at the centre of the universe.

3 **A** The lawyer advised that he should be open with his partners.

    B The lawyer advised that he was open with his partners.

    C The lawyer advised that he be open with his partners.

4 **A** I haven't heard if I have to go or stay.

    B I've just heard that I have to go.

    C I've yet to hear whether I can stay.

5 **A** The football coach insisted that the players follow a strict diet.

    B The football coach insisted that the players followed a strict diet.

    C The football coach insisted that the players must on a strict diet.

PRACTICE **B** Underline the correct words in the brackets.

1 He demanded that the board of directors (resign / resigned).

2 The zoo-keeper told her that not all snakes (are / were) deadly.

3 Let Rachel decide for herself (if / that) she wants to stand for the post of president.

4 We're wondering if (may we / we may) see your new baby.

5 The members of the team (feel / feels that) they lack practice.

6 The old man claimed that he (had / has) once fought a bear single-handedly.

7 I suggest that the documents (are / be) shredded.

8 She has to decide (if / whether) she's taking arts or science courses.

9 In 1994, he said (he would / that he will) complete his thesis in a year.

10 They're trying to guess whether (are those diamonds / those diamonds are) real.

PRACTICE **C** Rearrange the underlined words to complete the sentences.

1 I told our neighbour <u>been — considerate — had — always — that — he.</u>

    I told our neighbour _____

2 I haven't decided <u>any — has — if — merit — proposal — the.</u>

    I haven't decided _____

3 The speaker pointed out <u>being — every — has — human — that — weaknesses.</u>

    The speaker pointed out_____

4 He vowed <u>family's — he — his — fortune — restore — would.</u>

    He vowed _____

5 She can sense <u>happy — is — not — or — someone — whether.</u>

    She can sense _____

PRACTICE $\boxed{D}$ Rewrite the sentences correctly.

1 They're speculating whether will the market recover soon.
They're speculating whether the market will recover soon.

2 All his friends reminded him that the future was unpredictable.

3 I suggest that your sister takes a long holiday.

4 You must find out if have you been immunised.

5 The millionaire agree that riches didn't guarantee happiness.

6 We enquired if could we fly direct to Atlanta.

YOUR SCORE

10

PRACTICE $\boxed{E}$ Underline the incorrect sentences and rewrite them correctly.

I can't recall or not I've told you this story. You've often said that I'm the world's most absent-minded person. You've even suggested that I carried photos to help me remember my friends! Well, a month ago I thought I'd caught a glimpse of a friend at a supermarket. I ran after him, complaining loudly that he has been neglecting me.

A smiling stranger turned round and asked I would forgive him. Still apologetic about not contacting me all these years, he insisted that I joined him for coffee so that we could catch up on old times. To my delight I realised that I am finding someone even more absent-minded than me.

I can't recall whether or not I've told you this story.

YOUR SCORE

10

149

UNIT 11.2 REPORTED CLAUSES

with wh-words

Look at the **A** and **B** sentences below. Find out why **B** is correct and **A** is wrong in the **Grammar Points** section.

			GRAMMAR POINTS
1A	I realised what **would life be** like without friends.	✗	
1B	I realised what **life would be** like without friends.	✓	1
2A	She guessed **who** I wanted and offered to help me get it.	✗	
2B	She guessed **what** I wanted and offered to help me get it.	✓	2
3A	They've discovered **who's** incompetence ruined the company.	✗	
3B	They've discovered **whose** incompetence ruined the company.	✓	3
4A	The shopkeeper asked **what** material she preferred, silk or cotton.	✗	
4B	The shopkeeper asked **which** material she preferred, silk or cotton.	✓	4

GRAMMAR POINTS

1 We use a clause beginning with a wh-word to report a wh-question. But we use the word order for a statement, not a question, in the reported clause.

EXAMPLES:

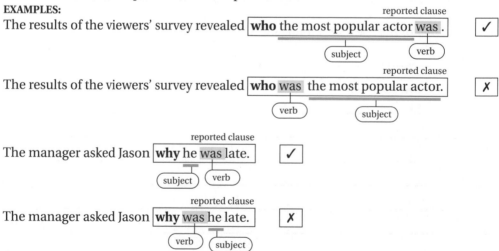

2 We must use the appropriate wh-word to begin the reported clause, depending on whether we are referring to a person, thing, place, time, reason, etc.

EXAMPLES:

reported clause

I know **who** you are trying to impress.

referring to a person

reported clause

I know **what** you are trying to prove.

referring to a thing

> **REMEMBER!**
>
> ■ These are some common wh-words:
>
> | wh-word | refers to |
> |---------|-----------|
> | who | a person |
> | what | a thing |
> | where | a place |
> | when | a time |
> | why | a reason |
> | how | a manner |
>
> **EXAMPLES:**
> They've established **where** the crime was committed.
> They've established **when** the crime was committed.
> They've established **why** the crime was committed.
> They've established **how** the crime was committed.

3 We use a clause beginning with **whose** + noun to refer to a relationship such as ownership or a connection between the noun and the subject of the reported clause.

EXAMPLE:

reported clause

He's just learnt **whose** signature that is.

referring to ownership

We must not confuse **whose** with **who's**. **Who's** is the short form of **who is** or **who has**.

EXAMPLES:

He's just learnt **who's** (who is) signing the pay cheques. ✓

He's just learnt **who's** (who has) been signing the pay cheques. ✓

He's just learnt **who's** pay is the highest. ✗

4 We use a clause beginning with **which** + noun to refer to a person or thing to be chosen from a group or list.

EXAMPLE:

reported clause

She was asked **which** instrument she played, the violin or the cello.

which + noun

> **REMEMBER!**
>
> ■ To avoid repetition, the noun after **which** or **whose** at the beginning of a reported clause is dropped.
> **EXAMPLES:** Of your three novels, you can guess **which** ~~novel~~ I like best.
> He noticed a bicycle and wondered **whose** ~~bicycle~~ it was.
>
> ■ **One** can be used to replace the noun after **which** but not the noun after **whose**.
> **EXAMPLES:** Of your three novels, you can guess which **one** I like best. ✓
> He noticed a bicycle and wondered whose **one** it was. ✗

PRACTICE *A* Underline the reported clauses in the sentences and write in the brackets what they refer to: person, thing, time, place, reason or manner.

1 The editors can't always publish <u>what the correspondent sends them</u>. (*thing*)

2 The engineer has estimated when the dam will be completed. ( )

3 I want to learn how a computer programme is written. ( )

4 We are planning where we should spend the next holidays. ( )

5 He's wondering who he can approach for help to solve his problem. ( )

6 I can't understand why you want to see that movie again. ( )

PRACTICE **B** Cross out the incorrect words in the boxes to complete the sentences.

1 The personnel officer will show you which cubicle │ have you │ you have │ been allocated.

2 Richard doesn't know │ when │ what │ his company will be sending him to France.

3 You won't believe │ who's │ whose │ car is parked next to ours.

4 I understand │ how │ why │ you sometimes shun company.

5 Of the two strategies, we can tell you │ which │ which strategy │ is better.

6 He described what │ did he see │ he saw │ as vividly as possible to the police officer.

7 She found a slipper and realised │ whose │ whose one │ it must be.

8 Ian hasn't decided │ what │ which │ route he will take, the inland or the coastal one.

9 Her memoirs will reveal │ who's │ whose │ been financing her plays.

10 We can't imagine how │ the old man coped │ did the old man cope │ all these years.

PRACTICE **C** Tick the correct sentences.

1 Kelvin has always done what seems right and fair to him.

2 This cardigan's not mine. I wonder whose one it is.

3 The reporter wouldn't disclose who had given him the story.

4 Their expressions don't indicate which of the three accounts they believe.

5 I enquired when would the manager be able to see me.

6 He needs to recommend who's banking privileges should be increased.

7 They demanded to know why had their petition been ignored.

8 We cannot understand how you came to that conclusion.

9 Of the two scenarios, I can't say which one is more attractive.

10 Now I recall where did I first see that tattoo.

PRACTICE **D** Fill in the blanks with the words in the boxes.

1 I'll explain _____ kind of assistance I need.

what	how

2 The consultants explained _____ they thought the plan wouldn't work.

how	why

3 She's never forgotten _____ support won her that seat.

who's	whose

4 We're wondering when _____ face the truth.

he will	will he

5 Lisa has confided _____ she feels about this.

how	which

6 I can sense _____ of the two men is more competent.

which	which one

7 Nobody suspects where _____ going.

are we	we are

8 Of all your souvenirs, I know _____ you treasure most.

which souvenir	which one

9 Mr Long asked who _____ from.

the hamper was	was the hamper

10 She grabbed the bouquet without checking _____ it was.

whose	whose one

YOUR SCORE
10

PRACTICE **E** Underline the correct words in the brackets.

I don't remember **1** (how / where) I came to be so busy. I don't know when **2** (will I / I will) have some leisure. Every moment, I have to decide **3** (which / which task) of my many tasks **4** (should I / I should) tackle. The people in my life clamour to have their needs met and it's hard to tell **5** (whose / whose is) the most urgent. Sometimes I wonder hazily **6** (what / why) I am doing this. I ask myself **7** (how / where) I am heading. Then, one day, I suddenly see **8** (what / which) is happening to me. I need a break to find out **9** (what / which) I want to do in the coming months and how **10** (can I / I can) achieve a better balance in life.

YOUR SCORE
10

PRACTICE **F** Rewrite the sentences correctly.

1 These tests show which talent of your many talents is the most developed.
These tests show which of your many talents is the most developed.

2 He likes to mention who does he know in high places.

He likes to mention _____
3 She tried to explain how she meant by those words.

She tried to explain _____
4 They can predict whose going to win the championship at this stage.

They can predict _____
5 I understand why did you feel sad.

I understand _____
6 We can demonstrate to you what method is the better of the two.

We can demonstrate to you _____

YOUR SCORE
10

UNIT 11.3 REPORTED CLAUSES

that-clauses with subjunctives

Look at the **A** and **B** sentences below. Find out why **B** is correct and **A** is wrong in the **Grammar Points** section.

			GRAMMAR POINTS
1A	Mrs Ingram insisted that the company **apologises** to her.	✗	
1B	Mrs Ingram insisted that the company **apologise** to her.	✓	1
2A	It is important that Fiona **will see** a doctor as soon as possible.	✗	
2B	It is important that Fiona **see** a doctor as soon as possible.	✓	2
3A	The lecturer said it was necessary that all students **attended** the workshops.	✗	
3B	The lecturer said it was necessary that all students **attend** the workshops.	✓	3

GRAMMAR POINTS

1   A **subjunctive** is a special verb that is the same as the base form of a verb. We can use it in a **that**-clause when we want to state what should be done. We use it when the **that**-clause comes after reporting verbs like the following:

agree	ask	command	demand	insist
order	propose	recommend	request	suggest

EXAMPLES: *Direct Speech:*   Adam said, "Mary **should lead** the way."

Reported Speech: Adam **suggested** that Mary **should lead** the way. ✓

    reporting verb   modal   base form

Adam **suggested** that Mary **lead** the way. ✓

    reporting verb   subjunctive

Adam **suggested** that Mary **leads** the way. ✗

    reporting verb   3rd person singular form

Note: The subjunctive can take the place of **should** + base form in sentences with the above reporting verbs. We usually use the subjunctive in a more formal context.

- The subjunctive is often used to state advice, instructions, suggestions, etc, and to refer to actions that may or may not take place.

  EXAMPLE: Mr Lawson recommended that Eileen **sit** for her Grade 8 music exam this year.
  Did Mr Lawson recommend something? Yes. *(His recommendation is a past action.)*

  Will Eileen sit for her Grade 8 music exam this year? We do not know.
  She may sit for the exam. *(possible future action)*

- A subjunctive has only the base form. The rules for subject-verb agreement are not observed when the subjunctive is used.

EXAMPLES:	Subjunctive form of the verb 'to be'	Subjunctive form of a main verb
Singular nouns	John **be**, the office **be**	John **leave**, the office **close**
Plural nouns	the boys **be**, the offices **be**	the boys **leave**, the offices **close**
1st person	I **be**, we **be**	I **stay**, we **stay**
2nd person	you **be**	you **stay**
3rd person	he/she/it **be**, they **be**	he/she/it **stay**, they **stay**

- The subjunctive is usually used in formal situations such as when writing reports and letters.

  EXAMPLE: I asked the shop to give me a refund immediately. *(in a conversation or a letter to a friend)*
  I request that the shop **give** me a refund immediately. *(in a letter of complaint)*

- A few reporting verbs like **ask**, **command** and **order** can be immediately followed by a **that**-clause containing a subjunctive or an object + infinitive .

  EXAMPLES: *David to Elaine:* Could we get Mary to select the venue for the company dinner?

  David **asked** that Mary **select** the venue for the company dinner.
  (reporting verb) (subjunctive) **that**-clause

  David to Mary: Could you select the venue for the company dinner?

  David **asked** Mary to select the venue for the company dinner.
  (reporting verb) (object) (infinitive)

2 When we use the expression **it is** + adjective in sentences containing advice, suggestions, etc, the **that**-clause which follows the expression must contain a subjunctive.

EXAMPLES:

It is **necessary** that he **inform** the police immediately. ✓
(adjective) (subjunctive)

It is **necessary** that he **informs** the police immediately. ✗

We think it is **important** that you **be** on time. ✓
(adjective) (subjunctive)

We think it is **important** that you **are** on time. ✗

3 When the verb in the main clause is in the past tense, the verb in the **that**-clause remains in the subjunctive form.

EXAMPLE: The president **ordered** that his private jet **be** on standby. ✓
(adjective) (subjunctive)

The president **ordered** that his private jet **was** on standby. ✗

1 It is imperative that the soldiers cross the bridge before dawn.

2 Henry's father demanded that the principal saw him immediately.

3 The committee proposed that their club organised a regional quiz in April.

4 The judge asked that the defence attorney rephrase his question to the witness.

5 It was essential that all the exhibits displayed price tags.

6 The director announced that everyone should attend the latest training session.

7 It is vital that the blood bank have sufficient blood to cope with emergencies.

8 Sue prefers that we holds the meeting in her house after dinner.

9 The counsellor advised that I take up engineering in university.

10 The Sports Council says it is advantageous that every student plays at least two games per week.

YOUR SCORE
10

PRACTICE $\boxed{B}$ Underline the correct verb forms in the brackets.

1 Our lecturer recommended that we (subscribe / subscribed) to the magazine 'Voices'.

2 The architect advised Mr Chambers (extend / to extend) his back terrace.

3 Maisie prayed that her garden (survived / would survive) the harsh winter.

4 It is important that you (do / did) extensive research before you write your historical novel.

5 The villagers urged the authorities (stop / to stop) the indiscriminate logging in their area.

6 Dad intends that we (spend / spent) a weekend on a farm during our vacation in Australia.

7 The prime minister said it is vital that we (respect / will respect) all our fellow citizens.

8 The stewardess ordered the unruly passenger (return / to return) to his seat immediately.

9 She proposed that the kindergarten children (be /are) in their classrooms until their parents arrive to take them home.

10 The manager stipulated that every employee (abides / should abide) by the rules or face disciplinary action.

YOUR SCORE
10

PRACTICE $\boxed{C}$ Circle the letters of the correct sentences. There may be more than one answer for each question.

1 A The manager asked our group to take the initiative in keeping our city clean.

  B It is necessary that everyone must participates in keeping the environment clean.

  C The Environment Society asked that every group attend its workshop on keeping the environment clean.

2 A My mother said it is important that John has confidence in himself.

  B My mother said it was important that I have confidence in myself.

  C My mother suggested that Fiona read a book on how to gain self-confidence.

3 **A** My sister thinks it is important that we follow the latest fashions.

  B My sister recommends that I should colour my hair burgundy red.

  C I think it is necessary that my sister stop following fashions blindly.

4 **A** The company directed all its employees to submit the completed questionnaire by Friday.

  B The company directed that its employees submitted the completed questionnaire by Friday.

  C The company directed that its employees will submit the completed questionnaire by Friday.

5 **A** The police ordered the motorists move to the side of the road.

  B The police ordered that the motorists move to the side of the road.

  C The police ordered the motorists to move to the side of the road.

YOUR SCORE
10

PRACTICE **D** Rewrite the sentences using subjunctives, **that**-clauses and the words in the brackets.

1 Our captain : Please act more responsibly.

  (asked — we) *Our captain asked that we act more responsibly.*

2 Matthew : Why doesn't Katy apply for a scholarship since her exam results are outstanding?

  (recommended — Katy) _____

  _____

3 Police Commissioner : Arrest all those breaking the curfew!

  (commanded — his policemen) _____

  _____

4 Speaker : It is vital for you to understand what drug addiction can lead to.

  (vital — we) _____

  _____

5 Larry : I asked Steven to assist me in the project.

  (asked — Steven) _____

  _____

6 Katy : Let's hold the wedding reception by the poolside.

  (suggested — they) _____

  _____

YOUR SCORE
10

UNIT 11.4 REPORTED CLAUSES AND CONDITIONAL CLAUSES

that-clauses with subjunctives and if-clauses

Look at the **A** and **B** sentences below. Find out why **B** is correct and **A** is wrong in the **Grammar Points** section.

				GRAMMAR POINTS
1A	Mrs Lee requested that the decorations **will be taken down** by tomorrow.	✗		
1B	Mrs Lee requested that the decorations **be taken down** by tomorrow.	✓		1
2A	Stanley ordered **don't include his name** in the letter of complaint. / Stanley ordered that his name **be not included** in the letter of complaint.	✗		
2B	Stanley ordered that his name **not be included** in the letter of complaint.	✓		2
3A	If I **am** the prime minister, I would make further education compulsory for all.	✗		
3B	If I **were** the prime minister, I would make further education compulsory for all.	✓		3

GRAMMAR POINTS

1 We use the subjunctive **be** + the past participle in the **that**-clause when the clause is in the passive voice.

EXAMPLES:

Active Voice:

that-clause

The hijackers demanded | that the government **provide** a car for their getaway. |

         reporting verb   subjunctive

Passive Voice:

that-clause

The hijackers demanded | that a car **be provided** by the government for their getaway. |

      reporting verb   subjunctive   past participle

Active Voice:

that-clause

It is imperative | that the military commandos **overpower** the hijackers before dawn. |

    adjective   subjunctive

Passive Voice:

that-clause

It is imperative | that the hijackers **be overpowered** by the military commandos before dawn. |

    adjective   subjunctive   past participle

This type of usage normally occurs when the **that**-clause comes after certain reporting verbs and adjectives, and it points to a possible future action.

EXAMPLES:

Reporting verbs					Adjectives (It is / was ...)		
agree	ask	beg	demand	direct	appropriate	critical	crucial
insist	intend	order	plead		essential	imperative	important
prefer	propose	request	suggest		necessary	vital	

2 When we want to show that we are not in favour of a likely future action, we can use a subjunctive and the word **not** in this way:

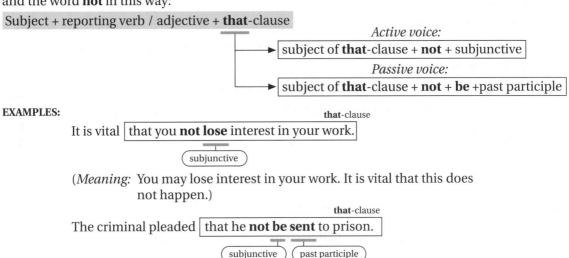

Subject + reporting verb / adjective + **that**-clause

Active voice:
subject of **that**-clause + **not** + subjunctive

Passive voice:
subject of **that**-clause + **not** + **be** +past participle

EXAMPLES:

that-clause

It is vital | that you **not lose** interest in your work.

subjunctive

(*Meaning:* You may lose interest in your work. It is vital that this does not happen.)

that-clause

The criminal pleaded | that he **not be sent** to prison.

subjunctive   past participle

(*Meaning:* The criminal may be sent to a prison. He hopes that this does not happen.)

3 We use the subjunctive **were** in **if**-clauses when talking about future events which are not likely to take place. We use it for all subjects, whether nouns or pronouns.

EXAMPLES: If **I ~~was~~** / **were** a millionaire, I **would** buy myself an island.

If **Adam ~~was~~** / **were** here, he **would** help me with this problem.

REMEMBER!

■ When the expression **If I were you** is used to give advice, **should** and not **would** is usually used in the second part of the sentence.

EXAMPLE: **If I were you**, I **should** pay more attention to my health. (same meaning as 'You should pay more attention to your health.')

■ When the expression **I wish** is used to express hope, regret or desire, both the subjunctive **were** and the singular verb **was** can be used for singular subjects and singular third person pronouns.

EXAMPLES: I wish Lara **were** / **was** my elder sister.
I wish it **were** / **was** my turn to plan an outing.
I wish they **were** / ~~**was**~~ more considerate towards others.

PRACTICE *A* Underline the correct words in the brackets.

It is recommended that a well-received article on child abuse **1** (be read out / not be read out) in community groups. This article stresses the following parts:

- It is necessary that there **2** (be / not be) greater public awareness about the problem.
- It is imperative that parents **3** (neglect / not neglect) their duties towards their children.
- It is vital that children **4** (be protected / not be protected) from violence.
- It is critical that an abused child **5** (be separated / not be separated) from his or her abusive parent.
- It is necessary that the government **6** (delay / not delay) the enforcement of legislation dealing with children's rights.
- It is crucial that schools **7** (consider / not consider) child abuse to be solely a family matter.
- It is important that teachers **8** (ignore / not ignore) remarks or complaints by students about beatings they receive at home.
- It is appropriate that child abusers **9** (be treated / not be treated) like criminals.
- It is essential that convicted abusers **10** (be let off / not be let off) with a light sentence by the courts.

YOUR SCORE
10

PRACTICE *B* Circle the correct words to complete the sentences.

1	The captain said it was necessary that passengers _____ warned about the delay.	be	were
2	If Emma _____ a politician, she would create more job opportunities for senior citizens.	was	were
3	Janice requested that her interview _____ for Tuesday.	be not scheduled	not be scheduled
4	If I were you, I _____ ask the receptionist for a room with better lighting.	should	would
5	The elderly man requested that he _____ an aisle seat on the plane.	be given	give
6	The bus driver asked that we _____ such a noise at the back of the bus.	make not	not make
7	I wish I _____ a brilliant surgeon like my uncle.	am	were
8	It is important that factories _____ their chemical wastes into streams and rivers.	don't dump	not dump
9	The editor intends that every case of racism _____ in his newspaper.	be highlighted	is highlighted
10	If I were an architect, I _____ build myself a house overlooking the sea.	should	would

YOUR SCORE
10

PRACTICE *C*   Some of the underlined words contain mistakes. Write the correct words in the boxes provided.

1 The contractor proposed that our family <u>built</u> a pond to beautify the garden.

2 Hussein prefers that we <u>stay</u> close to him during our trek into the jungle.

3 The king intends that the law <u>obeyed</u> by one and all.

4 If I <u>were</u> you, I should replant those rose bushes away from the entrance.

5 It is imperative that racial prejudice <u>not be prevailed</u> in our society.

6 The distressed woman pleaded that she <u>be allowed</u> to use our telephone.

7 I wish Richard <u>were</u> more thoughtful in his behaviour towards others.

8 It is appropriate that they <u>be informed</u> of your intended visit ahead of time.

9 If Anne <u>was</u> an actress, she would only want to work with the Academy Award winning director Joe Stenson.

10 The chairperson insisted that the meeting <u>not adjourned</u> until all matters arising had been dealt with.

YOUR SCORE

/10

PRACTICE *D*   Rewrite the sentences correctly.

1 If I the mayor, I would encourage the city to have a Speakers' Corner.
   If I were the mayor, I would encourage the city to have a Speakers' Corner.

2 John requested that we don't tell Betty about the present he had bought for her.

3 Our neighbours suggested that we paid half the cost of the wall between our houses.

4 It is important that the fine print in legal documents read carefully.

5 I wish Mr Lee is our neighbour because he is so understanding.

6 Jessie begged that she not required to give a speech before the large audience.

YOUR SCORE

/10

161

UNIT 12.1 ADJECTIVAL PHRASES

with prepositions

Look at the **A** and **B** sentences below. Find out why **B** is correct and **A** is wrong in the **Grammar Points** section.

1A	That oil tycoon possesses riches **are beyond** imagination.	✗	
1B	That oil tycoon possesses riches **beyond** imagination.	✓	1
2A	She noticed a suspicious-looking man **who in** the lobby.	✗	
2B	She noticed a suspicious-looking man **in** the lobby.	✓	2
3A	**The tension** between the two factions **have** worsened.	✗	
3B	**The tension** between the two factions **has** worsened.	✓	3

GRAMMAR POINTS

1 An adjectival clause has a finite verb. An adjectival phrase does not have a finite verb.

EXAMPLES:

He dreaded the task [that **was** before him.]

adjectival clause

noun described

finite verb

adjectival phrase

He dreaded the task [before him.]

2 An adjectival phrase does not begin with **who**, **which** or **that**. It can begin with a preposition.

EXAMPLE:

He dreaded the task [before him.]   ✓

adjectival phrase

He dreaded the task **that** before him.   ✗

These are some examples of adjectival phrases beginning with prepositions:

against the law	down the lane	in front of me
next to the station	opposite the gallery	over the mountains
under surveillance	up the street	within our capacity

3 When an adjectival phrase describes the subject of the sentence, it comes between the subject and the finite verb. We must take special care that the finite verb agrees with the subject.

EXAMPLES:

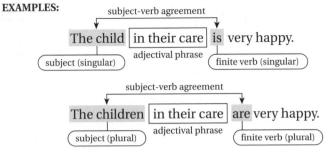

subject-verb agreement

The child | in their care | is very happy.

subject (singular) — adjectival phrase — finite verb (singular)

subject-verb agreement

The children | in their care | are very happy.

subject (plural) — adjectival phrase — finite verb (plural)

REMEMBER!

■ An adjectival phrase beginning with a preposition is used after a noun to give more information about the noun.

EXAMPLE: The man | with the untidy beard | plays the guitar beautifully. ✓

noun described — adjectival phrase describing **the man**

adjectival phrase describing **the man**

The man plays the guitar beautifully | with the untidy beard. ✗

Take note that the adjectival phrase must come immediately after the noun it describes.

PRACTICE *A* Underline the adjectival phrases.

1 She is staring at the photo on her table again.

2 We finally saw the light at the end of the tunnel.

3 He was honoured for his contribution towards peace.

4 Her dispute with the company is still unresolved.

5 The fingerprints on the glass belong to the murder suspect.

6 Her house is full of junk from various sales.

7 The close bond between the twins is something I wish I had with my sister.

8 Our new employee is the man with the cheerful grin.

9 Hazel's hard work behind the scenes helped a lot.

10 I like the sense of satisfaction after finishing a task.

YOUR SCORE

10

PRACTICE *B* Rearrange the words to form sentences with adjectival phrases.

1 a — along — beach — relax — stroll — the — will — you.

_____

2 a — he — is — of — rights — supporter — women's.

_____

3 above — hundred — is — metres — resort — sea level — the — two.

_____

163

4 do — his — in — mind — nobody — right — that — would.

_____

5 behind — mask — now — person — see — the — the — we.

_____

PRACTICE $\boxed{C}$ Tick the correct sentences.

1 The ground beneath his feet shook violently.

2 We noticed the ladder which against the wall.

3 The boat belongs to a pirate alongside ours.

4 Designing a web page is a task beyond my capability.

5 Walter frequents the mall opposite the cinema.

6 Conversations within earshot of strangers should be guarded.

7 The demonstrators are on a rampage were rounded up by the police.

8 Any sum over ten thousand dollars have to be declared.

9 Everything on those shelves is made by our craftsmen.

10 Everyone for the motion were asked to say 'aye'.

PRACTICE $\boxed{D}$ Circle the letters of the suitable items in the boxes and mark with $\wedge$ where they should be added to the sentences.

1 The debate$\wedge$was very heated .

Ⓐ	on the proposed new tax.
B	that on the proposed new tax.

2 This famous magician has performed feats .

A	are beyond belief.
B	beyond belief.

3 The difficulties before her final triumph .

A	has matured her.
B	have matured her.

4 Killing is not murder .

A	during a fit of insanity.
B	which during a fit of insanity.

5 Letters of complaint without the writers' names or addresses .

A	not to be given consideration.
B	are not to be given consideration.

6 Viewers enjoyed the programme .

A	all over the world.
B	who all over the world.

PRACTICE *E* Underline the correct words in the brackets.

A recent article on 'Unidentified Flying Objects' or 'UFOs' **1** (are / is) refreshingly sceptical. The author says that creatures **2** (from / that from) other planets are being unfairly suspected of wanting to invade Earth. Reports **3** (are without / without) sound evidence are eagerly believed.

Our faith is reinforced by science fiction **4** (in / on) television. The pseudo-scientific jargon **5** (in / which in) these series can be very convincing. So can the scenes **6** (for / with) their special effects.

These factors blur the line **7** (between / is between) fact and fiction. Indeed, modern-day enthusiasm **8** (after / for) anything remotely scientific has made us vulnerable **9** (for / to) high-tech hoaxes. This article **10** (by / of) an educational psychologist gives some interesting new information.

YOUR SCORE
10

PRACTICE *F* Rewrite the sentences correctly using adjectival phrases beginning with prepositions.

1 Travelling is with the wrong companion can be a miserable experience.

Travelling with the wrong companion can be a miserable experience.

2 If the ambassador and his wife come, there must be perfect behaviour around their presence.

_____

_____

3 Hit songs are becoming popular again from old musicals.

_____

_____

4 This movie is not recommended for viewers who below 18.

_____

_____

5 The enormous lady is in front of me blocked my view.

_____

_____

6 She realised behind his gruff manner the kindness.

_____

_____

YOUR SCORE
10

UNIT 12.2 ADJECTIVAL PHRASES

with present and past participles

Look at the **A** and **B** sentences below. Find out why **B** is correct and **A** is wrong in the **Grammar Points** section.

CHECKPOINT

1A	She has many problems **are weighing** her down.	✗	
1B	She has many problems **weighing** her down.	✓	1
2A	Donations started pouring in for the farm **that struck** by lightning.	✗	
2B	Donations started pouring in for the farm **struck** by lightning.	✓	2
3A	**The tank** containing the goldfish **are** too small.	✗	
3B	**The tank** containing the goldfish **is** too small.	✓	3

GRAMMAR POINTS

1 Unlike an adjectival clause, an adjectival phrase does not have a finite verb. It can have a non-finite verb, for instance a present participle or a past participle.

EXAMPLES:

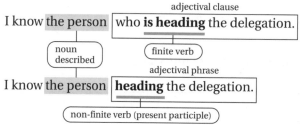

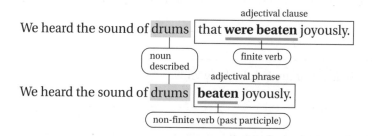

2 An adjectival phrase does not begin with **who**, **which** or **that**. It can begin with a present participle or a past participle.

EXAMPLES:

adjectival phrase

I know the person heading the delegation. ✓

I know the person **who** heading the delegation. ✗

adjectival phrase

We heard the sound of drums **beaten joyously.** ✓

We heard the sound of drums **which** beaten joyously. ✗

3 When an adjectival phrase describes the subject of the sentence, it comes between the subject and the finite verb. We must take special care that the finite verb agrees with the subject.

EXAMPLES:

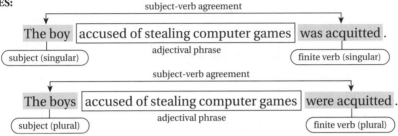

subject-verb agreement

The boy | accused of stealing computer games | was acquitted .

subject (singular)   adjectival phrase   finite verb (singular)

subject-verb agreement

The boys | accused of stealing computer games | were acquitted .

subject (plural)   adjectival phrase   finite verb (plural)

REMEMBER!

■ An adjectival phrase beginning with a present participle or past participle is used after people or things to describe or identify them by saying what they are doing or what happens to them.

EXAMPLE: adjectival clause describing **the girl**

The girl | dancing gracefully on the stage | can also swim well. ✓

noun described   adjectival phrase describing **the girl**

The girl can also swim well | dancing on the stage. ✗

Take note that the adjectival phrase must come immediately after the noun it describes.

■ An adjectival phrase beginning with a present participle has an active meaning.

EXAMPLE:

We marvelled at the child | painting the picture. ✓

We marvelled at the child | painted the picture. ✗

■ An adjectival phrase beginning with a past participle has a passive meaning.

EXAMPLE:

We marvelled at the picture | painted by the child. ✓

We marvelled at the picture | painting by the child. ✗

PRACTICE *A* Underline the adjectival phrases.

1 The workers evacuating the flood victims are volunteers from the community.

2 The visitors taken to see the sights were unimpressed.

3 I felt grief mixed with exhaustion.

4 He beckoned to the boy hesitating in the doorway.

5 The bells chiming so clearly brought back her childhood.

6 A chair flung out of a window hit a passer-by.

7 You have a son blessed with a happy nature.

8 I love to hear these voices harmonising so well.

9 The lawyer cross-examining the witness is formidable.

10 He strikes me as a man disillusioned with his profession.

YOUR SCORE

10

B Tick the correct sentences.

1 Marks can pull your percentage down deducted for spelling.

2 She was lulled by the breeze fanning her face.

3 The man spoken rather brusquely apologised at once.

4 They're showing signs of nerves are frayed by anxiety.

5 The equipment arriving today is of top quality.

6 The portrait is of his grandfather hanging on the wall.

7 The quilt woven by our group won first prize.

8 The girl masquerading as a fairy had paper wings.

9 People who hurrying by are not likely to notice us.

10 These are some figures queried by the auditor.

YOUR SCORE
10

PRACTICE **C** Rearrange the words to form sentences with adjectival phrases.

1 children — detest — forced — it — may — music — study — to.

_____

2 grilled — he — loves — perfection — steaks — to.

_____

3 a — a — girl — greeted — kimono — me — wearing.

_____

4 aside — for — insufficient — is — France — money — our — set — the — trip — to.

_____

5 a — as — backyard — child — climbing — her — I — in — our — remember — trees.

_____

_____

YOUR SCORE
10

PRACTICE **D** Fill in the blanks with suitable words in the boxes.

1 The man _____ the labourers is fussy.

| hiring | who hiring |

2 Restaurants _____ excellent can be disappointing.

| are rated | rated |

3 People facing worse hardship _____ kept calm.

| has | have |

4 We spoke to passengers _____ by the cable car accident.

| shaken | were shaken |

5 Only members _____ to secrecy know the truth.

| sworn | that sworn |

168

6 He was unmoved by the tears _____ in their eyes.

glistening	which glistening

7 Strange noises in the middle of the night _____ scare her.

doesn't	don't

8 He was a boy _____ by his family.

overprotected	was overprotected

9 The sun is now a red ball _____ into the sea.

is sinking	sinking

10 Next, I'll introduce a lady _____ a great deal for us.

done	who's done

YOUR SCORE
10

PRACTICE **E** Rewrite the sentences correctly using adjectival phrases beginning with present participles or past participles.

1 A candidate fared very badly expected to win the election.

A candidate expected to win the election fared very badly.

2 She looked disdainfully at the youth who approaching her.

_____

3 Overseas students yearn for home need help to deal with the loneliness.

_____

4 The person is very experienced chosen for the post.

_____

5 They came in carrying cameras were slung on their shoulders.

_____

6 The Master of Ceremonies gave a speech which filled with anecdotes.

_____

YOUR SCORE
10

PRACTICE **F** Underline the correct words in the brackets to complete the passage.

Articles **1** (are appearing / appearing) in newspapers and magazines sometimes **2** (offer / offers) tips on learning. According to one writer, a nose **3** (buried / is buried) in a book will not sniff out much knowledge. Hours **4** (have been spent / spent) studying non-stop are so many hours wasted. A tactic **5** (becoming / which becoming) popular with students is to stop studying every hour and jump about for five minutes.

If jumping about is not acceptable in your family, think of something **6** (deem / deemed) less inappropriate. You may have read a piece **7** (recommending / was recommending) that you glance at a book of jokes or cartoons. Humour is an element **8** (known / that known) to help learning. However, the risk **9** (are / is) that you'll scare everyone with a sudden cackle of laughter. Perhaps slow, wordless music **10** (keep / keeping) you company is a safer aid.

YOUR SCORE
10

UNIT 12.3 ADJECTIVAL PHRASES

with adjectives

Look at the **A** and **B** sentences below. Find out why **B** is correct and **A** is wrong in the **Grammar Points** section.

CHECKPOINT

				GRAMMAR POINTS
1A	We can't find anyone **is competent** to do the job.	✗		
1B	We can't find anyone **competent** to do the job.	✓		1
2A	I'm a man **who content** with simple pleasures.	✗		
2B	I'm a man **content** with simple pleasures.	✓		2
3A	People tired of the city **comes** here to relax.	✗		
3B	People tired of the city **come** here to relax.	✓		3

GRAMMAR POINTS

1 Unlike an adjectival clause, an adjectival phrase does not have a finite verb.

EXAMPLE:

This is a country **that is** rich in traditions. — adjectival clause / noun described / finite verb

This is a country rich in traditions. — adjectival phrase

2 An adjectival phrase does not begin with **who**, **which** or **that**. It can begin with an adjective. (The adjective is followed by a preposition.)

EXAMPLE:

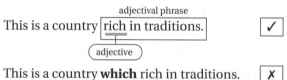

This is a country rich in traditions. — adjectival phrase / adjective ✓

This is a country **which** rich in traditions. ✗

3 When an adjectival phrase describes the subject of the sentence, it comes between the subject and the finite verb. We must take special care that the finite verb agrees with the subject.

EXAMPLES:

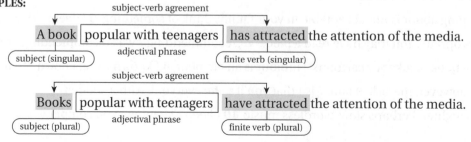

A book popular with teenagers has attracted the attention of the media.
subject (singular) / adjectival phrase / finite verb (singular) — subject-verb agreement

Books popular with teenagers have attracted the attention of the media.
subject (plural) / adjectival phrase / finite verb (plural) — subject-verb agreement

PRACTICE | *A*   Underline the adjectival phrases.

1 The boys found themselves staring at a farmer's face red with anger.

2 A child forlorn in a corner caught my eye.

3 Rice fields golden in the sun make me think of home.

4 She has skin allergic to nylon.

5 We were a group of students ready for adventure.

6 A policy brilliant in conception will fail if poorly implemented.

7 Her smile hid a heart heavy with anxiety.

8 A guest reluctant to depart was straining our patience.

9 The racing car was watched by boys green with envy.

10 Children eager to learn are a delight to teach.

YOUR SCORE

10

PRACTICE | *B*   Rearrange the words to form sentences.

1 a — bright — future — have — promise — they — with.

_____

2 alive — faces — interest — saw — we — with.

_____

3 adept — are — at — managers — motivating — needed — people.

_____

_____

4 a — choose — close — place — to — we'll — you.

_____

5 by — expedition — join — jungle — keen — must — our — register — students — to — tomorrow.

_____

_____

YOUR SCORE

10

PRACTICE $\boxed{C}$ Circle the letters of the correct sentences.

1 **A** He spoke in tones firm with conviction.
   B He spoke in tones that firm with conviction.
   C He spoke in tones that were firm with conviction.

2 **A** Places free from pollution are getting fewer.
   B There are fewer and fewer places free from pollution.
   C Places free from pollution is getting fewer.

3 **A** The man has a fleet of them crazy about cars.
   B The man crazy about cars has a fleet of them.
   C The man who is crazy about cars has a fleet of them.

4 **A** We gazed at the meadows serene in the moonlight.
   B We gazed at meadows that lay serene in the moonlight.
   C Meadows serene in the moonlight lay before us.

5 **A** A child wise beyond his years have helped us.
   B A child has helped us wise beyond his years.
   C A child wise beyond his years has helped us.

YOUR SCORE
10

PRACTICE $\boxed{D}$ Fill in the blanks with suitable words in the box.

are	beautiful	eyes	easy	is
sickness	need	painful	proud	requires

1 We are a nation _____ of our heritage.
2 The shop famous for its noodles _____ over there.
3 Children shy in adult company _____ careful handling.
4 She is a lady _____ beyond compare.
5 They were a family _____ to like.
6 People hungry for knowledge _____ waiting to be educated.
7 The toddler looked at us with _____ full of wonder.
8 A student able to motivate himself _____ little help.
9 His is a difficult _____ to cure.
10 It was a scene _____ to witness.

YOUR SCORE
10

172

Join the sentences under **A** to those under **B**. Change the sentences under **B** into adjectival phrases beginning with adjectives.

A		B
1	People tend to avoid cakes and pastries.	They are conscious of their weight.
2	She touched a forehead.	It was clammy with cold sweat.
3	We entered rooms.	They were bare of furniture.
4	A boy may become a fine man.	He is thoughtless during childhood.
5	A pet is full of energy.	It is sure of its master's love.
6	I watched the tailor.	He was busy at work.

1 *People conscious of their weight tend to avoid cakes and pastries.*

2 _____

_____

3 _____

_____

4 _____

_____

5 _____

_____

6 _____

_____

YOUR SCORE

10

PRACTICE F Underline the correct words in the brackets.

I once asked my grandfather what it had been like for him to be a teenager **1** (eager / that eager) to grow up and be accepted as an adult **2** (is responsible / responsible) for his own life. He smiled and gave an answer **3** (different / was different) from anything I had expected. He said that adolescence as a time **4** (filled / full) of conflict **5** (was / were) a concept foreign to his generation. "In fact, a childhood **6** (free / which free) of serious responsibilities **7** (are / is) a modern notion," he said.

At the age of six, he was already a 'big boy' with three younger siblings **8** (depend / dependent) on him for safety and early education. At 14, he was a young man **9** (certain / who certain) of his place in society. The values dominant in that society **10** (was / were) a part of him and rebellion was out of the question.

YOUR SCORE

10

UNIT 13.1 ADVERBIAL PHRASES

with **because of**

Look at the **A** and **B** sentences below. Find out why **B** is correct and **A** is wrong in the **Grammar Points** section.

				GRAMMAR POINTS
1A	I would not change my plan because of **I am extremely stubborn**.	✗		
1B	I would not change my plan because of **my extreme stubbornness**.	✓		1
2A	We like climbing with him because of **he is agile**.	✗		
2B	We like climbing with him because of **his agility**.	✓		2

GRAMMAR POINTS

1 Unlike an adverbial clause, an adverbial phrase does not have a finite verb. The adverbial phrase contains either a noun alone or a noun phrase.

EXAMPLES:

adverbial clause

The children are irritable **because** they lack sleep.

finite verb

adverbial phrase

The children are irritable **because of** their lack of sleep.

noun phrase

2 An adverbial phrase beginning with **because of** often contains:

(a) a noun

noun

EXAMPLE: He got into mischief **because of** boredom.

(b) adjective + noun

adjective　　noun

EXAMPLE: He got into mischief **because of** intolerable boredom.

(c) article + noun

article noun

EXAMPLE: Our flight is delayed **because of** the fog.

(d) article + adjective + noun

article adjective noun

EXAMPLE: Our flight is delayed **because of** the dense fog.

(e) possessive pronoun + noun

possessive
pronoun　　noun

EXAMPLE: The villagers prevailed **because of** their solidarity.

(f) possessive pronoun + adjective + noun

possessive
pronoun　　adjective　　noun

EXAMPLE: The villagers prevailed **because of** their tremendous solidarity.

(g) article / possessive pronoun + adjective + noun with 'ing'

EXAMPLE:

possessive
pronoun　adjective　noun with 'ing'

Their house deteriorated **because of** their regular absences.

174

PRACTICE A Underline the adverbial phrases.

1 Our report was commended for its accuracy.

2 For their persistence in upholding justice, they will always be remembered.

3 Because of the elegance of its furnishings, this hotel is our first choice.

4 He almost ruined his fishing rod because of a momentary carelessness.

5 For your generosity when we were in serious trouble, you've earned our gratitude.

6 A curfew has been imposed because of the riots.

7 Because of his sad experiences in childhood, he is very compassionate.

8 Children love her for her affectionate nature.

9 For the incisive humour of his lectures, Professor Lee is much admired.

10 That building has been restored and preserved because of its historical value.

PRACTICE B Tick the correct sentences.

1 Some cancers of the skin can develop because of prolonged exposure to the sun.

2 For his repeated failure to comply with the club rules, he was suspended for two months.

3 They are being criticised because of they are narrow-minded.

4 Because of he's a judge, he must be careful in social situations.

5 She suspects that men want to marry her for her money.

6 Because of their vigilance, three lives were saved.

7 For your lack of cooperate, we cannot have you on our team.

8 We won our case because of you were persuasive.

9 I admire them for resilient.

10 For her remarkable ability to deal with people, Sue was promoted to the position of Human Resource Manager.

Underline the correct words in the brackets.

1 They were late for work (because / because of) the heavy snowing.

2 For (his compassion / his compassionate) towards the poor, he was warmly received.

3 Because of (his / the) obvious inexperience, he did not obtain respect.

4 We chose this machine for (its / it's) versatility.

5 Those buildings are in bad shape because of (a poor / poor) maintenance.

6 For (good / the good) of mankind, some scientists devote their lives to research.

7 She won a prize for exemplary (behaviour / she behaved).

8 Because of his (fails / failure) to conform to club rules, he was asked to resign.

9 For (their / they) help on that occasion, they were given the day off.

10 He found himself speechless because of sheer (terror / terror-stricken).

YOUR SCORE
10

PRACTICE **D**   Rearrange the words in the boxes to complete the sentences.

1   because — her — of — responsibility — shirk — tendency — to , we daren't trust her yet.

Because of her tendency to shirk responsibility, we daren't trust her yet.

2 He is disliked by some   conform — for — his — refusal — to .

_____

3 The universe is beyond our grasp   awesome — because — its — of — vastness .

_____

4   beauty — for — its — lyrics — of — the , the song stayed at the top of the charts for 10 weeks.

_____

5   a — because — misunderstanding — of — silly , we lost contact for years.

_____

6 The entire platoon was punished   for — its — obey — orders — slowness — to .

_____

YOUR SCORE
10

PRACTICE **E**   Circle the letters of the correct sentences.

1 A   For their selfless dedication, they've won a place in our history.
   B   They've won a place in our history because of their selfless dedication.
   C   They've won a place in our history because of their selfless dedicated.

2 A   Because of his good nature, he was taken advantage of by some people.
   B   He was taken advantage of by some people because of good-natured.
   C   He was taken advantage of by some people of his good nature.

3 A They were enchanted with her because of their beautiful voice.

   B They were enchanted with her because of her beautiful voice.

   C They were enchanted with her because she had a beautiful voice.

4 A We value this work for its artistic excellence.

   B We value this work because of its artistic excellence.

   C We value this work because of artistically excellent.

5 A Because his love of money, he sacrificed his free time.

   B For his love of money, he sacrificed his free time.

   C He sacrificed his free time because of his love of money.

PRACTICE *F*   Some of the adverbial phrases in the passage are incorrect. Underline them and rewrite the adverbial phrases beginning with **because of** or **for** correctly.

    It was the junior college prize-giving ceremony and Lisa felt happy <u>because of the college's recognise of its students' achievements</u>. From Lisa's group, Julia received the prize for the best overall result. Because of her performed outstandingly in sports, Asha won the title 'College Sports Star'. The 'Best Speaker' title went to Fara for a brilliance of her debating. Sally, the new student, was the winner of the art prize because of the striking originality of her work. For their excellent in the science subjects, Andy and Sheila shared a prize.

    Lastly a new prize was announced. It was awarded to Lisa for her kind to other students. This unexpected appreciate almost made Lisa cry.

1   *It was the junior college prize-giving ceremony and Lisa felt happy because of the college's*
    recognition of its students' achievements.

2 _____

    _____

3 _____

    _____

4 _____

    _____

5 _____

    _____

6 _____

    _____

UNIT 13.2 ADVERBIAL PHRASES

with **in order to**, **so as to** and **to**

Look at the **A** and **B** sentences below. Find out why **B** is correct and **A** is wrong in the **Grammar Points** section.

GRAMMAR POINTS

				GRAMMAR POINTS
1A	The police ransacked the suspect's house **to looked** for drugs.	✗		
1B	The police ransacked the suspect's house **to look** for drugs.	✓	1	
2A	I wrote it down **in order to not forget** .	✗		
2B	I wrote it down **in order not to forget** .	✓	2	
3A	He packed sandwiches **not to miss** dinner.	✗		
3B	He packed sandwiches **in order not to miss** dinner. He packed sandwiches **so as not to miss** dinner.	✓ ✓	3	

GRAMMAR POINTS

1   In an adverbial phrase, **in order to**, **so as to** or **to** must be followed by the base form of a verb.
EXAMPLE:

adverbial phrase

The government is developing the beach resort in order to / so as to / to **attract** tourists.   ✓

base form of verb

adverbial phrase

The government is developing the beach resort in order to / so as to /to **attracting** tourists.   ✗

present participle

2   We cannot add **not** immediately after **in order to** or **so as to**. For a negative phrase, we must use **in order not to** or **so as not to**.

EXAMPLE: They checked his credentials **in order not to** / **so as not to** be cheated.   ✓

They checked his credentials **in order to not** / **so as to not** be cheated.   ✗

3   We do not normally begin a negative phrase with **not to**.
EXAMPLES: She made up a story **not to** do the night shift.   ✗

She made up a story **in order not to** / **so as not to** do the night shift.   ✓

We can begin a negative phrase with **not to** when it is accompanied by a positive phrase.
EXAMPLE: I joined the society not to jostle for leadership but to contribute.   ✓
negative phrase   positive phrase

I joined the society to contribute and not to jostle for leadership.   ✓
positive phrase   negative phrase

PRACTICE | *A* | Underline the adverbial phrases that show purpose.

1 To heighten environmental awareness, the minister suggested launching a publicity campaign.

2 My uncle is saving as much money as he can in order to retire in comfort.

3 She chose her words carefully so as not to offend her client.

4 In order to increase your chances of a promotion, you should work extra hard.

5 I'm practising conscientiously so as to become a good violinist.

6 We'll work extra hours to make sure the goods are ready on time.

7 In order to earn the respect of your team members, you must be a firm and fair leader.

8 She lets her children share in the housework so as to teach them useful skills.

9 They quickly settled the issue out of court in order not to attract media attention.

10 The computer system will be improved so as to protect it against hackers.

PRACTICE | *B* | Rearrange the words in the boxes to complete the sentences.

1 | bankrupt — go — in — not — order — to, | they're cutting costs drastically.

_____

2 He'll try to persuade everybody | contest — for — him — in — 'Most Popular Resident' — the — to — vote. |

_____

3 We'd better tell the truth | suspense — as — the— not — prolong — so — to. |

_____

4 | a — child's — develop — to — self-esteem, | parents should not be afraid to provide challenges.

_____

5 He keeps quiet most of the time | arguing — avoid — in — his — order — to — roommate — with. |

_____

PRACTICE $\boxed{C}$ Tick the correct sentences.

1 The doctor prescribed an antibiotic to control the infection.

2 In order not to seemed too eager, he sauntered in late.

3 The manager pointed out the new employee's strength so as to boost his morale.

4 To arouse my curiosity, the children deliberately spoke in whispers.

5 So as to not make expensive mistakes, Julie takes professional advice on legal matters.

6 We're interviewing the victims of the fire not to meddle but to find out their needs.

7 In order get a promotion, most people have to work hard.

8 The prisoners conforming to the ways of his group so as not to be ostracise.

9 To equip students for the IT age, our schools have included computer lessons in the curriculum.

10 We've been learning the latest dances in order not to felt awkward at the next ball.

YOUR SCORE
10

PRACTICE $\boxed{D}$ Underline the correct words in brackets.

1 The dentist made small talk with Sally so as to (put / puts) her at ease.

2 To (galvanise / galvanised) his soldiers into action, the captain said the high command might make an unscheduled inspection.

3 In order not (seem / to seem) inexperienced, he told us that he had been in the industry for many years.

4 They studied the map carefully so as (not / not to) take a wrong turn along the way.

5 Jane wandered around the new house in order to (get / got) the feel of the place.

6 So as to (ensure / ensured) he assembled the cabinet correctly, he studied the diagrams in the do-it-yourself manual.

7 He has come not to complain but to (help / helping) us learn from our mistakes.

8 He kept his problems to himself so as (not to / to not) upset us.

9 In order to (ran / run) unencumbered up the steep slope, he threw down his backpack.

10 She told us everything (not / so as not) to be blamed.

YOUR SCORE
10

PRACTICE $\boxed{E}$ Join the sentences. Change the underlined ones into adverbial phrases beginning with the words in brackets.

1 He wants to hone his debating skills (in order to). He often practises speaking before a mirror.

   In order to hone his debating skills, he often practises speaking before a mirror.

2 You are saying these things. You want to humour me (to).

3 <u>She doesn't want to be outdone (in order)</u>. She's attempting the highest peak when we go mountain-climbing.

_____

_____

4 <u>I wanted to let Susan know when I'll be back (to)</u>. I left a note on the refrigerator door.

_____

_____

5 Ben stood still, hardly daring to breathe. <u>He didn't want to awaken the sleeping tiger (in order)</u>.

_____

_____

6 <u>Nancy does not want to forget important dates (so as)</u>. Nancy always carries a notebook with her.

_____

_____

YOUR SCORE
10

PRACTICE | *F* | Rewrite the paragraph correctly using adverbial phrases showing purpose.

In order to overcame her paralysing shyness, Diana tried various techniques from magazine articles. One involved imagining the people she was shy of in their pyjamas so as to lost her awe of them. Unfortunately, this made her even more nervous and she hastily reclothed them in proper clothes to restoring her composure. Another technique was rather more successful. In order to not be tongue-tied, she asked people questions about themselves, their families, schools or jobs, hobbies, favourite colours and so on. The people responded happily but she had to keep on asking them questions so as not to gave them a chance to question her back. To copes with this need, Diana compiled a list of questions long enough to qualify for the Guinness Book of World Records.

In order to overcome her paralysing shyness, Diana tried various techniques from

magazine articles.

_____

_____

_____

_____

_____

_____

_____

_____

YOUR SCORE
10

UNIT 13.3 ADVERBIAL PHRASES

with present participles

Look at the **A** and **B** sentences below. Find out why **B** is correct and **A** is wrong in the **Grammar Points** section.

**CH**ECKPOINT

				GRAMMAR POINTS
1A	Lynn's car broke down yesterday, **causes** her to be late for work.		✗	
1B	Lynn's car broke down yesterday, **causing** her to be late for work.		✓	1
2A	**Giving Gary an excuse to tease me**, I was late for our appointment.		✗	
2B	I was late for our appointment, **giving Gary an excuse to tease me**.		✓	2

GRAMMAR POINTS

1 We can use an adverbial phrase beginning with the 'ing' (present participle) form when describing an action done by or an event caused by the same subject in the main clause.

EXAMPLE:

adverbial phrase showing result

The tornado swept through the town, | **leaving** a trail of destruction. |

(present participle)

2 We put the adverbial phrase after the main clause if the action or event is the result of the action in the main clause.

EXAMPLE:

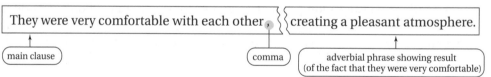

They were very comfortable with each other, } } creating a pleasant atmosphere.

(main clause)   (comma)   (adverbial phrase showing result (of the fact that they were very comfortable))

We can place the adverbial phrase before the main clause if the action or event takes place before the action in the main clause.

EXAMPLE:

adverbial phrase

| Sensing her growing displeasure, | I quickly changed the subject.

REMEMBER!

■ A comma is usually placed between the main clause and the adverbial phrase beginning with an 'ing' form.

EXAMPLE:

He often makes tactless remarks, hurting other people's feelings as a result.

(comma)

■ **Hence**, **therefore** or **thus** can be added immediately before an adverbial phrase showing result. However, they should not be added before words like **causing** or **resulting in**, which already indicate very clearly that the phrase shows result.

PRACTICE *A*   Underline the adverbial phrases of result.

1 The demonstrators refused to disperse, leaving the police no choice but to arrest them.

2 The lecture had been well-advertised, drawing a large crowd.

3 A fresh breeze blew, tempering the heat of noon.

4 Two friends joined us, making up a foursome for a game.

5 The speaker kept contradicting himself, bewildering the audience.

6 Someone yawned, causing the rest of us to do the same.

7 He acted swiftly and wisely, preventing a crisis.

8 We left the building unlocked last night, exposing it to vandals.

9 Finally the rains came, enabling the farmers to plough their lands.

10 Her grandchildren arrived, making her much more cheerful.

YOUR SCORE

10

PRACTICE *B*   Circle the letters of the correct sentences.

1 A   We celebrated from dusk to dawn, turning night into day.

  B   We celebrated from dusk to dawn, thus turning night into day.

  C   We celebrated from dusk to dawn, turned night into day.

2 A   He had excellent scores in the game, thus qualified for inclusion in the next round.

  B   He had excellent scores in the game, hence qualifying for inclusion in the next round.

  C   He had excellent scores in the game, therefore qualifying for inclusion in the next round.

3 A   Cycling furiously, Joe and I arrived well before the others.

  B   Arriving well before the others, Joe and I cycled furiously.

  C   Joe and I cycled furiously, hence arriving well before the others.

4 A   Showing no signs of a thaw, the ice forced us to stay at home.

  B   The ice showed no signs of thawing, thus forcing us to stay at home.

  C   The ice showed no signs of thawing, hence forced us to stay at home.

5 **A** The play was deeply moving, thus making some of the audience cry.

     B The play was deeply moving, was making some of the audience cry.

     C The play was deeply moving, making some of the audience cry.

PRACTICE **C** Tick the correct sentences.

1 Feeling himself exhausted, he had fallen asleep.

2 They cleared the rainforests recklessly, thus losing their heritage.

3 The river overflowed its banks, flooding the plain.

4 She hung up two paintings, brighten the room.

5 His efforts were fuelled by pride, therefore resulting in failure.

6 Your proposal is highly original, hence meriting serious consideration.

7 Dawn broke, awakened birds and babies.

8 Causing a lot of debate, she set one idea against another.

9 We had been slackening, therefore getting poor results.

10 A group of revellers gatecrashed our party, creating real confusion.

PRACTICE **D** Cross out the incorrect words in the boxes to complete the sentences.

1 Brownie jumped onto the table, | toppled | toppling | a statuette.

2 He promoted his friends, | causing | hence causing | much resentment.

3 The humidity is high, | make | making | us feel lethargic.

4 Her outlook on life is positive and dynamic, | resulting | therefore resulting | in success.

5 Our action proved wise, | break | breaking | the deadlock.

6 Their strategy | failed | worked | , filling them with despair.

7 Ted's business grew, bringing him | affluence | poverty | .

8 The organisers kept changing the rules, | upsets | upsetting | the participants.

9 I overspent, | eaten | eating | into my pension fund.

10 She works steadily, | meeting | meets | all deadlines.

PRACTICE _E_   Rewrite the sentences correctly using adverbial phrases showing result.

1 Her articles were witty and concise, thus attracted more discerning readers.
   Her articles were witty and concise, thus attracting more discerning readers.

2 Their attempts at covering up were useless, therefore resulting in ugly paintwork.

3 Those opal earrings suit her, enhance her delicate beauty.

4 Delighting the youngsters, the idea of the trip was suggested last night.

5 He kept losing at cards, ends up with nothing.

6 This morning's exertion was too much for him, trigger a bad headache.

PRACTICE _F_   Rewrite the paragraph. Change each of the sentences in the brackets into an adverbial phrase showing result and join it to the sentence before it.

Driving a car can change a person. (It makes a monster out of a man or woman.) It exposes you to spicy language. (It widens your vocabulary greatly.) Soon you are an expert at exchanging insults. (You shock family and friends travelling with you.) You cannot bear to be overtaken. (You often break the speed limit to even the score.) After some time, you may realise the lunacy of it all. (You revert to your sane self.) You start to drive sensibly. (You learn to return rudeness with courtesy.)

Driving a car can change a person, making a monster out of a man or woman.

UNIT 13.4 ADVERBIAL PHRASES

with **after**, **before**, **when**, **while**

Look at the **A** and **B** sentences below. Find out why **B** is correct and **A** is wrong in the **Grammar Points** section.

				GRAMMAR POINTS
1A	He has returned to work after **lazes** on the beach.	✗		
1B	He has returned to work after **lazing** on the beach.	✓		1
2A	The grenades exploded while **transported** out of the country.	✗		
2B	The grenades exploded while **being transported** out of the country.	✓		2

GRAMMAR POINTS

1 We can begin an adverbial phrase with **after**, **before**, **when** or **while** followed by a present participle but not a finite verb.

> **EXAMPLE:** He had a drink | while **chatting** with me. | ✓
>
> *adverbial phrase*
> *present participle*

> He had a drink | while **was chatting** with me. | ✗
>
> *adverbial phrase*
> *finite verb*

2 We can begin an adverbial phrase with **when** followed by a past participle. **After**, **before** or **while** cannot be followed by a past participle.

> **EXAMPLES:** Most people try to give compliments
> **when shown** around friends' new homes. | ✓
>
> They were bored **while shown** around the house. | ✗
> They were bored **while being shown** around the house. | ✓
>
> They were tired **after shown** around the house. | ✗
> They were tired **after being shown** around the house. | ✓
>
> They were curious **before shown** around the house. | ✗
> They were curious **before being shown** around the house. | ✓

PRACTICE A Underline the adverbial phrases indicating time.

1 While travelling in Africa, we took some splendid pictures.

2 She let me down badly after promising to help me.

3 He showed no fear when threatened by the robber.

4 Before accepting the offer, you should consider it carefully.

5 When bargaining at a bazaar, some people are very successful.

6 We had a brief problem before landing safely in Madrid.

7 After graduating from college, he set up a business.

8 I was daydreaming while watching the documentary.

9 When given a free hand, you did a good job.

10 Ada looks chic after having her hair styled.

YOUR SCORE
10

PRACTICE B Underline the correct words in the brackets.

1 The matador never regained his strength after (being gored / gored) by a bull.

2 While (loitered / loitering) in the street, he was scrutinising every passer-by.

3 When (complimented / complimenting) for being elegant, she just laughed.

4 I sat by the river for hours before (catch / catching) one tiny fish.

5 After (mastering / was mastering) the technique of roller-blading, she bought a pair of skates.

6 You need patience and perception when (handled / handling) people.

7 Laura added two points while (keyed / keying) in her report.

8 Before (commit / committing) ourselves to any investment, we must evaluate the risks.

9 She gets flustered when (hurried / hurry) into giving an answer.

10 After (sending / sent) my family an e-mail, I gave way to jet lag.

YOUR SCORE
10

Tick the correct sentences.

1 She fell asleep while tried to study the new book.

2 When practised faithfully, good values become a part of us.

3 He learnt to be tough while sailing alone.

4 We are going to try everything before given up hope.

5 After looking through an encyclopaedia, we solved the puzzle.

6 While were cruising down the river, they saw a crocodile.

7 The bull chased the boys when madden by their teasing.

8 Before fleeing the country, he said 'goodbye' to only one person.

9 He broke down in court when found guilty.

10 After realise the seriousness of my mistake, I apologised.

YOUR SCORE

10

PRACTICE *D* Complete the sentences by rearranging the words in the boxes to form adverbial phrases indicating time.

1 You should have consulted us | an — before — decision — important — making — such |.

You should have consulted us before making such an important decision.

2 | an — as — excuse — used — when, | a headache sometimes becomes real.

_____

_____

3 | after — all — analysing — errors — our — tactical, | we made a new plan.

_____

_____

4 He worked seven days a week | being — for — prepared — job — the — top — while |.

_____

_____

5 We are giving him a last chance | action — before — legal — taking |.

_____

_____

6 | disappearance — investigating — millionaire — of — the — the — while, | the inspector himself vanished.

_____

YOUR SCORE

10

_____

188

Change each of the underlined sentences into an adverbial phrase beginning with the word in brackets. Join the phrase to the sentence before or after it.

1 You are born with certain talents (when). You should develop them.

2 The princess was smiling and waving. She was passing by in her chauffeured limousine (while).

3 He pursued his dream for years (after). He suddenly lost interest.

4 She wanted to see her son. She was going on a long journey (before).

5 They were exploring the cave (while). They found a strange object.

6 I plan to hitchhike around the world. I'll graduate from college (after).

1 *When born with certain talents, you should develop them.*

2 _____

_____

3 _____

_____

4 _____

_____

5 _____

_____

6 _____

_____

YOUR SCORE

10

Rewrite the paragraph correctly using adverbial phrases showing time.

A Hollywood star once gave a strange reply when asking the secret behind her unlined face. She said: 'While am acting, I portray emotions through my eyes and not my facial muscles.' She added this piece of advice: 'In everyday life too, you must think before you allow yourself to smile. The loveliest woman will look a wreck after smiled recklessly over the years. When smiled into the camera or at anyone, I never let my eyes crinkle up at the corners.' After read this, are you prepared to give up 'smiling recklessly' to avoid wrinkles?

A Hollywood star once gave a strange reply when asked the secret behind her

unlined face.

_____

_____

_____

_____

_____

YOUR SCORE

10

UNIT 14.1 NOUN PHRASES

with infinitive (with and without **to**) and present participle

Look at the **A** and **B** sentences below. Find out why **B** is correct and **A** is wrong in the **Grammar Points** section.

CHECKPOINT

GRAMMAR POINTS

1A	I don't intend **ask** for assistance.	✗	
1B	I don't intend **to ask** for assistance.	✓	1
2A	He considered **to join** the air force.	✗	
2B	He considered **joining** the air force.	✓	2
3A	Our guide let us **to plan** our own itinerary.	✗	
3B	Our guide let us **plan** our own itinerary.	✓	3

GRAMMAR POINTS

1 A noun phrase does not have a finite verb. It can have a non-finite verb, for instance, an infinitive (the 'to' form) or a present participle (the 'ing' form).

EXAMPLE:

noun phrase

We love **to watch / watching** sunsets.

non-finite verb (infinitive)   non-finite verb (present participle)

> **REMEMBER!**
> ■ A noun phrase answers the question "What?". When it is used as the object of the main clause, it occurs after the verb in the main clause.
>
> EXAMPLE: He **mentioned** seeing her at the conference.
> subject   verb   object (noun phrase)
>
> What did he mention? Seeing her at the conference.
>
> The noun phrase is said to be the object of the verb **mentioned**.

2 Some verbs can have as objects
(a) noun phrases beginning with **infinitives** and **present participles**, for instance:

begin	continue	hate	like	love	prefer	remember	start	try

EXAMPLE: They **began** to work / working for the software company in 1999.
noun phrase

(b) noun phrases beginning with **infinitives** but not **present participles**, for instance:

choose	decide	demand	hope	manage	need	offer
plan	promise	refuse	seek	want	wish	

EXAMPLE: He **hoped** to work for his uncle after graduation.
noun phrase

(c) noun phrases beginning with **present participles** but not **infinitives**, for instance:

admit	avoid	consider	deny	detest	endure	enjoy
finish	imagine	mention	miss	postpone	practise	recall
resent	resume	stop	suggest	take		

EXAMPLE: We can no longer **endure** | **working** for this company. |
                                              noun phrase

3 Sometimes another object is placed between the verb in the main clause and the noun phrase in these ways:

(a) verb + other object + noun phrase beginning with infinitive (with **to**)

ask	allow	beg	encourage	expect	force
help	like	need	persuade	prefer	request
require	teach	tell	want	warn	

EXAMPLE: I **encouraged** her | **to speak** her mind. |
                                        noun phrase

(b) verb + other object + noun phrase beginning with infinitive (without **to**)

feel	have	help	let	make
notice	observe	overhear	see	watch

EXAMPLE: She **made** the boys | **wash** their own clothes. |
                                        noun phrase

(c) verb + other object + noun phrase beginning with present participle

have	hear	notice	observe
overhear	see	sense	watch

EXAMPLE: He **overheard** his manager | **applying** for another job. |
                                              noun phrase

PRACTICE | *A* | Underline the noun phrases in the sentences.

1 We were laughing happily when she walked in.

2 They forgot to tell me about it.

3 This doesn't entitle you to speak at meetings.

4 She no longer avoids singing in public.

5 He expects to be served immediately.

6 The mountaineers climbed to the summit.

7 Lily sometimes hears them chatting amicably.

8 I don't intend to get myself poisoned by this food.

9 He is going abroad for a few weeks.

10 Suddenly I saw her fall to the ground.

YOUR SCORE

10

PRACTICE **B** Complete the sentences by rearranging the words in the boxes to form noun phrases.

1 Sorelle and I have arranged | after — seminar — Thailand — the — to — tour | .

Sorelle and I have arranged to tour Thailand after the seminar.

2 She did not fancy | a — beach — crowded — on — such — sunbathing | .

_____

3 I beg you | a — chance — give — plan — second — this — to | .

_____

4 He must not let this | ability — confidence — in — shatter — his — his | .

_____

5 We saw the barrels | day — downhill — rolling — that | .

_____

6 The boy wants | tutored — be — by — teacher — particular — that — to | .

_____

YOUR SCORE
10

PRACTICE **C** Fill in the blanks with suitable words in the boxes.

going	to go
make	to make
teaching	to teach
control	to control
worry	worrying
be	being
followed	following
face	faced
blinding	to blind
dressing	is dressing

1 You have allowed your garden _____ to seed.

2 She watched me _____ a fool of myself.

3 The inspector came to observe Judy _____ the class.

4 Shane has learnt _____ his temper.

5 They have stopped _____ about silly things.

6 Nobody can persuade him to _____ less serious.

7 I could sense friendly eyes _____ me.

8 He made us _____ certain hard facts.

9 Lara chooses _____ herself to her house's flaws.

10 My father detests _____ up for formal functions.

YOUR SCORE
10

PRACTICE **D** Tick the correct sentences.

1 They started importing our goods long ago.

2 The irate customer demanded seeing the manager.

3 After a short break, we resumed our reading.

4 The police warned the public to beware of pickpockets.

5 She'll soon have all of them to do as she say.

6 It's so noisy I can't hear myself to think.

7 We overheard them wondering about the holiday plans.

8 I regret to inform you that your application has not been approved.

9 He has requested us keeping this confidential.

10 You should not delay to have some car repairs.

YOUR SCORE

10

PRACTICE *E* Rewrite each sentence expressing the same meaning in a slightly different way.

1 She helped me to come to terms with my problem.

She helped me come to terms with my problem.

2 We saw him flinch at the sight of the letter.

3 Some people won't even try understanding how to use the Internet.

4 The neighbours often hear her talking to her plants.

5 At his birth, his parents started to save for his education.

6 I don't want you sacrificing your free time for this project.

YOUR SCORE

10

PRACTICE *F* Rewrite the paragraph correctly using noun phrases.

Laura wanted to work with animals so her friends persuaded her phoning the famous animal hospital in the next town. She asked spoke to the chief administrator and began explain she was willing to work as a volunteer to gain experience. He listened for a while and then told her the hospital had a vacancy for a trainee and she only needed applying. She felt herself to skipping with delight as she ran to tell her friends and she started wrote her application letter that afternoon.

Laura wanted to work with animals so her friends persuaded her to phone the famous

animal hospital in the next town.

YOUR SCORE

10

UNIT 14.2 **NOUN PHRASES**

as complements and objects of prepositions

Look at the **A** and **B** sentences below. Find out why **B** is correct and **A** is wrong in the **Grammar Points** section.

			GRAMMAR POINTS
1A	The boy's guardian **appeared being** a pleasant man.	✗	
1B	The boy's guardian **appeared to be** a pleasant man.	✓	1
2A	They petitioned **against to demolish** the old buildings.	✗	
2B	They petitioned **against demolishing** the old buildings.	✓	2

GRAMMAR POINTS

1 A noun phrase can be the complement of the verb before it. Verbs that take complements are called link verbs. They include the verbs **appear**, **be**, **came**, **grow**, **prove**, **seem** and **turn out**.
EXAMPLE:

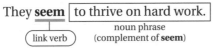

They **seem** | to thrive on hard work. |
　　　(link verb)　　noun phrase
　　　　　　　(complement of **seem**)

A noun phrase beginning with a **present participle** can be the complement of the verb 'to be' but not of other link verbs.
EXAMPLES:

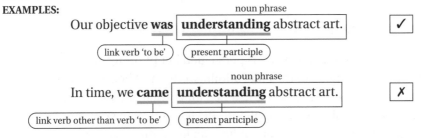

Our objective **was** | **understanding** abstract art. | ✓
　　(link verb 'to be')　(present participle)

In time, we **came** | **understanding** abstract art. | ✗
　(link verb other than verb 'to be')　(present participle)

A noun phrase beginning with an **infinitive** can be the complement of the verb 'to be' and other link verbs.
EXAMPLES:

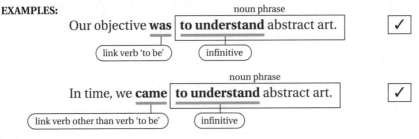

Our objective **was** | **to understand** abstract art. | ✓
　(link verb 'to be')　(infinitive)

In time, we **came** | **to understand** abstract art. | ✓
　(link verb other than verb 'to be')　(infinitive)

2 A noun phrase beginning with a present participle can be the object of the preposition before it.

EXAMPLE:

We'll work **towards** [**having** a just society.]

preposition   noun phrase
(object of the preposition **towards**)

A noun phrase beginning with an infinitive cannot be the object of a preposition.

EXAMPLE:

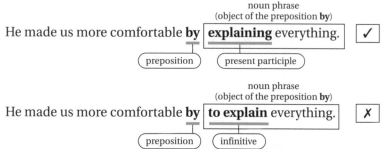

noun phrase
(object of the preposition **by**)

He made us more comfortable **by** [**explaining** everything.]   ✓

preposition   present participle

noun phrase
(object of the preposition **by**)

He made us more comfortable **by** [**to explain** everything.]   ✗

preposition   infinitive

REMEMBER!

- A noun phrase answers the question "What?". When it is used as a complement, it occurs after a link verb. When it is used as the object of a preposition, it occurs after the preposition.

  EXAMPLES: Her aim **was** [to learn the trumpet.]

  link verb 'to be'   noun phrase (complement)

  What was her aim? To learn the trumpet.

  John is good **at** [repairing electrical appliances.]

  preposition   noun phrase (object of preposition)

  What is John good at? Repairing electrical appliances.

- A noun phrase does not have a finite verb. It can have a non-finite verb, for instance, an infinitive or a present participle.

  EXAMPLES: I've grown [**to like** the climate here.]   This must be done without [**hurting** anyone.]

  infinitive   present participle

PRACTICE [*A*]   Underline the noun phrases.

1 Your candidate has proved to be a dedicated party member.

2 He disappointed us after raising our hopes.

3 We congratulated her on her being elected president of the Nature Society.

4 The mysterious visitor turned out to be an old friend.

5 Their business seemed to prosper despite the recession.

6 She is committed to improving the services in this city.

7 They will not succeed in intimidating that girl.

8 I always do a sketch before painting a landscape.

9 The children came to love the trips to the city.

10 Our greatest joy will be to see the garden flourishing.

YOUR SCORE

10

PRACTICE **B** Complete the sentences by rearranging the words in the boxes to form noun phrases.

1 One of my interests is | athletes — collecting — of — pictures — promising — young |.

One of my interests is collecting pictures of promising young athletes.

2 Gradually they came | country — culture — of — the — the — to — understand |.

_____

3 She charmed them into | a — interesting — number — of — revealing — secrets |.

_____

4 You don't appear | about — care — club's — to — future — your |.

_____

5 He is not above | his — on — using — party — a — savings — all |.

_____

6 We soon gave up fantasies of | armour — being — in — knights — shining |.

_____

PRACTICE **C** Cross out the incorrect words in the boxes to complete the sentences.

1 Everyone in this firm seems | nursing | to nurse | a hope of promotion.

2 Sally reproached me for | forgetting | forgotten | to send the application.

3 The bane of my life is | have | having | to live in this suburb.

4 The pizza proved | to be | was | the best we had ever tasted.

5 She does the most daring things | not | without | turning a hair.

6 I've grown to | love | loves | the whirl of activity here.

7 You are very good | at | in | making people feel successful.

8 The sight of you | appear | appears | to encourage him.

9 He'll join the family business | in | upon | completing college.

10 They would never agree to | being | have | questioned by journalists.

PRACTICE **D** Tick the correct answers.

1 The black sheep of my family turned out being a fine person.

2 In our desperate situation, we were past bothering about appearances.

3 I was entrusted with took them home safely.

4 In due course, they came to realise their good fortune.

5 Our nation's aspiration is to be a model for racial harmony.

6 They'll soon resort to threaten that country with sanctions.

7 We had the humbling experience of playing against a superb team.

8 He seemed regarded everyone as a potential rival.

9 Losing is far less unpleasant than winning through trickery.

10 Their choice of a leader has proved is a mistake.

PRACTICE E Change **B** into noun phrases to complete **A**.

A	B
1 Over the years we have come . . .	We rely on your guidance.
2 He won the boys' confidence by . . .	He treated them as adults.
3 The root of her troubles was . . .	She had a very bad memory.
4 I can't get over . . .	I saw her in such a predicament.
5 Every mannerism of his seems . . .	It irritates the audience.
6 They are obsessed with . . .	They maintain their old sports car.

1 *Over the years we have come to rely on your guidance.*

2 _____

3 _____

4 _____

5 _____

6 _____

PRACTICE F Rewrite the paragraph correctly using noun phrases.

As a teenage girl, I often received odd looks from a neighbour for came home after dark. She always seemed being worried even when my friends insisted on seeing me safely home after extra science classes. One night, when my family was away at a wedding, the lady next door saw what must have appeared was thieves hiding in my backyard. She hurried over to check. She looked rather disappointed when the burglary turned out being three schoolgirls organising 'Operation Catch Toads' for the next day's biology class.

As a teenage girl, I often received odd looks from a neighbour for coming home after dark.

_____

_____

_____

_____

_____

UNIT 14.3 NOUN PHRASES

as subjects

Look at the **A** and **B** sentences below. Find out why **B** is correct and **A** is wrong in the **Grammar Points** section.

GRAMMAR POINTS

1A	To become an astronaut **my little brother's dream**.	✗	
1B	To become an astronaut **is my little brother's dream**.	✓	1
2A	Watching horror movies **giving** us nightmares.	✗	
2B	Watching horror movies **gives** us nightmares.	✓	2
3A	To serve the people **were** her aim in life.	✗	
3B	To serve the people **was** her aim in life.	✓	3

GRAMMAR POINTS

1 A noun phrase can be used as the subject of the verb after it. The verb must not be dropped. The noun phrase can begin with an infinitive or a present participle.

EXAMPLE:

noun phrase (subject of **was**)

To meet him / **Meeting** him | **was** a privilege.   ✓

infinitive   present participle   verb

noun phrase (subject)

To meet him / Meeting him | a privilege.   ✗

2 The verb after a noun phrase subject must be **finite**.

EXAMPLE:

Working with you | **has been** a great pleasure.   ✓
noun phrase
(subject of **has been**)   finite verb

Working with you | **been** a great pleasure.   ✗
noun phrase (subject)

3 A noun phrase subject is considered singular. Therefore, the verb after it must be singular too.

EXAMPLE:

Listening to my favourite songs | **relaxes** my mind.   ✓
noun phrase (subject)   singular verb

Listening to my favourite songs | **relax** my mind.   ✗
noun phrase (subject)   plural verb

PRACTICE $\boxed{A}$ Some of these sentences contain noun phrases used as subjects. Underline these noun phrases.

1 Rushing around makes me feel dizzy.

2 To organise all these books won't be easy.

3 To keep them amused, she told them stories.

4 Talking about the past can be fascinating.

5 Feeling miserable, I went away quietly.

6 To avoid bankruptcy seemed impossible.

7 Being self-sufficient, he will be happy living alone.

8 To pre-empt rumours, we made everything public.

9 Confronting him would probably be best.

10 To satisfy everyone, we'll discuss it thoroughly.

PRACTICE $\boxed{B}$ Rearrange the words to form sentences whose subjects are noun phrases.

1 can — cancer — cause — protection — skin — sun-tanning — without.
Sun-tanning without protection can cause skin cancer.

2 global — is — mission — peace — promote — their — to.

_____

3 fight — him — lose — this — to — upset — would.

_____

4 needs — rehabilitating — skills — special — stroke — victims.

_____

5 country — decision — his — leave — own — the — to — was.

_____

6 in — indulging — jealousies — our — petty — time — wasted.

_____

PRACTICE $\boxed{C}$ Circle the letters of the correct sentences.

1 A   Smoothing over problems appears to be his role.
   B   To smooth over problems appears to be his role.
   C   Smoothing over problems appear to be his role.

2 A   To find a cure for cancer the aim of much painstaking research.
   B   To find a cure for cancer is the aim of much painstaking research.
   C   Finding a cure for cancer is the aim of much painstaking research.

3 A   To be charged with speeding would mean a fine.
   B   Being charged with speeding to mean a fine.
   C   Being charged with speeding would mean a fine.

4 A   To hitchhike around the world must be very exciting.
   B   Hitchhiking around the world must be very exciting.
   C   To hitchhike around the world very exciting.

5 A   Winning that prize was his fondest hope.
   B   To win that prize being his fondest hope.
   C   To win that prize was his fondest hope.

YOUR SCORE
10

PRACTICE $\boxed{D}$ Underline the correct words in the brackets.

1   Exercising regularly (help / helps) build strong muscles.

2   To live in luxury (is not / not) the top priority for me.

3   Bringing up six children alone (has / having) made her strong.

4   Meeting new people (will / will be) good for you.

5   To see every new film (remain / remains) his obsession.

6   To find her in a bad mood (a / was a) rare event.

7   Meddling in other people's affairs (seeming / seems) a huge waste of time.

8   To make him a supervisor (may be / maybe) a good idea.

9   Attending cocktail parties (bores / to bore) me greatly.

10 To attend all his grandchildren's graduation ceremonies (was / were)
    Mr Lee's dearest wish.

YOUR SCORE
10

PRACTICE `E` Rewrite the sentences correctly using noun phrases as subjects.

1 Mixing with people from all walks of life have made him broadminded.
   Mixing with people from all walks of life has made him broadminded.

2 Collecting Asian proverbs my late uncle's pastime.

   _____

3 To make money being once his reason for living.

   _____

4 Face their disapproval doesn't frighten her in the least.

   _____

5 To help the community develop been our concern all these years.

   _____

6 To go on doing this a sheer waste of time.

   _____

YOUR SCORE
/ 10

PRACTICE `F` Fill in the blanks with suitable words from the box to complete the passage.

been	growing	hugging	prepared	turned
bring	had	kissing	see	was

From the time my grandfather was a little boy, to study abroad had (1) _____ his

dream. However, adjusting to a new way of life in a foreign country (2) _____ out to be

a nightmare. (3) _____ up in an isolated village in the Middle East (4) _____

made him a stranger to Western ways. Watching the occasional romantic scene in a cowboy film had

not (5) _____ him for similar scenes in everyday life. To (6) _____ real

live couples embrace in public was a great shock to him. Back home in his village, even for engaged

couples to be seen just holding hands would (7) _____ shame on both families. He was

always aware that to walk alone with a girl was to start gossip. On the other hand, in the university,

Grandpa soon learnt that to hug another boy in gratitude for his help (8) _____ not quite

the thing to do. Grandpa explained that in his country, (9) _____ between men was

perfectly proper. He did not add that (10) _____ on the cheek was the traditional

greeting between men, most of whom had full beards.

YOUR SCORE
/ 10

UNIT 15.1 SENTENCE STRUCTURE

joining two simple sentences with **either ... or**
and **neither ... nor**

Look at the **A** and **B** sentences below. Find out why **B** is correct and **A** is wrong in the
Grammar Points section.

1A	You **either can** come with us **or** stay here.	✗	
1B	You **can either** come with us **or** stay here.	✓	1
2A	Someone **either** borrowed my dictionary **or** I dropped it on the bus.	✗	
2B	**Either** someone borrowed my dictionary **or** I dropped it on the bus.	✓	2
3A	I didn't order the steak and neither **she didn't** ask for the lamb chop.	✗	
	I didn't order the steak and neither **she did** ask for the lamb chop.	✗	
3B	I didn't order the steak and neither **did she** ask for the lamb chop.	✓	3

GRAMMAR POINTS

1 We can use **either ... or** / **neither ... nor** to join two simple sentences that have the same
modals but different main verbs. We usually put the modal before **either/neither**.

EXAMPLES: Dan **would** speak sensibly. He **would** keep quiet.
Dan **would either** speak sensibly **or** keep quiet.
⎵
(modal)

Mary is a strict vegetarian. She **will not** eat meat. She **will not** order fish.
Mary is a strict vegetarian. She **will neither** eat meat **nor** order fish.
⎵
(modal)

The two simple sentences should have subjects referring to the
same person or thing, and they should have the same tense.

2 We can also use **either ... or** to join two simple sentences that
have subjects referring to different people or things, and
different verbs.
We place **either** before the first subject and put **or** before the
second subject.

EXAMPLES: Strong winds wrecked the ship. It ran into a rock.
Either strong winds wrecked the ship **or** it ran into a rock.
⎵   ⎵
(subject)   (subject)

> **REMEMBER!**
> ■ Join two simple sentences
>   with **either ... or** to indicate
>   that one out of the two
>   choices or events is possible.
>
> ■ Join two simple sentences
>   with **neither ... nor** to
>   indicate that both choices or
>   events are not possible.

In commands (such as **Come here / Help me / Take this**), the hidden subject is **you**.

EXAMPLE: Keep quiet. I won't tell you the story.

Either you keep quiet **or** I won't tell you the story.

$\underset{\text{subject}}{}$ $\underset{\text{subject}}{}$

Note that we do not usually apply this rule for negative sentences.

EXAMPLE: He didn't contact us. We didn't call him.

Either he didn't contact us **or** we didn't call him.   ☒

3 We can use **either/neither** to join two negative sentences that have subjects referring to different people or things in these ways:

(a) 1st sentence + **and** + 2nd sentence + **either**.
EXAMPLE: He didn't contact us. We didn't call him.
He didn't contact us **and** we didn't call him **either**.

(b) 1st sentence + **and neither** + 2nd sentence with inversion*.
EXAMPLE: He didn't contact us. We didn't call him.
He didn't contact us **and neither** did we* call him.

(*After inversion, the auxiliary verb comes before the subject, just like in a question.)

REMEMBER!

■ When two sentences are joined with **either...or / neither...nor / either / neither**, repeated parts are sometimes left out in the second sentence.
EXAMPLES:
You can have coffee. You can have tea.   Jon didn't contact us. Audrey didn't contact us.
You can **either** have coffee **or** (have) tea.   Jon didn't contact us **and** Audrey didn't (contact us) **either**.

$\underset{\text{can be left out}}{}$ $\underset{\text{can be left out}}{}$

PRACTICE $\boxed{A}$ Complete the sentences with the words in the boxes by writing their numbers in the correct circles.

1 Rosemary ⟨2⟩ register and neither ⟨1⟩ I.

2 The grass didn't wither ◯ the flowers didn't ◯.

3 We can ◯ protest or ◯.

4 ◯ the motorist or the cyclist ◯ at fault.

5 The mangoes ◯ ripened and ◯ have the papayas.

6 He ◯ either ◯ or cry on hearing this.

1	did	2	didn't
1	and	2	either
1	disobey	2	either
1	either	2	is
1	haven't	2	neither
1	will	2	laugh

YOUR SCORE
/10

PRACTICE $\boxed{B}$ Rearrange the words in the boxes and complete the sentences.

1 The sunrise didn't interest them | and — did — neither — sunset — the |.

2 You either stop wasting time | or — straight — go —home |.

_____

3 The dress may neither fit her | her — nor — suit |.

_____

4 That grandfather clock either stops | fast — goes — or — really |.

_____

5 Our parent company has not made any profit this year | and — have — neither — our — subsidiaries |.

_____

_____

PRACTICE *C* Some of the sentences contain words that can be dropped without changing the meaning. Bracket the words.

1 This piece of news will either make you pleased or make you angry.

2 I wouldn't deceive anyone and neither would you deceive anyone.

3 Either he gives them what they want or they will pester him.

4 The roses haven't bloomed and the chrysanthemums haven't bloomed either.

5 Either his hearing is poor or he is pretending not to hear you.

6 I could neither restore his trust in us nor revive his faith in our organisation.

7 Age has not dimmed the castle's splendour and neither has neglect dimmed the castle's splendour.

8 Usually Ted either looks excited or speaks excitedly.

9 They don't resent us and neither do we bear them a grudge.

10 We can either go to the book fair with our friends or go to the book fair with our parents.

PRACTICE *D* Join the sentences using the words in the boxes.

1 I can't remember when we first met. I can't remember where we first met. | neither, nor |
I can neither remember when we first met nor where we first met.

_____

2 He works reasonable hours. His health suffers. | either, or |

_____

3 They aren't prepared. I'm not prepared. | and, either |

_____

4 We shouldn't be difficult. They shouldn't be difficult. | and, either |

_____

5 My parents don't like my music. I don't enjoy their old tunes. | and, neither |

_____

204

6 The hotel manager didn't understand my instructions. The receptionist is forgetful.

either, or

_____

_____

PRACTICE E Fill in the blanks with suitable words in the box. Each word may be used more than once.

bother	chides	did	do	either	have	join
joined	neither	nor	or	plunge	plunging	would

On leaving secondary school, I will either go on to further education or (1) _____

into the job market. My father did not have the opportunity of a college education and neither

(2) _____ my mother. They are therefore anxious that I should either go to

university or (3) _____ a polytechnic. Unfortunately, neither my marks

(4) _____ my application has been impressive. My friends are not interested in

studying and I am not (5) _____ .

On the other hand, the thought of joining the work force so soon (6) _____

attracts nor excites me. Moreover, with just my present certificate I wouldn't get a high salary and

neither (7) _____ the working conditions be very good. Above all, (8) _____

my parents or my own conscience would (9) _____ me. No, I must

neither disappoint (10) _____ hurt my family.

PRACTICE F Complete the **B** sentences to give the same meaning as the **A** sentences.

1 A The pilot couldn't stop the dive and the co-pilot couldn't either.

B The pilot couldn't stop the dive and neither _could the co-pilot_____ .

2 A Either a fireman rescued the baby or a neighbour did.

B Either a fireman or _____ .

3 A Neither the dialogue nor the acting is convincing.

B _____ and neither is the acting.

4 A Your son will do well or he will perhaps perform brilliantly.

B _____ do well or perhaps perform brilliantly.

5 A Neither the soldiers nor the officers knew anything about the terrain.

B _____ and the officers didn't either.

6 A Your friends shouldn't waste time and neither should you.

B Your friends shouldn't waste time _____ either.

UNIT 15.2 SENTENCE STRUCTURE

sentence adverbials (**as a result**, **besides**, **moreover**)

Look at the **A** and **B** sentences below. Find out why **B** is correct and **A** is wrong in the **Grammar Points** section.

CHECKPOINT

			GRAMMAR POINTS
1A	He is an efficient boss. **Moreover** he is generous.	✗	
1B	He is an efficient boss. **Moreover,** he is generous.	✓	1
2A	Kate exercises regularly. **As the result**, she is healthy.	✗	
2B	Kate exercises regularly. **As a result**, she is healthy.	✓	2
3A	It's late so I must go. **Beside**, it's going to rain.	✗	
3B	It's late so I must go. **Besides**, it's going to rain.	✓	3
4A	It was a satisfying meal. **Some more**, it was cheap.	✗	
4B	It was a satisfying meal. **Moreover**, it was cheap.	✓	4

GRAMMAR POINTS

1　We use sentence adverbials to link ideas between two sentences. Sentence adverbials usually come at the beginning of a sentence, and we usually place a comma after the sentence adverbial.
EXAMPLE:

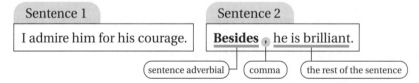

Sentence 1 — I admire him for his courage.　Sentence 2 — **Besides** , he is brilliant.

sentence adverbial　comma　the rest of the sentence

2　We use **as a result** as a link to show that what follows is caused by the idea in the previous sentence.
EXAMPLE:　Fred was caught bullying. **As a result**, he was punished.

3　We use **besides** as a link to show that we are adding an idea to the idea in the previous sentence. We must not confuse **besides** as a sentence adverbial with the word **beside**. **Beside** is used only as a preposition.
EXAMPLES:　Television is entertaining. **Besides**, it is educational.
　　　　　　　We stayed in a chalet **beside** a lake.

4　We use **moreover**, like **besides**, as a link to show that we are adding an idea to the idea in the previous sentence.
EXAMPLE:　I believe that our secretary is efficient. **Moreover**, she is always cheerful.

Circle the letters of the correct items to complete the sentences. There may be more than one answer for each question.

1 He sprained his ankle. As a result,
  A he cannot take part in the soccer match tomorrow.
  B it happened while he was playing soccer.
  C it is required a lot of rest.
  D he has to miss soccer practice for two weeks.

2 I'm too tired to go for a walk. Besides,
  A I didn't walk this morning.
  B it's going to rain.
  C there's a horrible movie on television.
  D my walking shoes are worn out.

3 I'd like to buy this kite because it's colourful. Moreover,
  A it can't fly very high.
  B it isn't expensive.
  C it has an attractive shape.
  D it's a present from my Dad.

4 Last year, our Science Society was very active. As a result,
  A we were praised by the mayor.
  B we attracted more members to our club this year.
  C we were warned by the authorities.
  D we are less active this year.

5 He is a successful salesman because he speaks well. Besides,
  A he forces people to buy his goods.
  B he is dishonest and unreliable.
  C he is always friendly.
  D he is very knowledgeable about his products.

PRACTICE B Tick the sentences where the sentence adverbials are used correctly.

1 The little girl cried because she was tired. Beside, she was thirsty.
2 He walked fast on the slippery floor. As a result, he fell.
3 I like Lynn for her honesty. Besides, she is amusing.
4 Derek seldom to draw. Moreover he isn't good at it.
5 Ted played in the rain. As the result, he caught a cold.
6 Fried food makes me fat. Some more, it spoils my skin.
7 A tree fell across the road. As a result, there was a traffic jam.
8 This house is comfortable. Moreover, the rent is reasonable.
9 Our library is too small. Besides, the books are dull.
10 The bus overturned. Some more, some passengers were hurt.

PRACTICE *C* Underline the correct words in the brackets.

CEO	: Danny Winters has accepted a job with another company. **1** (As a result, /Moreover,) we need to appoint a new branch manager to replace him. Who would you recommend?
Accountant	: I think Bill would make a good branch manager. He has shown leadership qualities when left in charge of a project. **2** (Beside, / Besides,) he's popular with everybody.
Company Secretary	: That's true but he is rather exuberant. **3** (As a result, / As the result,) the atmosphere in the office is too light-hearted when he is in charge.
Accountant	: He has become much quieter lately. **4** (As the result, / Moreover,) he is encouraging the other staff to work quietly.
Company Secretary	: I think Eugene deserves a promotion. He has always behaved appropriately in the office. **5** (As a result, / Besides,) he reports are always excellent.
Accountant	: Eugene works a bit too hard. **6** (As a result, / Moreover,) he does not have enough time for social life or sports. **7** (Beside, / Moreover,) he doesn't always get on well with the rest of the staff.
CEO	: What about Harry? He's a reliable worker. **8** (As a result, / Besides,) he is generally popular. **9** (Moreover, / Some more,) he did well on the management course.
Accountant	: I know that after the course Harry suggested some changes in the general office. **10** (As a result, / Besides,) the staff there seem much happier.

YOUR SCORE
10

PRACTICE *D* Which words in the boxes would you use at the places marked ⋏ ?
Write their numbers in the circles above the sentences.

1 That vegetable seller is friendly. ③ ⋏ , her vegetables are fresh. ① ⋏ , she has many customers.

1 As a result	2 Beside	3 Besides

2 Francis acted well in the play. ◯ ⋏ , he won tremendous applause. ◯ ⋏ , he was offered a part in a film.

1 As a result	2 As the result	3 Moreover

3 Pat was sleepy. ◯ ⋏ , the street had no lights. ◯ ⋏ , Pat drove into a ditch.

1 As a result	2 Besides	3 Some more

4 I saw nothing attractive at the sale. ◯ ⋏ , the prices were not really low. ◯ ⋏ , I did not buy anything.

1 As a result	2 Moreover	3 Some more

5 The man walked very fast. ◯ ⋏ , I could not catch up with him. ◯ ⋏ , I was not well that day.

1 As a result	2 As the result	3 Besides

6 The weather was fine. ◯ ⋏ , we had good seats at the stadium. ◯ ⋏ , we enjoyed ourselves.

1 As a result	2 Beside	3 Moreover

YOUR SCORE
10

Rewrite the sentences using sentence adverbials correctly.

1 The room was crowded. Beside, the air-conditioning was not working. As a result, we
were very uncomfortable.

_____

_____

2 Some picnickers litter the beaches. As a result, the beaches are dirty and unattractive.
Some more, our country gets a bad name.

_____

_____

3 This airline has a good safety record. Besides, it offers excellent service. As the result,
it is very popular.

_____

_____

4 The neighbourhood is very noisy. As a result, the residents' hearing may be affected.
They become nervous and irritable, moreover.

_____

_____

5 I did not join them for the movies besides. I had read the book. Some more, the
reviews were no good.

_____

_____

YOUR SCORE
10

PRACTICE _F_ Underline the sentences which use sentence adverbials incorrectly and
rewrite them correctly.

Nita felt awkward because she was a new student in the college. Some more she was from another
country and she was a shy girl. As the result, she was very unhappy.

Fortunately, a popular girl called Kate sat next to Nita in lectures. Kate was intrigued by Nita's
quiet manner. Beside, she liked Nita although she hardly talked. Kate told the other students that she
found Nita to be very pleasant. Then they too made friends with Nita. Beside, Nita was really a nice
girl. Moreover, after losing her shyness she began telling her friends interesting stories about her
country. As the result, she became quite popular. She even won a prize in that year's story-telling
contest.

1 _____

2 _____

3 _____

4 _____

5 _____

YOUR SCORE
10

UNIT 15.3 SENTENCE STRUCTURE

sentence adverbials (**first / firstly**, **after that / next / then**, **finally / lastly**)

Look at the **A** and **B** sentences below. Find out why **B** is correct and **A** is wrong in the **Grammar Points** section.

			GRAMMAR POINTS
1A	**At first**, dust the room. **Next** sweep it.	✗	
1B	**First, / Firstly,** dust the room. **Next,** sweep it.	✓	1
2A	Jasmine fed the hungry puppy. **After**, she bathed it.	✗	
2B	Jasmine fed the hungry puppy. **After that**, she bathed it.	✓	2
3A	Bob made the curry. Then, he cooked the rice. **At last**, he fried the fish.	✗	
3B	Bob made the curry. Then, he cooked the rice. **Finally, / Lastly,** he fried the fish.	✓	3

GRAMMAR POINTS

1 We use the sentence adverbials **first / firstly** to show that the action in the sentence comes at the beginning of a series of sentences.

EXAMPLE: **First, / Firstly,** he learnt to float. Next, he learnt to swim. Lastly, he learnt to dive.

> **REMEMBER!**
> - Some sentence adverbials like **first**, **next**, **finally**, are used to link a series of sentences and show the sequence of the actions. They are often used when describing a string of events or when giving instructions to others.

2 We use the sentence adverbials **after that / next / then** to show that the action in the sentence comes immediately after the action in the previous sentence.

EXAMPLE: Samuel greeted me in the hallway. **After that, / Next, / Then,** he chatted with me.

3 We use the sentence adverbials **finally / lastly** to show that the action in the sentence comes at the end of a series of sentences.

EXAMPLES: First, I locked the doors. After that, I shut the windows. **Finally, / Lastly,** I switched on the alarm system.

First, she soaped the dishes. After that, she rinsed them. **Finally, / Lastly,** she dried them.

> **REMEMBER!**
> - **First / Firstly** must not be confused with **at first**. **At first** shows that something is true only at the beginning.
>   EXAMPLE: **At first** I hated Science. Later, I learnt to like it.
> - **Lastly** must not be confused with **at last**. **At last** shows that something took a long time to happen.
>   EXAMPLE: I waited for hours. **At last** I got a taxi.
> - **Second / secondly** and **third / thirdly** are sentence adverbials which are often used with **first / firstly**.
>   EXAMPLE: **Firstly**, I'll find a place to stay. **Secondly**, I'll look for a job. **Thirdly**, I'll buy a car.

PRACTICE *A* Cross out the incorrect words in the boxes to complete the sentences.

1 First, wash the carrots. | At last, | Next, | slice them.

2 | At first | Firstly | they disliked the cold weather. Then, they began to have fun in the snow.

3 First, load the clothes into the washing machine. Second, sprinkle some detergent on them.
| After, | Third, | close the lid.

4 The voice teacher taught us scales at the beginning. Then, she made us practise them.
| After that, | Thirdly, | she moved on to simple songs.

5 | At first, | First, | fertilise the soil. Next, dig a hole in the soil. Then, put the seeds in.

6 Firstly, my flight was delayed. Then, I had a problem going through the Customs.
| At last | Lastly | I'm here.

7 First, wash your face with the foaming cleanser. Next, pat some skin toner on your face.
| Next, | Then, | apply moisturiser.

8 | At first, | Firstly, | I chose one of the hairstyles in her book. Next, she studied my face. After that,
she suggested changing the hairstyle a little to suit my face.

9 First, the planes flew in formation. | After, | After that, | they did rolls and loops in the air.

10 Firstly, she watched the exercise video. Then, she exercised along with the video.
| At last, | Lastly, | she did the exercises on her own.

YOUR SCORE
10

PRACTICE *B* Circle the letters of the correct sentences. There may be more than one answer
for each question.

1 **A** First, greet the guests. Then, usher them to their seats.
   B Firstly, greet the guests. Then, usher them to their seats.
   C At first greet the guests. Then, usher them to their seats.

2 **A** First, they tuned their instruments. After, they practised the difficult parts of the musical piece.
   B First, they tuned their instruments. Next, they practised the difficult parts of the musical piece.
   C First, they tuned their instruments. Then, they practised the difficult parts of the musical piece.

3 **A** Firstly, the doctor asked about my symptoms. Then, he examined me. Lastly, he prescribed
   some medicine for me.
   B Firstly, the doctor asked about my symptoms. Then, he examined me. At last he prescribed
   some medicine for me.
   C Firstly, the doctor asked about my symptoms. Then, he examined me. Finally, he prescribed
   some medicine for me.

4 **A** First, do your homework. Second, do your chores.
   B First, do your homework. Last do your chores.
   C Firstly, do your homework. Secondly, do your chores.

5 **A** First, I enjoyed video games. Next, I found them boring.
   B At first I enjoyed video games. Then, I found them boring.
   C Firstly, I enjoyed video games. Then, I found them boring.

6 **A** First, he wanted to go by taxi. Then, he decided to wait for the bus. At last he agreed to get a lift from me.

     B At first, he wanted to go by taxi. Then, he decided to wait for the bus. Finally, he agreed to get a lift from me.

     C Firstly, he wanted to go by taxi. Secondly, he decided to wait for the bus. Thirdly, he agreed to get a lift from me.

PRACTICE C   Fill in the blanks with the words in the box. You may use each item more than once.

After that,	At first	At last	Firstly,
Lastly,	Secondly,	Then,	Third,

1 At first I only dared to cycle around my garden. Then, I cycled around my neighbourhood.

   _____ I cycled all over my hometown.

2 At first they were shy. Then, they exchanged a few words. _____ they laughed together. Finally, they became friends.

3 Firstly, fill half the baby's training cup with grape juice. _____ top up with water. Thirdly, close the cup tightly.

4 _____ we did light exercises to warm up. Next, we jogged three miles. Lastly, we rested for a few minutes to cool down.

5 First, I spoke to them in English but they did not understand me. After that, I tried three other languages. Then, I used sign language. _____ they understood me.

6 Firstly, the queen in the kindergarten play dropped her crown. After that, one of the fairies lost a wing. _____ the king's moustache fell off. Finally, both the audience and the actors burst out laughing.

7 _____ I didn't want to join the sea cruise. Then, I realised it would be fun.

8 First, heat some butter in a pan. Second, break an egg gently into the pan. _____ turn the egg over after two minutes. Finally, scoop the egg onto a plate.

9 Firstly, he bowed to the audience. Then he sang a song. _____ he bowed again.

10 First, he taught me how to draw a circle without using an instrument. Then, he made me do it again and again. _____ he was satisfied.

PRACTICE D   Underline the correct words in the brackets.

Dear Ken,

    I'm sorry I won't be able to come on the trip. Let me explain why. **1** (Firstly, / Secondly,) I need to work really hard. **2** (After, / Secondly,) I don't want to go out of town until I have cleared my desk.

    This is because I got into a lot of trouble last week. You won't believe what happened. **3** (At first / Firstly,) my sales figures were bad. **4** (Next, / Some more,) I crashed my manager's car into a gate. **5** (Lastly, / Then,) they caught me swimming when I should have been at work. **6** (At last / Lastly,) a customer complained to the office that I had been rude.

    So that's why I have to stay here. **7** (At first / Firstly,) I hated having to sit and write.

8 (Lastly, / Then,) I told myself to try to enjoy my work. **9** (After, / After that,)
I wrote the reports much more easily. **10** (At last / Next,) I have found an effective way
of doing my work. How about discussing it when we can get together again?

Joe

PRACTICE *E* Rewrite the sentences correctly.

1 To make banana fritters, you need to buy some fresh bananas. Then, you peel the
   bananas. Next, coat them with flour. At last fry them.

   _____

2 Firstly, he ordered mushroom soup. After, he changed his mind and said he wanted
   tomato soup. Finally, he settled for chicken soup.

   _____

3 At first, shampoo your hair. Then, rinse it. After that, dry it. Lastly, comb it.

   _____

4 First, wash the towels. Then, hang them up to dry. Fold them.

   _____

5 First, Jack looks at the cartoons in the newspaper. He reads the sports pages. Lastly, he
   scans the front page news.

   _____

PRACTICE *F* Arrange the sentences in the correct order and use suitable words from the
boxes to create a sequence of actions.

1 Fill in your particulars. Post the form to the given address. Get a form.

at last	first	lastly	next

   First, get a form. Next, fill in your particulars. Lastly, post the form to the given address.

2 Use the points to write a summary of the passage. Jot down the important points.
   Read the passage.

after that	at first	last	firstly	lastly

   _____

3 I passed it on my fourth attempt. I could drive around town. I kept failing my driving
   test.

at first	at last	lastly	then

   _____

4 The whole family was ill. Mum caught it from him. Dad had the flu.

at first	first	finally	then

   _____

5 Switch on the electricity to check the new bulb. Switch off the electricity. Change the
   bulb.

at first	first	lastly	then

   _____

6 I applied some ointment on it. I cleaned the cut on my finger. I put a plaster over it.

after that	at last	firstly	lastly

   _____

UNIT 16 CHANGING WORD ORDER

with adverbs, **had**, **should**, **were**

Look at the **A** and **B** sentences below. Find out why **B** is correct and **A** is wrong in the **Grammar Points** section.

GRAMMAR POINTS

1A	**Never we dreamt** we would become champions.	✗	
1B	**Never did we dream** we would become champions. / **We never dreamt** we would become champions	✓	1
2A	**If were he** on guard, he wouldn't have run away.	✗	
2B	**Were he** on guard, he wouldn't have run away. / **If he were** on guard, he wouldn't have run away.	✓	2

GRAMMAR POINTS

1 We sometimes change the normal word order in a sentence for emphasis. We move the word to be emphasised to the beginning of the sentence. We can, for example, emphasise the adverbs **barely**, **hardly**, **never**, **no sooner**, **rarely** and **seldom** in these ways:

(a) *Normal word order :* subject + adverb +verb comprising one word
     Changed word order : adverb +verb 'to do' + subject + base form of verb

   EXAMPLE: It **seldom** fails. ⟶ **Seldom** does it fail.

(b) *Normal word order :* subject + first word of verb comprising two words or more + adverb + the rest of the verb
     Changed word order : adverb + first word of verb comprising two words or more + subject + the rest of the verb

   EXAMPLE: It **has seldom** failed. ⟶ **Seldom has** it failed.

2 We sometimes drop **if** from a conditional clause containing **had**, **should** or **were** and change the word order in the clause in these ways:

(a) *Normal word order :* **if** + subject + **had / were** (verbs by themselves)
     Changed word order : **had / were** + subject

   EXAMPLES: If **we had** the time ⟶ **Had we** the time
                  If **it were** true ⟶ **Were it** true

(b) *Normal word order :* **if** + subject + **had / should / were** + the rest of the verb
     Changed word order : **had / should / were** + subject + the rest of the verb

   EXAMPLES: If you **had been chosen** ⟶ **Had** you **been chosen**
                  If I **should succeed** ⟶ **Should** I **succeed**
                  If it **were done** ⟶ **Were** it **done**

PRACTICE *A*   Circle the numbers of the sentences with parts that do not follow the normal word order.

1 Rarely do we come across such talent.

2 Success has sometimes made people complacent.

3 No sooner did she run out of the house than it collapsed.

4 I had barely completed the paper when the invigilator told us to stop writing.

5 She would never have known about it if you hadn't told her.

6 Hardly had she recovered when she went back to work.

7 We rarely get a chance to relax together.

8 Lydia no sooner graduated than she got a job.

9 Seldom does a book remain a bestseller for so long.

10 Never will this incident be erased from their minds.

YOUR SCORE

10

PRACTICE *B*   Rearrange the words in the brackets to complete the sentences.

1 (for — help — it — not — were — your), we might have failed.

Were it not for your help, we might have failed.

2 (an — accepted — author's — first — is — novel — seldom) by this publisher.

_____

3 (fail — if — should — strategy — this), we'd have to give up.

_____

4 Generally, (a — be — decision — I — make — reluctant — so — soon — to — would).

_____

5 (advice — had — listened — my — to — you), you would have done brilliantly.

_____

6 She (barely — breath — caught — had — her) when she rushed off again.

_____

YOUR SCORE

10

PRACTICE $\boxed{C}$ Underline the correct words in the brackets.

1   Never (I would / would I) sell my books.

2   (If should / Should) he come, please give him this note.

3   Hardly (had she / she had) apologised when she dropped another cup.

4   Rarely (does he open / he opens) up to someone so readily.

5   Sometimes (do they expect / they expect) too much from our department.

6   (Was / Were) it safe, we would certainly let you come with us.

7   Seldom could they (get / got) away for a real holiday.

8   (Had / Have) you been my professor, I would have enjoyed studying history.

9   If (she were / were she) coming this evening, I would bake a cake.

10 Should (be he / he be) willing, we'd love to have him as our patron.

YOUR SCORE

10

PRACTICE $\boxed{D}$ Tick the correct sentences.

1   Occasionally do we go out and see a film.

2   Were I a fisherman, I would spend all my days by the lake.

3   Usually she is reasonable and open-minded.

4   Had been the drivers alert, the accident wouldn't have occurred.

5   No sooner did he appear on stage than the audience clapped.

6   Should Zena proved to be right, we'd regret our stubbornness.

7   Never I could have accomplished that without your support.

8   If Sally were to join us, we'd be a formidable team.

9   Seldom is a great artist appreciated in his lifetime.

10 If had they used their common sense, they would have found our house.

YOUR SCORE

10

PRACTICE $\boxed{E}$ Rewrite the sentences without changing the meaning. Use the words provided.

1   Jane had barely finished cooking when her guests arrived.

    Barely _had Jane finished cooking when her guests arrived._

2   If it were just a question of courage, you'd win.

    Were _____

    _____

3   Had I controlled my temper, I would have won the match.

    If _____

    _____

4 Rarely does a woman reach the top rung of the corporate ladder.

A woman _____

_____

5 They would never be able to go sailing again.

Never _____

_____

6 If he should find the treasure, he'd definitely tell the police.

Should _____

_____

PRACTICE *F* Rewrite the underlined words correctly in two different ways. You may need to change the word order, delete words, or add the verbs 'to be' or 'had'.

(1) <u>Never I had had</u> such a grand reception as I did when I went to spend a month with a friend of my late grandmother's in a little village. (2) <u>No sooner I stepped</u> into her house than a crowd came to welcome me. I thought happily: (3) <u>If had I known</u> I'd receive so much attention, I'd have come sooner. The friendly interest did not flag. (4) <u>Seldom I got</u> a moment to dream by the quiet river or roam around by myself. (5) <u>Was I</u> to explain my need for solitude, I would have hurt the villagers' feelings. Yet, now that I'm back in the city, (6) <u>rarely a day passes</u> without my longing to visit the village again.

1 (a) *Never had I had* _____

(b) *I had never had* _____

2 (a) _____

(b) _____

3 (a) _____

(b) _____

4 (a) _____

(b) _____

5 (a) _____

(b) _____

6 (a) _____

(b) _____

UNIT 17 REDUNDANCY

Look at the **A** and **B** sentences below. Find out why **B** is correct and **A** is wrong in the **Grammar Points** section.

GRAMMAR POINTS

1A	We **rushed quickly** out of the house.	✗	
1B	We **rushed** out of the house.	✓	1
2A	**At last**, I **finally** found a tennis partner.	✗	
2B	**At last** I found a tennis partner. / I **finally** found a tennis partner.	✓	2

GRAMMAR POINTS

1 A word or phrase is redundant (unnecessary) and should be deleted from a sentence when its meaning is part of another word or phrase in the sentence.

> EXAMPLE: The balloon **rose up** into the air.　☒
>
> > **rose = went up**
> > **Up** is part of the meaning of rose.
> > Therefore, **up** is redundant and should be deleted.
>
> The balloon **rose** into the air.　✓

2 When two words or phrases of similar meaning are in a sentence, one of them can be deleted as it is redundant.

> EXAMPLE: **Without saying a word**, she **silently** showed her disapproval.　☒
>
> > **without saying a word = silently**
> > Therefore one of them should be deleted as it is redundant.
>
> **Without saying a word**, she showed her disapproval.　✓
>
> She **silently** showed her disapproval.　✓

REMEMBER!

■ A sentence may have more than one redundant word or phrase which should be deleted or left out.

> EXAMPLE: One day tigers may **become totally extinct** and **vanish from the face of the earth**.　☒
>
> > **Extinct** contains the idea of **totally**.
> > ∴ **totally** should be deleted.
> > **become extinct = vanish from the face of the earth**
> > One of them should be deleted.
>
> One day tigers may **become extinct**.　✓
> One day tigers may **vanish from the face of the earth**.　✓

PRACTICE **A**   Strike out the words that are redundant and should be left out of the sentences.

1 I'll read out the question and then I'll repeat it ~~again~~.

2 We walked all the way there on foot.

3 You are behaving like a crazy lunatic.

4 The pearl diver plunged down into the sea.

5 She gently coaxed her little son to finish his porridge.

6 A car hurtled down the road at great speed.

7 Your sister will grow up to be a gorgeous beauty.

8 Soon Yoshiko will be returning back to Japan.

9 The fire razed the planetarium completely.

10 The prices of goods are soaring up.

11 I've finished my assignment but I may have to redo it again.

YOUR SCORE

10

PRACTICE **B**   Underline the correct words in the brackets.

1 They (entered / entered into) the building through the roof.

2 We (starved / went) without food for five days.

3 Without wasting a moment, she (dash / immediately dashed) in to save the child.

4 I hope those (silly / young) fools will come to their senses.

5 The battlefield was littered with (corpses / corpses of the dead).

6 He is remembered as a (man / very brave man) of great courage.

7 (Speaking / Speaking in a rage) will only earn you their contempt for lack of self-control.

8 In the end, the rebels (eventually surrendered / surrendered).

9 We were (delayed / unavoidably delayed) by circumstances beyond our control.

YOUR SCORE

10

10 The country sent (seasoned troops / troops) with a lot of experience on the peacekeeping mission.

PRACTICE **C**   Fill in the blanks with suitable words in the boxes.

1 You and I will _____ about this later.
| discuss | talk |

2 In no time they'll _____ of it.
| soon tire | tire |

3 We are fighting for a _____ cause.
| lost | totally lost |

4 Furious, the delegates walked _____ .
| out | out angrily |

5 He was advised to _____ there by plane.
| fly | go |

6 Bobby is a _____ with good manners.
| child | polite child |

7 Albert Einstein was definitely a _____ .
| brilliant genius | genius |

8 Without hesitation, they _____ to join us. | agreed | readily agreed |

9 My hopes _____ at the news. | plummeted | plummeted down |

10 I'm sure you'll _____ with flying colours. | certainly pass | pass |

PRACTICE **D** Tick the sentences that are correct.

1 Little by little, the youngsters gradually gained confidence.

2 We are moved by her kindness and generosity.

3 All of you must continue on the good work.

4 I waited impatiently as they ambled leisurely into the hall.

5 He suspected that we had invented the whole story.

6 The news was received with sighs of disappointment.

7 She was thrilled at the unexpected surprise.

8 In a moment, his wealth was gone.

9 The child's eyes were shining and sparkling with excitement.

10 Asha firmly declined the offer of a quick promotion.

PRACTICE **E** Rewrite the sentences correctly.

1 He helped you sincerely, with no ulterior motive.
He helped you sincerely. / He helped you with no ulterior motive.

2 The bullets could not penetrate through these walls.

_____

_____

3 Without shedding a tear, she walked dry-eyed through the departure gate.

_____

_____

4 The rich old man is known to be a stingy miser.

_____

_____

5 Feeling miserable, I lay staring unhappily at the ceiling.

_____

_____

6 Carl was extremely overjoyed to hear of your success.

_____

_____

PRACTICE *F* Cross out the incorrect words in the boxes to complete the passage.

Sally enjoyed having her face **1** | made | made up | for television. A 17-year-old
2 | girl | teenager |, she felt **3** | fortunate | fortunate and lucky | to be asked to join a television
forum. Of the four **4** | participants | people | taking part, she was the only one under 21.
A **5** | secret worry | worry | which she kept to herself was that her round face on the screen might
look **6** | childishly chubby | chubby | like a little girl's.

To Sally's delight, she **7** | noticed | noticed joyfully | that the make-up artist had given her face an
oval shape. When he had finished with her, she was **8** | totally transformed | transformed |. The adult
look **9** | added | added extra | credibility to the opinions she expressed. Alas, when the show was
finally aired, her family and friends **10** | hated | unfortunately hated | the look and
wailed, "That wasn't you!"

YOUR SCORE
/10

PRACTICE *G* Rewrite the conversation correctly, leaving out redundant words.

Lady : Don't look now, but the woman in dark glasses alone at that table is a famous celebrity.
Friend : Actually, I spotted her when she entered the restaurant, in fact.
Lady : Why did you keep quiet and not say anything?
Friend : I always feel sorry for stars trying to escape from their fans.
Lady : Okay, we'll leave her alone to enjoy her meal undisturbed.

1 Lady : _____

_____

2 Friend : _____

_____

3 Lady : _____

_____

4 Friend : _____

_____

5 Lady : _____

_____

YOUR SCORE
/10

UNIT 18 REFERENCE

Look at the **A** and **B** sentences below. Find out why **B** is correct and **A** is wrong in the **Grammar Points** section.

			GRAMMAR POINTS
1A	Sarah's igloo won first prize in a 'Build Your Own Home' competition. **Sarah's igloo** was made of cardboard and cotton wool.	✗	
1B	Sarah's igloo won first prize in a 'Build Your Own Home' competition. **It** / **The igloo** / **The prize-winning entry** was made of cardboard and cotton wool.	✓	1
2A	You may not believe but I can sing Korean songs.	✗	
2B	You may not believe **it** / **this** but I can sing Korean songs.	✓	2

GRAMMAR POINTS

1 When we write an essay, a letter, an article, etc, we have to make sure the text has unity and the sentences and paragraphs are connected in ideas. We can establish links in meaning between sentences and between paragraphs by using words like the following:

(a) pronouns – to point back to a noun or noun phrase

> **EXAMPLE:**
> subject
> Tiger Woods is one of the biggest names in the world of golf. **He** is recognised for **his** brilliant achievements and the style that **he** brings to **his** game.

Tiger Woods is the subject of this article. The words **He** and **his** in the second sentence refer back to **Tiger Woods** and therefore help to connect sentence 2 to sentence 1.

REMEMBER!

■ When we use a pronoun to refer back to a noun or a noun phrase, we must make sure it agrees with the noun in person, gender and number.

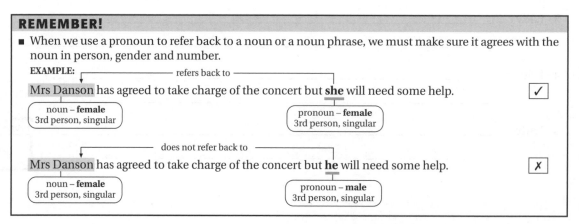

(b) the article **the** together with the same noun or noun phrase used earlier or with a different noun or noun phrase which is linked in meaning to the original words

   EXAMPLES:
   (1) Mrs Croft was in a queue at **her** bank when a man came and stood in front of **her**.
   (2) **She** told **him**[1] politely that **he**[1] should not queue-jump but **the man** just glared at **her**.
   (3) **The spirited lady** then marched up to a security guard and complained to **him**[2].
   (4) **The guard** went up to **the unpleasant person** and made **him**[1] apologise to **Mrs Croft**.
   (5) Then **he**[2] directed **him**[1] to stand at the back of the queue, which **he**[1] promptly did.

   Words that refer back to Mrs Croft   = her, She, The spirited lady, Mrs Croft

   Words that refer back to a man   = he[1], him[1], the man, the unpleasant person

   Words that refer back to a security guard = he[2], him[2], The guard

(c) demonstrative adjectives and pronouns (**this**, **that**, **these**, **those**) – to refer back to nouns, noun phrases, parts of sentences, whole sentences or paragraphs

   EXAMPLE:

   > Linda and I hurried over to Grand Central Department Store on the second day of **their** sale, hoping to buy their coffee percolaters. Unfortunately, **those** were already sold out.

   The word **those** refers back to their coffee percolaters.
   The word **their** in the phrase their coffee percolaters refers back to Grand Central Department Store .

   EXAMPLE:

   > Sam and Helen told their father that it was not his presents they wanted but his presence. They said they missed him and wanted him to spend more time with them. Mr Bala finally understood **this** and made sure he devoted his weekends to his family.

   The word **this** refers back to everything said in the earlier sentences.

2 We can also connect sentences and paragraphs by using words that point forward to what is said in later sentences. For this purpose, we use words like **it**, **this**, **that**, **these** and **those**.

   EXAMPLE:

   > John may not like **it** but he has to sell his car to pay his debts.

   The word **it** points forward to John's having to sell his car to pay his debts.

   EXAMPLE:

   > Did you hear **that**? Faizal scored all five goals in our match against United College and after that a manager of a local club who was at the game approached him about playing professionally.

   The word **that** points forward to the whole of the next sentence.

   REMEMBER!
   - **This** and **these** are used to indicate closeness to the speaker, and **that** and **those** are used to indicate distance.
     EXAMPLE:
     A: Do you like **these** oil paintings on **this** wall?
     B: I don't like **these**. I like **that** painting on the other side of the room.

PRACTICE A Cross out the incorrect words in the boxes to complete the passage.

Dear Aunt Debbie,

I've read your advice column for teenagers and what **1** | they | you | say is sensible and helpful to **2** | it | them | so I'd like to share **3** | this | these | problem with you even though I am 21 years old. I have known Kay for three years now. **4** | We | They | do many things together and I truly enjoy **5** | her | their | company. However, she has **6** | this | those | annoying habit which is beginning to spoil our friendship. She gets angry whenever I go out with Janet and Wendy, two of our office colleagues, because she does not like **7** | them | us |. I have assured her time and again that she means more to me than they do but **8** | that | those | has not changed her attitude. She is being childish and I don't know how to deal with **9** | it | them |. I don't want to lose our friendship but **10** | her | its | sulks are driving me crazy. Please help.

Yours sincerely,
Sue-Ann

YOUR SCORE
10

PRACTICE B What do the words in bold point back to? Underline your answers.

1 We'll be holding an education fair next weekend. **It** will be open to the public from 9 a.m. to 6 p.m.

2 An old movie, *House of Wax*, is having a rerun on TV. I remember after I watched **that thriller** years ago, I could not sleep for several nights.

3 Some city officials visited the site of an old disused mining pool last week. They decided **it** was an ideal place for a nature park because of its vegetation and abundance of wildlife.

4 John phoned to say he was not coming to work because his mother is seriously ill. **This** means I have to give our product presentation to our clients by myself.

5 Members of the public enjoyed the Environment Carnival yesterday. Among the activities **they** participated in were the forest canopy walks and the 'Plant a Tree' competition.

6 The lady selling cosmetics said that women should always use a facial wash, a toner and a moisturiser. I told her I did not use **those** but relied on soap and water instead.

7 **This** should surprise you. Jennifer is going to marry Steve in a month's time!

8 When the doctors examined my brother just before the operation, they found that the problem had disappeared. **It** is something they have not been able to explain to this day.

9 Mum said that our neighbour could take care of our cats and dogs while we were away but **she** could only do it for a week.

10 I want you to realise **these things**: I am studying for an exam so you need to lower the volume of your music. When you don't do your chores properly, Mum gets me to finish your work. That's not fair.

YOUR SCORE
10

PRACTICE C Tick the sentences in column B that can come after the sentences in column A.

A		B
1 John Cooper began acting at the remarkable age of four.	A ☐	The talented actor says it is his first love and he has no intention of quitting.
	B ☐	The film 'Sandstorm' was made when Mr Cooper was 20.

224

2 I liked the openness of the participants on the latest episode of 'Teen Talk'.

A ☐ They shared their worst experiences with the audience.

B ☐ The episode had five teens facing an audience of 50.

3 Millions of sharks are killed yearly to satisfy man's appetite for shark's fin soup.

A ☐ The soup is very much in demand in restaurants the world over.

B ☐ This has caused a drastic worldwide decline in their numbers.

4 Tom and I got to know an amazing cab driver called Mehmet in Turkey.

A ☐ He was not only a cab driver but also a tour guide, a chef and a storyteller.

B ☐ Tom was working in a shipping company and I was in a manufacturing firm then.

5 Mum and I have written down a few things you need to do in the university.

A ☐ You're going to university to get a degree so please work hard.

B ☐ Study hard. Budget wisely. Don't go out with strangers. Phone home once a week.

YOUR SCORE 10

PRACTICE **D** Read the passage and state what the underlined words refer back to or point forward to.

I remember very well the first law conference I attended. (1) It was in the 1990s. The conference had many outstanding speakers but only one of (2) them left a lasting impression in my mind.

(3) That speaker, a law lecturer, had just finished answering a number of questions on the paper he had presented when an elderly gentleman in the audience asked him (4) this: "If your father committed a murder and he confessed the crime to you, what would you do?"

The speaker smiled and said, "Sir, you have asked me a very difficult question. I need time to answer (5) that, but I will, after the tea-break."

When the session resumed, the speaker took his place on the stage. "I would like to answer the gentleman's question now," he said calmly. "As my father's son, I would do (6) these for (7) him. I would listen to him. I would hold his hand. I would put my arms around him. I would even cry with him. As his lawyer, I would advise him to confess to (8) the crime and I would go with him to the police station."

His answer received what (9) it deserved — thunderous applause.

1 it – *the first law conference I attended*

2 them – *the* _____ [1 *mark*]

3 That speaker – _____ [1 *mark*]

4 this – _____ [2 *marks*]

5 that – *the* _____ [1 *mark*]

6 these – _____ [2 *marks*]

7 him – _____ [1 *mark*]

8 the crime – _____ [1 *mark*]

9 it – _____ [1 *mark*]

YOUR SCORE 10

TEST 1

Units 1 – 4

A   Ten of the underlined verbs are incorrect. Write the correct verbs in the boxes.

Larry : Do you <u>remembered</u> which lift we came out of?   line 1

Emma : No, I don't. I was busy with Jimmy so I <u>didn't took note</u>   2
of where we were.

Larry : <u>I know</u> each of the sections on this floor has a lift — one   3
in the north wing, one in the east wing, one in . . .

Jimmy : Daddy, I can show you the lift. We <u>must finding</u> the man   4
<u>wears</u> a spacesuit. He was next to the lift just now.   line 5

Larry : Emma, I think Jimmy <u>has been watch</u> too many   6
cartoons lately. We <u>needs</u> to wean him off TV.   7

Jimmy : But Daddy, there <u>was</u> a spaceman there. He was . . .   8

Emma : Jimmy, <u>don't disturb</u> your father.   9

Larry : Let's try <u>to retraced</u> our steps.   line 10

Jimmy : Daddy, we can go to every lift and check where the
spaceman is.

Larry : We <u>can't be looking</u> in every section, Jimmy. This mall is   11
huge. Let's check with the information booth. There is
one <u>locates</u> near the seafood restaurant.   12

Emma : Larry, wait a minute. I <u>notice</u> that pretty dress in the   13
showcase earlier, just after we stepped out of the lift. We
must have <u>took</u> the lift along this corridor.   14

Jimmy : Daddy! Mummy! The spaceman's still there.

Larry : Oh my goodness! Jimmy's spaceman is on the billboard
advertisement next to the lift!

YOUR SCORE

10

B   Tick the correct verbs in the boxes to complete the sentences.

1 Something [ ] seem / [ ] seems to be bothering Anna. Can you find out what's troubling her?

2 The number of participants who have signed up for this year's marathon [ ] are / [ ] is relatively small.

3 Bitterness between the two major factions in the country [ ] has been building up / [ ] have been building up tremendously in this past decade.

226

4 Vicki's sense of responsibility and commitment always [| inspire / inspires] her team members to do their best.

5 All the time we spent interviewing people for the newspaper article [| was / were] worth it.

6 Neither the chairman of the board nor its other members [| are willing / is willing] to talk to the press.

7 In many countries, the people [| are / is] barely able to survive on the daily wage.

8 Dejection [| was written / were written] all over Adam's face when our opponents scored point after point against the home team.

9 The disabled [| receive / receives] little public consideration in some communities.

10 Most of the news aired on TV nowadays [| focus / focuses] on crime and calamities.

YOUR SCORE

10

C Fill in the blanks with the correct forms of the words in the brackets.

Megan (1) _____had promised_____ (promise) to join her friends for a weekend retreat at Heron's Peak before going abroad. She (2) _____ (decline) their offer of a lift as she (3) _____ (already make up) her mind to climb the peak. When she was a child, she (4) _____ (often use to go) to the log cabin up there among the pine trees so she (5) _____ (not forsee) any problems in finding the place once again.

"If I swing right at the signboard, I (6) _____ (be) at the cabin in no time," she thought, as she made her way up.

But something was wrong. She (7) _____ (trudge) along the steep mountain trail for more than two hours but there (8) _____ (not be) even the remotest sign of the cabin anywhere. Megan (9) _____ (drenched) with perspiration. She (10) _____ (squint) up at the sky. The sun (11) _____ _____ (slowly move) to its highest point.

"I hope I (12) _____ (not take) the wrong turn just now," she said to herself.

Her muscles (13) _____ (ache) and her throat (14) _____ (parch) from the heat.

"If I had listened to John and accepted a ride up, I (15) _____ (not be) in this situation," she muttered to herself.

Her compass (16) _____ (indicate) that she (17) _____ (head) north-east. Then she realised why she was lost. The compass needle (18) _____ _____ (jam).

"Why (19) _____ (I not see) this earlier?" she cried.

The sudden crunch of tyres on gravel made her whirl around. What she saw made her heart jump with joy. John, Amy and Sue (20) _____ (wave) at her from their jeep. Anxious because there was no sign of her, they (21) _____ (decide) to drive down to look for her.

D Rewrite the sentences in either the active voice or the passive voice.

1 One of us usually takes the dog out in the evening for a walk.

_____

_____

2 We were thoroughly shocked by the group's rowdy behaviour.

_____

_____

3 The women of that community have practised traditional methods of weaving and dyeing for hundreds of years.

_____

_____

4 Wilson will have completed the renovations to the house just before Christmas.

_____

_____

5 A police car and a helicopter were tailing the red van all the way from the airport.

_____

_____

TEST 2

Units 5 – 11

A   Underline the correct words in the brackets.

1   Emily (ought not to be divulging / shouldn't divulging) confidential office matters to her friends.

2   Can these sequins (be sewn / sew) onto my black evening gown?

3   He (might resort / might resorted) to fixing an alarm system in his house if the break-ins continue.

4   (Could they be waiting / Could be they waiting) for us outside the ballroom instead of in the hotel foyer?

5   The issues (should have been raised / should have raised) earlier before the management came to a decision this morning.

B   Insert ⟨ where prepositions are missing. Write the correct prepositions in the boxes.

1   She is a person who everyone finds easy to confide.

2   Nicole is an efficient executive assistant. She is capable of running the whole office when her boss is away.

3   The president listened to all the complaints that the club members brought regarding the sports facilities.

4   The nurses were unable to tell the patient where the basket of fruit had come from.

5   Maisie doesn't care that she is always late appointments.

6   Our plane arrived at Amsterdam airport on time despite encountering technical problems before take-off.

7   Please inform your group that they have to attend an orientation course next Monday.

8   The preliminary investigations the disappearance of the well-known businessman did not provide any leads.

9   Mr Cole was thrilled at my being able to communicate with his overseas guests in Spanish.

10   She is filled remorse because she had seriously misjudged somebody.

C Complete the following sentences.

1 The prime minister said, "Stand together in unity and strength so that no one can divide us."

The prime minister advised the people _____

_____

2 The senior manager said, "Jennifer, I'm caught in a traffic jam so I will be a little late for the meeting."

The senior manager told Jennifer _____

_____

3 "Don't you find the book fascinating?" said Sean.

Sean asked me _____

_____

4 Jean said to Mary, _____

_____

Jean asked Mary if Bill was performing at the musical concert on Saturday.

5 Mrs Reed said to Jean and Diana, _____

_____

Mrs Reed told Jean and Diana to concentrate on their work and not on the fashion news.

YOUR SCORE
10

D Rearrange the words to form correct sentences.

1 Adam — don't — from — let — remove — reports — table — the — the.

_____

_____

2 chemical — company — engineer — in — is — Sarah — that — the — youngest.

_____

_____

3 credentials — envoy — his — king — presented — the — the — to.

_____

_____

4 a — convictions — grandfather — man — my — of — strong — was.

_____

_____

5 elderly — help — let's — in — those — wheelchairs — women.

_____

_____

YOUR SCORE
10

230

E Circle the letters of the items that go in the places marked with ⋀ .

1 This is an airline ⋀ pilots are very experienced.

A	which
B	whose

2 The team ⋀ trounced us had a good strategy.

A	that
B	who

3 We gave some homemade soup to the lady next door ⋀

A	whose husband is unwell.
B	, whose husband is unwell.

4 The handicraft ⋀ was made of rubber bands and scraps of cloth.

A	that intrigued everyone
B	which everyone intrigued

5 The residents of Lavender Grove ⋀ may appoint a committee to ensure no more condominiums are built.

A	, who is a quiet residential area,
B	, which is a quiet residential area,

YOUR SCORE

5

F Rewrite the sentences correctly.

1 I don't know if that is a Portuguese, Spanish or Italian song.

_____

_____

2 It is imperative that every passenger is screened before being allowed to enter the departure lounge.

_____

_____

3 I fail to see why is this so important to you.

_____

4 If I am Marie, I would ask about the warranty period before buying the electric mixer.

_____

_____

5 His secret wish was that would he make it to the top of his profession.

_____

_____

YOUR SCORE

10

TEST 3

A Mark with ⟨ where the words in the boxes should be in the sentences.

1 Sam has charisma and he's very helpful . He is very popular in school .

as a result,

2 Can we take a cab there ? The bus ride is terribly bumpy. I feel a little unwell .

besides,

3 Firstly, it's not right to tell a lie. You may be forced to tell another lie to cover up the first lie .

secondly,

4 I was unable to balance myself on the ice skates. Later, I found I was able to move without holding on to the side of the rink .

at first

5 They post their entry forms to our office or hand them in personally .

can either

YOUR SCORE

5

B Fill in the blanks with the correct words in brackets.

1 The enemy's plan was _____ (strike / to strike) during the night and catch us unawares.

2 _____ (Winning / Won) the first match gave them confidence.

3 Furniture fine enough to please them _____ (are / is) hard to find.

4 They dropped several hints, _____ (caused / causing) great excitement.

5 He was a child _____ (deprived / who deprived) of affection.

6 She was intent _____ (on / with) buying the apartment.

7 Joe became more anxious after _____ (being made / made) a manager.

8 _____ (Leave / To leave) her now would be unkind.

9 Rivers _____ (teemed / teeming) with fish are a common sight in this unspoilt countryside.

10 Mr Horne's willingness _____ (relinquish / to relinquish) his prize earned him a lot of respect.

YOUR SCORE

10

C Circle the letters of the correct sentences.

1 A Because of your vigilance, lives were saved.
  B Because vigilant, lives were saved.
  C Because of your vigilant, lives were saved.

2 A People who under stress tending to act irrationally.
  B People under stress tend to act irrationally.
  C People under stress tending to act irrationally.

3 **A** To know her is to love her.

  B To know her to love her.

  C To know her is love her.

4 **A** We made her to blush by lavishing praise on her.

  B We made her blush by we lavished praise on her.

  C We made her blush by lavishing praise on her.

5 **A** I secretly admired his bravery when loudly deplored his impulsiveness.

  B While loudly deploring his impulsiveness, I secretly admired his bravery.

  C I secretly admired his bravery while loudly deplored his impulsiveness.

6 **A** He apologised to Macy in order to end the quarrel.

  B He apologised to Macy to in order end the quarrel.

  C He apologised to Macy in order that to end the quarrel.

7 **A** Give feedback needs both honesty and tact.

  B Giving feedback needs both honesty and tact.

  C Giving feedback needing honesty and tact.

8 **A** Her main aim is earn enough to pay for her son's college education.

  B Her main aim to earn enough paying for her son's college education.

  C Her main aim is earning enough to pay for her son's college education.

9 **A** I spoke frankly not to upset you but help you.

  B I spoke frankly not to upset you but to help you.

  C I spoke frankly not to upset you to help you.

10 **A** The library stayed open till 9 p.m. every day so enable working adults to enjoy its facilities.

  B The library stayed open till 9 p.m. every day so that enable working adults to enjoy its facilities.

  C The library stayed open till 9 p.m. every day so as to enable working adults to enjoy its facilities.

YOUR SCORE
10

D Cross out the incorrect words in the boxes so that the **B** sentences mean the same as the **A** sentences.

1 **A** He often wished that he had chosen a different career.

  B | Often did he wish | Often wished he | that he had chosen a different career.

2 **A** If a riot had broken out, you would have been trapped in the city.

  B | A riot had | Had a riot | broken out, you would have been trapped in the city.

3 **A** We rarely see a hand plough nowadays, even in remote villages.

  B Rarely | do we | we do | see a hand plough nowadays, even in remote villages.

4 **A** If she were to enter the contest, all of us would be outclassed.

  B | Had | Were | she to enter the contest, all of us would be outclassed.

5 **A** I will never forget the useful lesson I learnt that day.

  B | Never will | Will never | I forget the useful lesson I learnt that day.

YOUR SCORE
5

233

1 In my opinion, I think that this company needs young people with a fresh outlook
        A   B
to change its image.
        C

2 Harmony among the ethnic groups must be maintained since political stability is essential
                    A
if the economy is to continue to progress forward.
                    B   C

3 Certainly, you may have my permission to interview the inmates on life in this prison.
        A   B   C

4 At around 12:00 midnight I was jolted awake by the sound of a car alarm, which shattered my
                A   B   C
hopes of a restful sleep.

5 He is a Punjabi boy who is often mistaken for a Caucasian because his skin is very fair and his eyes
                    A   B
are bluish green in colour.
                C

YOUR SCORE

10

1 Have you visited John and Janice's new home? I like the unusual way **they** furnished their living room and bedroom.

2 Not everyone has the ability to be discerning. I think **that** comes with wisdom and experience.

3 I can never understand **this** about you. You dislike Monica yet you spend a lot of time with her.

4 Jill was going to buy her favourite cheese tartlets at Kay's Café but Stan persuaded her to try **those** at Lily's Deli.

5 The phenomenal success of Andy Jenkins' latest novel *Rising Roar* has led to several offers to buy the film rights to **it**.

YOUR SCORE

10

TEST 4

A Fill each blank with the most suitable word.

Dearest Mum,

    The first two weeks here have been hectic and I am still trying to get used to many things.

    The way of life here is so different (1) _____ back home. You and Dad always emphasised the (2) _____ of discipline. I must also account for what (3) _____ spend on.

    Here, college students generally live on (4) _____ own, away from their parents. They drive to (5) _____ , do their own shopping and laundry at weekends (6) _____ they usually have more free time, and generally (7) _____ independent lives. Many of them even work part-time (8) _____ support themselves.

    When I talk to them, I (9) _____ amazed. I have been so protected at home (10) _____ I was in 'culture shock' for a while.

YOUR SCORE

10

B Circle the letters of the correct words to complete the dialogue.

Mr Smith : Good morning, Miss Vaz. Please take a seat.

Olivia : Thank you, Sir.

Mr Smith : I (1) _____ through your personal file. I (2) _____ that you have a degree in communications from UCLA. (3) _____ any working experience?

Olivia : Yes, I do. I (4) _____ in a private college near San Diego after graduation. A year later I (5) _____ an excellent offer from a television network to work as a news editor. After I (6) _____ with the network for two years, I resigned and moved to Seattle.

Mr Smith : If you found the job challenging, why (7) _____ ?

Olivia : There was only one reason. I (8) _____ some problems with the hectic schedule that I (9) _____ . I (10) _____ to travel extensively, meet people and edit the news clips. At times, I (11) _____ to get four hours of sleep. My health (12) _____ . If I had continued with the station, I (13) _____ in charge of my unit. Instead, I (14) _____ to quit before I (15) _____ ill.

Mr Smith : I see. (16) _____ you can manage the post of a public relations executive? It (17) _____ some degree of stress too.

Olivia : I'm sure I (18) _____ to do the job competently. I (19) _____ there will be difficult times but I (20) _____ problems as you can see from my curriculum vitae. I would appreciate it if you could give me a chance to prove my capability.

1	A	was read	11	A	barely manage
	B	have been reading		B	was barely managed
	C	had read		C	barely managed

2	A	understand	12	A	were affected
	B	understood		B	was being affected
	C	was understanding		C	was affecting

3	A	Do you have	13	A	would be put
	B	Did you have		B	would been put
	C	Are you having		C	would have been put

4	A	was lecturing	14	A	chose
	B	have lectured		B	was choosing
	C	am lecturing		C	have chosen

5	A	had received	15	A	become
	B	have received		B	had become
	C	received		C	became

6	A	am	16	A	Are you thinking
	B	had been		B	Do you think
	C	was		C	Did you think

7	A	did you leave	17	A	will involve
	B	do you leave		B	will be involving
	C	were you leaving		C	will be involved

8	A	did encounter	18	A	be able
	B	encountered		B	will be able
	C	have encountered		C	would be able

9	A	am assigned	19	A	am knowing
	B	was assigned		B	will know
	C	were assigned		C	know

10	A	was expected	20	A	am used to handling
	B	were expected		B	was used to handling
	C	were expecting handling		C	will be used to handling

YOUR SCORE
20

C Rewrite the sentences without changing the meaning. Use the words provided.

1 The motivation course has proved to be effective. They attended it.

_____ which

_____

2 He signed the contract. His fingers trembled.

_____ as _____

_____

3 The big question is when our project will be completed.

When _____

_____

4 I can't imagine from where you got that silly idea.

_____ imagine where _____

_____

5 If he lost everything tomorrow, he would start afresh cheerfully.

Should _____

_____

D Rewrite the sentences using the correct verbs.

1 Dealing with criminals have affected you.

_____

_____

2 He is discovering facts forgot by the people.

_____

_____

3 While they happy with our work, they still have to make us redundant.

_____

_____

4 His speech seems having galvanised them into action.

_____

_____

5 The tears glistening in her eyes belies her cheerful smile.

_____

_____

TEST 5

A   Fill each blank with the most suitable word.

Tour guide : Mr Manas, it is essential that you not delay us tomorrow.

Mr Manas : We're on holiday. I don't understand why we have (1) _____ board the bus at 8 a.m.

Mr Lee : We've to leave (2) _____ in order to complete everything on our itinerary (3) _____ the day.

Mrs Roy : Mr Manas, don't you think you (4) _____ go to bed early? You said you were (5) _____ TV till about 1 a.m. this morning.

Mr Manas : If I (6) _____ you, Mrs Roy, I should stop giving advice. (7) _____ wish I were back home and not on (8) _____ silly tour.

Tour guide : My dad was right to worry (9) _____ me!

Mr Manas : Huh?

Tour guide : My dad was certain I would (10) _____ driven insane by my tour group.

YOUR SCORE

10

B   Circle the letters of the correct words to complete the passage.

I like the place I live. This apartment block (1) _____ interesting. At street level, there (2) _____ several small businesses and language schools. I see children (3) _____ for their class and later (4) _____ by their parents. Sometimes the families stay to (5) _____ in the little restaurant at the back of the building. When I have a free evening, I go down there to eat and (6) _____ a video or buy a book from the bookshop. From my window, I can (7) _____ a park quite near the tennis courts. My friends and I (8) _____ there most weekends and the winner (9) _____ everybody lunch. A lovely river (10) _____ through the park and we (11) _____ of the fine trees and new fountain.

It (12) _____ take more than ten minutes to reach the city centre. I enjoy the old street market where (13) _____ bargainers can buy goods very cheaply. Our city (14) _____ a theatre and concert hall and I often (15) _____ them with my family. We also have good street entertainers and some evenings the city seems (16) _____ of music and dance.

I don't often (17) _____ time to travel, but I (18) _____ to visit the mountains once a year. It feels good to (19) _____ the mountain air and (20) _____ at my home.

238

1 A are
   B is
   C being

2 A are
   B have
   C is

3 A are arrived
   B arriving
   C will arrive

4 A picking up
   B were picked up
   C being picked up

5 A have dinner
   B having dinner
   C dinner

6 A have rented
   B rented
   C rent

7 A saw
   B see
   C have seem

8 A play
   B playing
   C was playing

9 A has bought
   B is buying
   C buys

10 A ran
    B runs
    C running

11 A has been proud
    B are proud
    C is proud

12 A have not
    B had not
    C does not

13 A skilled
    B are skilled
    C was skilled

14 A is
    B having
    C has

15 A am attending
    B attend
    C were attending

16 A is full
    B is filled
    C full

17 A am
    B have
    C had

18 A try
    B tried
    C trying

19 A breathing
    B were breathing
    C breathe

20 A to look down
    B looking down
    C was looking down

YOUR SCORE

20

C   Join the pairs of sentences. Turn the underlined ones into phrases beginning with the words in brackets. Then write out the sentences as a paragraph.

1 Yesterday, I looked at some photographs. <u>They were in a very old album.</u> (in)

2 <u>I saw my parents as college students.</u> (Seeing)   It was a revelation.

3 <u>They are serious and staid today.</u> (Though)   They were once lively teenagers.

4 I took out the best picture. <u>It showed them in comical costumes.</u> (showing)

5 They burst out laughing. <u>They caught sight of the funny old photograph.</u> (on)

239

D Underline the incorrect sentences and rewrite them correctly.

I've belonged to several choirs, but my best memories are of the first one I joined. We were a small group and only performed once a year, but we were very enthusiastic and we learnt a great deal about music from our leader.

A few weeks ago, a friend who was in that choir asked me I was interested in a reunion. I liked the idea very much and told her we could hold it at my house. Then I went to my storeroom to find the posters and programmes from our concerts together. I also found a rather tattered group photograph.

The next day, I decided to have copies made of the photograph because of they would be good to give as presents at the reunion. I went to the storeroom but the photograph was no longer with the posters neither it was anywhere in the room.

I was disappointed but forgot about the photograph until yesterday when I was preparing for the reunion party. I found the photograph on my table, restored and enlarged. Somebody in the family had done this that I would have a lovely centrepiece for the party. I asked as who had done it. Nobody would say and so I thanked them all.

1 _____

2 _____

3 _____

4 _____

5 _____

TEST 6

A Fill each blank with the most suitable word.

Arundathi Roy, an Indian national, won the Booker Prize in 1997 for her novel *The God of Small Things*. A tale of love and loss, the (1) _____ has sold more than six million copies. This (2) _____ not at all surprising, for the story, set (3) _____ India, mesmerises with its storyline and the power (4) _____ its innovative prose. The reader is likely (5) _____ find himself emotionally drained by the time he (6) _____ the end of the story. To his consternation, (7) _____ may also realise that even though the story (8) _____ over and the book is closed, the compelling (9) _____ tragic characters of Roy's imagination tend to linger (10) _____ his mind.

B Circle the letters of the correct words to complete the passage.

Ladies and gentlemen, it (1) _____ me great pleasure (2) _____ you on this auspicious occasion.

Before I (3) _____ , allow me to thank the chairman and organising committee (4) _____ me to open this Asian-Pacific Women Entrepreneurs' Conference. This day (5) _____ an indelible mark on the development of a new breed of businesswomen in our part of the world. The Asia-Pacific region (6) _____ a number of developing countries as well as Australia and New Zealand which (7) _____ a remarkable rate of growth these past 10 years. We (8) _____ tremendous improvements in the infrastructure of these nations. Our people now (9) _____ modern amenities and a standard of living higher than ever before. We (10) _____ to take a giant leap into the hi-tech era in the fields of business, media and communication. By the year 2010, we (11) _____ the goals set before us — to have a fully-developed nation status, to be self-reliant and economically strong.

To fulfil this vision, every individual (12) _____ his or her part. This is where our women come in. Traditional preconceptions and prejudice (13) _____ aside and women today (14) _____ a long way from where they (15) _____ 50 years ago. Significant numbers of women (16) _____ highly-qualified, highly-motivated and (17) _____ as equals with their male counterparts in the world of business and finance. Statistics (18) _____ that women have ventured into small businesses very successfully in our region. Some (19) _____ up the corporate ladder to become executives and managers. If the older generation of women had been given similar chances, I believe they (20) _____ as equally determined to succeed as their daughters and granddaughters.

1	A	gave	11 A	will have achieved
	B	is giving	B	have achieved
	C	gives	C	will be achieving
2	A	to address	12 A	have to play
	B	to be addressed	B	is having to play
	C	be addressing	C	has to play
3	A	am proceeding	13 A	have been cast
	B	proceeds	B	were casting
	C	proceed	C	was cast aside
4	A	to be inviting	14 A	come
	B	for inviting	B	have come
	C	to invite	C	will come
5	A	will leave	15 A	use to be
	B	will be leaving	B	used to been
	C	will have left	C	used to be
6	A	comprises	16 A	are
	B	comprised	B	were
	C	comprising	C	was
7	A	had experienced	17 A	are able to stand
	B	has experienced	B	was able to stand
	C	have experienced	C	has been able to stand
8	A	have seen	18 A	proves
	B	saw	B	prove
	C	are seeing	C	proved
9	A	enjoyed	19 A	had gradually climbed
	B	will enjoy	B	have gradually climbed
	C	enjoy	C	were gradually climbing
10	A	are daring	20 A	will have been
	B	have dared	B	would have been
	C	had dared	C	would be

YOUR SCORE
20

C Rewrite the underlined phrases in the passage turning them into clauses. Use the words provided.

For my friend Sonia, something (1) <u>beyond her means always</u> has a special attraction. (2) <u>When forced to accompany her to expensive shopping centres</u>, I watch her in amazement. She never looks uncertain about (3) <u>being able to afford the most fabulously expensive dress</u>. Somehow, she is invariably surrounded by shop assistants (4) <u>eager to let her try on numerous outfits</u>. (5) <u>Because of her charm</u>, they readily forgive her for not buying anything.

242

1 which _____

_____

2 When I _____

_____

3 whether she _____

_____

4 who _____

_____

5 Because _____ is _____

_____

D Rewrite the underlined clauses in the passage turning them into phrases.
Use the words provided.

(1) While I enjoy my first camping trip, I sometimes felt tired of the endless chores. (2) In order to pack the van properly, we lost the best part of the morning. (3) Before we cooked a meal, we had to light the stove and fetch water from the river. (4) I was called lazy because I suggested one night in a hotel. (5) My friends who were irritated by my idea, said I should take a luxury cruise for my next holiday.

1 While _____

_____

2 To _____

_____

3 Before _____

_____

4 for _____

_____

5 irritated _____

_____

··········· ANSWERS ···········

1.1 VERBS

Practice A

1   4   7   8   10

Practice B

1	didn't phone	5	can give	8	to be
2	to pose	6	inform	9	to go
3	have	7	need	10	Make
4	see				

Practice C

1	want	5	to cater	8	remove
2	write	6	go	9	audition
3	be	7	store	10	Sprinkle
4	must				

Practice D

1	to tell	5	listen	8	check
2	to perform	6	say	9	can call
3	know	7	didn't read	10	repeat
4	must see				

Practice E

2 Don't you has anything else to do? → Don't you have anything else to do?

3 You could earns some money for yourselves. → You could earn some money for yourselves.

4 After three hours of brainstorming, we decided to sets up 'Youth at Work'. → After three hours of brainstorming, we decided to set up 'Youth at Work'.

5 That afternoon, our phones didn't stopped ringing. → That afternoon, our phones didn't stop ringing.

6 We serves not just our neighbourhood but other areas as well. → We serve not just our neighbourhood but other areas as well.

1.2 VERBS

Practice A

1	create	5	wants	8	mutter
2	correct	6	specialises	9	operating
3	handles	7	lavish	10	protect
4	is slacken				

Practice B

1	(a) antagonises		(b)	antagonise
2	(a) making		(b)	are making
3	(a) reading		(b)	reads
4	(a) scrutinises		(b)	scrutinising
5	(a) entertaining		(b)	is entertaining

Practice C

1 Kathy / voluntary work at the hospital / once a fortnight.

2 The player / with the referee is / Alan.

3 Larry / the overhead bridge / to get to his office.

4 The athletes / impatiently / for the games to begin.

5 The expedition team / out earlier than the others wants to reach the village before / nightfall.

6 George / what you have done / for his family.

7 The government / a great deal of importance / on self-reliance.

8 The inhabitants / against / the logging activities in their area.

9 She / that Liz is the one who / deserves the praise.

10 The woman / to Samuel is / a TV reporter.

Practice D

1	running → runs	6	send → to send
2	manage → manages	7	packages → package
3	use → using	8	need → needs
4	is manage → is managing	9	demand → demands
5	having → have	10	recommends → recommend

Practice E

2 The road leads to Dolphin's Bay is under repair. → The road leading to Dolphin's Bay is under repair.

3 That road have a lot of potholes. → That road has a lot of potholes.

4 His phone is ring. → His phone is ringing.

5 On Saturdays he goes riding or he play a game of tennis at his club. → On Saturdays he goes riding or he plays a game of tennis at his club.

6 I wanted surprise the two of you. → I wanted to surprise the two of you.

1.3 VERBS

Practice A

1	was issued	5	was decided	8	was provided
2	exchanged	6	was offered	9	were noticed
3	was suffered	7	have arranged	10	served
4	was designed				

Practice B

1	designed	5	behaving	8	injured
2	providing	6	sprinting	9	honoured
3	marching	7	donated	10	surrounding
4	seated				

Practice C

1	huddled	5	was cleared	8	suggested
2	arrived	6	has recovered	9	made
3	was covered	7	have invested	10	loaded
4	was rushed				

Practice D

(line 2)   has capture → has captured

(line 3) called → is called
(line 5) to interviewed → to interview / interviewing
(line 6) were filmed → have filmed
(line 8) screened → was screened
(line 9) was featured → featured
(line 10) has retain → has retained
(line 11) was interviewed → interviewed
(line 15) I was agree → I agreed
(line 16) can learnt → can learn

2.1 SUBJECT-VERB AGREEMENT

Practice A

1 was used
2 were splashing
3 is
4 looks
5 is
6 were filming
7 has been used
8 was able to see
9 don't
10 is

Practice B

1 was
2 likes
3 has
4 was
5 participate
6 needs
7 is
8 annoys
9 has
10 has

Practice C

1 Everybody
2 A lot of
3 Everything
4 A number of
5 Somebody
6 The number of
7 anyone
8 Something
9 Nothing
10 Anything

Practice D

1 A number of customers were queuing to pay for their purchases.
2 I can't contact Sarah. Someone has damaged the public phone in this booth.
3 A lot of freshly grated cheese is used for this pizza topping.
4 The number of students in the literature class has increased dramatically.
5 Everything has been done to prevent the river from bursting its banks. Now we just have to wait and pray that all goes well.

Practice E

1 Nothing were in its usual place anymore. → Nothing was in its usual place anymore.
2 A number of her clothes was strewn on the floor. → A number of her clothes were / had been strewn on the floor.
3 All her jewellery were missing. → All her jewellery was missing.
4 The number of things stolen were not the only problem. → The number of things stolen was not the only problem.
5 Something inside Betty were deeply wounded. → Something inside Betty was/had been deeply wounded.

2.2 SUBJECT-VERB AGREEMENT

Practice A

1 is
2 makes
3 was
4 improvement
5 causes
6 has
7 is
8 changes
9 give
10 was

Practice B

1 were
2 are
3 were challenged
4 are
5 have been
6 discourage
7 have been
8 is
9 fill
10 were

Practice C

2   3   5   6   9

Practice D

1 chicken
2 distracts
3 make
4 has
5 were
6 leads
7 are
8 cost
9 has been
10 is

Practice E

1 has been
2 contributes
3 was
4 leads
5 are
6 goes
7 prevents
8 is
9 help
10 grips

Practice F

1 There is something on the table. Does it belong to you?
2 The weather has been so hot in the last few days that many people have suffered sunburn.
3 Tolerance plays an important role in making a happy community.
4 His obsession with house prices is often hard for his friends to bear.
5 The talents of the young musician were recognised by the music school.

2.3 SUBJECT-VERB AGREEMENT

Practice A

1 don't often receive
2 Skiing
3 was donated
4 was
5 Working
6 oppressed
7 is
8 educated
9 occupies
10 Tailoring

Practice B

2   4   5   7   8

Practice C

1 requires
2 relaxes
3 demand
4 are
5 helps
6 does
7 is
8 extend
9 are
10 causes

Practice D

1 makes
2 have
3 live
4 helps
5 is
6 was
7 shows
8 is
9 deserve
10 is

Practice E

2 are → is
4 Roasted → Roasting
5 was → were
9 Honest → Honesty
10 Famous → The famous

Practice F

1 The selfish seldom notice the pain and suffering of others.
2 Teaching children requires creativity and versatility.
3 More than a million dollars was spent by the government on improving the facilities in schools.
4 Working 48 hours without stopping has made him ill.
5 The underprivileged were treated to a special dinner last night.

3.1 SIMPLE PRESENT AND PRESENT CONTINUOUS TENSES

Practice A
1 is coming
2 kicks
3 is lecturing
4 accuses
5 patrol
6 promises
7 is seeing
8 keeps
9 is producing
10 is resting

Practice B
1 permeates
2 is setting off
3 train
4 worries
5 is vanishing
6 plays
7 are staying
8 denies
9 designs
10 objects

Practice C
1 are guaranteeing
2 makes
3 does
4 intend
5 is acting
6 takes
7 is repeating
8 map
9 spends
10 is bringing

Practice D
1 is calling
2 is looking
3 are opening
4 arrives
5 fight
6 bursts
7 is enrolling
8 creates
9 is hiring
10 are coming

Practice E
1 We are thinking of going to the flea market in the park this Sunday.
3 For the whole of next week, the college is organising career talks to give students an in-depth knowledge of the various professions.
4 Carol lectures in psychology at an institute of management. She has been there for five years.
5 Robin and his family are moving to an apartment in my area next month.

3.2 SIMPLE PAST TENSE

Practice A
2   4   7   8   10

Practice B
1 treated
2 set up
3 outstripped
4 tried
5 places
6 settle
7 made
8 overwhelms
9 live
10 used to sail

Practice C
1 shook
2 were
3 is still investigating
4 beat
5 were
6 is now thinking
7 scoffed
8 is beginning
9 surprised
10 stunned

Practice D
1 overturned
2 are pleading
3 used to recall
4 carried
5 tie
6 is spreading
7 thought
8 debated
9 advise
10 used to discipline

Practice E
1 Sam threatened to quit his job three days ago because he was bored.
2 In the spring, We usually plant rose bushes all along the garden wall so we can enjoy the blooms in the summer.

3 Rescue teams dug tirelessly last night to pull out the trapped miners from the pit.
4 Last year we frequently met at weekends and discussed common problems we faced.
5 Glen always takes charge of the office while Miss Richards is away and he ensures that everything runs smoothly.

Practice F
As I watched, the club members took out card tables and set them up. Tuesday was their games evening and most of them liked to play bridge or whist.

One woman played a game of solitaire. She sometimes got up to walk around and observe the games at the other tables.

Halfway through the evening there was a break for refreshments. A waiter served tea and coffee and everybody enjoyed conversation with their friends. Some people went home after this. but the enthusiastic players stayed until quite late

3.3 PAST CONTINUOUS TENSE

Practice A
3   4   6   8   9

Practice B
1 testify
2 polished
3 complain
4 are facing
5 are looking for
6 were fighting
7 were bringing
8 navigated
9 fills
10 dig

Practice C
2 ignored
3 was enjoying
4 was blaring
5 reached
6 were quarrelling
7 saw
8 was puffing
9 cut
10 flew
11 were crawling

Practice D
1 <u>cleared</u> → were clearing
2 <u>holding</u> → held
3 <u>coughing</u> → coughed / was coughing
5 <u>is very entertaining</u> → was very entertaining
7 <u>was mentioning</u> → mentioned

Practice E
1 We knew that everything in the report was grossly exaggerated.
2 Alice was thinking of leaving the company when someone approached her with an attractive job offer.
3 James was waiting for property prices to rise last month and he finally sold his house last week.
4 Peter and Lisa were going to get married in June but the wedding has been postponed.
5 Yesterday, the developers were trying to evict the squatters from the area but the people refused to move.

3.4 PRESENT PERFECT TENSE

Practice A
2   4   6   7   9

Practice B
1 has been
2 have found
3 inherited
4 hasn't paid
5 has forced
6 have hung
7 has become
8 has achieved
9 have resulted
10 observed

246

Practice C

1 have been
2 have used
3 want
4 recommended
5 have experienced
6 have asked
7 have talked
8 have never thought
9 discussed
10 have always wanted

Practice D

1 A surge of interest in of health and beauty / beauty and health has swept across the world.
2 We haven't found the cause of the failure of the security system yet.
3 Alice has spent the whole week getting everything ready for the meeting.
4 Since last month they have only gone out twice to the cinema.
5 He has already reprimanded us for the poor sales figures for last year.

Practice E

1 Five years ago, the two countries promised to work together to establish peace in the region.
2 The two motorcyclists have just broken traffic regulations by going against the lights.
3 I haven't made up my mind yet about which courses to do in college.
4 Haven't you ever gone bungee jumping before?
5 We have never learnt where our former colleagues are working now.

3.5 PAST PERFECT TENSE

Practice A

1 assembled
2 have sworn
3 had already destroyed
4 had just caught
5 have never said
6 had criticised
7 haven't heard
8 had seen
9 had searched
10 have asked

Practice B

1 had captured
2 has not / hasn't checked
3 had asked
4 had grown
5 has always craved
6 has forced
7 had never begged
8 was typing
9 have not / haven't seen
10 had just persuaded

Practice C

1 just finished → had just finished
4 grew → had grown
6 give rise → have given rise
7 lost → lost / had lost
8 has always enjoyed → had always enjoyed

Practice D

1 A, C   2 A, B   3 B, C   4 A, B   5 A, C

3.6 PRESENT AND PAST PERFECT CONTINUOUS TENSES

Practice A

1 have shown
2 had been requesting
3 have been polishing
4 hadn't expected
5 had angered
6 have gone
7 had been flouting
8 have violated
9 had been asking
10 have been appealing

Practice B

1   2   4   7   8

Practice C

1 has been looking
2 have been diving
3 has put / put
4 had been demonstrating
5 had already confirmed
6 has been affecting
7 had been spending
8 hadn't / had not arrived yet
9 have been holding
10 had been planning

Practice D

1 happened → had happened
2 had totter → had tottered
5 have bring → have brought
7 had questioned → have been questioning
10 have → had

Practice E

1 David has been smoking heavily these past two weeks.
2 The committee has been preparing for months for the charity bazaar.
3 The judge had been issuing strict warnings to both counsels throughout the trial.
4 We had been looking for Sheila all morning but couldn't find her in the crowd.
5 Mariko and I were tired because we had been baking pies all morning for the sale.

3.7 SIMPLE FUTURE AND FUTURE CONTINUOUS TENSES

Practice A

1 will assure
2 will be leaving
3 is going to be
4 has captured
5 will be participating
6 realised
7 is going to choose
8 are awaiting
9 will pass
10 will be coming

Practice B

1   3   4   7   10

Practice C

1 will be reaching
2 will leave
3 haven't yet decided
4 will give
5 had loved
6 was going to take up
7 hadn't realised
8 won't be facing
9 will be studying
10 will have

Practice D

1 A few years back, my uncle was going to set up his own business but he didn't have sufficient capital.
2 In a worldwide recession, developing countries will be hit the hardest because of falling demand for their exports.
3 I will return the money I owe you as soon as I receive my salary at the end of the month.
4 Jasmine will be expecting us to help her run the games stall at the funfair this Saturday.
5 I know it is going to rain this afternoon. The sky is overcast and gloomy.

Practice E

1 The cost of the new expressway will be far more than the council expected.
2 The company is going to increase productivity by implementing modern training methods.

3 Maria was going to perform at the dinner last night but she suddenly fell ill.

4 You don't have to worry as I will make sure the children are safe.

5 Ranjit will be in charge of the hockey team during the games in Manila.

3.8 FUTURE PERFECT AND FUTURE PERFECT CONTINUOUS TENSES

Practice A
1 have broken
2 will have been waiting
3 sacrificed
4 will have already received
5 will have been staying
6 was shocked
7 will have been managing
8 has just gone
9 will have been helping
10 will be submitting

Practice B
1   3   4   5   7

Practice C
1 had not heard
2 will have reached
3 will have been lecturing
4 will have occupied
5 have already visited
6 will have agreed
7 ordered
8 will have spoken
9 have been constructing
10 will have played

Practice D
1 She will have been teaching in our school for twenty years this November.

2 Angela will have already become the senior manager of the bank by June.

3 The monsoons have brought torrential rain and flooding to the Indian subcontinent.

4 Our faces will have frozen in this cold by the time we reach the cabin.

5 When we get home after the movie, everybody will have already gone to bed.

Practice E
1 Miss Cole will have been working as the executive secretary to the director for five years by this March.

2 The salaries commission will meet next week. We will have gathered more information about the expected pay rise by then.

3 The accounts department will have already checked the figures before submitting the reports next Monday.

4 The defence lawyers have requested a postponement of the trial until they get an expert medical opinion.

5 The anti-vice squad had been waiting all night for their man to give the signal before arresting the drugs syndicate.

3.9 CONDITIONALS – THE PRESENT TENSE

Practice A
1 B, C   2 A   3 B   4 B, C
5 A   6 A, C   7 B

Practice B
1 seeps   5 will take   8 won't
2 will laugh   6 will hurt   9 ends
3 will capsize   7 persists   10 is
4 will experience

Practice C
1 . . . you will expose them to danger.

2 . . . it will usually stalk a weak and helpless member of the herd.

3 . . . if she comes home before her mother.

4 . . . if there is any sign of an enemy attack.

5 . . . unless we improve the entertainment facilities in the town.

6 If the dog is disobedient, . . .

7 The manager will be furious . . .

8 . . . if you listen attentively.

9 . . . you know that winter is approaching.

10 Unless they give us some money . . .

Practice D
1 The tree is leaning precariously to one side. If there is a strong wind, it will fall on our rooftop.

2 The organisers of the games afternooon will wonder what happened to us unless we phone them to explain.

3 If you wish to continue with this discussion, you will have to listen to our point of view.

4 If deforestation proceeds at the present rate, it will have an adverse effect on the environment.

5 If we listen to the village elders, we will inherit a wealth of knowledge from them.

3.10 CONDITIONALS – SIMPLE PAST AND PAST PERFECT TENSES

Practice A
1   3   6   7   10

Practice B
1 would have been   7 would become
2 learned   8 had woken
3 would have told   9 would not have
4 would fight   postponed
5 were   10 hadn't appeared
6 would come

Practice C
1 would have done   6 would not suffer
2 knew   7 had bought
3 be   8 would have reached
4 had worked   9 granted
5 were   10 had

Practice D
1 would win → would have won

3 see → saw

4 would have forgot → would forget

6 bought → had bought

8 notice → had noticed

Practice E
1 If Tom had been here, he would have known what was wrong with the car.

2 The distinguished visitors would be delighted if they watched the tribal dances.

3 I wish I understood this problem. Then I would be able to help you.

4 Sue might have remembered the password if you had reminded her earlier.

5 If the prosecution lawyers had agreed, we would have called the children to be witnesses.

4.1 ACTIVE AND PASSIVE VOICE
Practice A
1 is believed	6 was diagnosed
2 were shown	7 cause
3 was selected	8 was suggested
4 think	9 will be provided
5 was welcomed	10 was set up

Practice B
1 B, C   2 A, C   3 A, C   4 B   5 B, C   6 A

Practice C
1 were shaken	4 is believed	7 was born
8 are saying	9 shocked	

Practice D
1 It is expected that new laws will be passed to curb drink-driving.
2 Sarah offered me a lift home as I didn't have my car.
3 Plans for the new extension will be discussed next week.
4 Suggestions for improving the hotel's services were accepted by the manager.
5 The lawyer questioned the two witnesses regarding the murder.

Practice E
It is generally thought that Angie is extremely good at organisation and decision-making. These skills were acquired during her six years as a junior executive at the firm. Her sound decisions and efficiency were noted by her bosses. She was promoted to office manager in her seventh year at the firm. The office is run with clockwork precision. Problems are solved quickly and firmly. She is respected by the rest of the staff because of her fairness, warmth and honesty.

4.2 ACTIVE AND PASSIVE VOICE
Practice A
1 A, C   2 C   3 B   4 A, C   5 A, B   6 A, C

Practice B
1 being criticise	6 often have advised
2 carefully is being arranged	7 being tell
3 are going to organising	8 have to warned
4 to be paid	9 to criticize
5 being treat	10 to be awarded

Practice C
1 to reward
2 to be posted
3 has finally agreed
4 have actually been done
5 will definitely tell
6 has already been informed
7 being taken
8 are to be recycled
9 being invited / to be invited
10 being disappointed / to be disappointed

Practice D
1 The hockey team wants to be given due recognition for winning the inter-state trophy.
2 I would like to apologise for my lateness last night.
3 These fine pieces of jewellery are to be handed down to your children when they are older.

4 Most of us hate to be humiliated in front of our friends.
5 Your parents have to be told about your decision to leave school and join a band.

Practice E
1 These parts will be assembled to form a bookcase.
2 Henry dislikes being treated like a fool.
3 I completely forgot to lock my car this morning.
4 Patrick is going to be made a senior partner in the firm.
5 Our guests loved being taken on a guided tour of the city.

4.3 ACTIVE AND PASSIVE VOICE
Practice A
1 A   2 B, C   3 B, C   4 A, B   5 A, B, C

Practice B
1 has the velvet cushion covers dry-cleaned	6 have had to battle
2 to write down	7 have had to send
3 is reported	8 had his leg broken
4 are said to have begun	9 is said to be
5 to be patient	10 to have my ears pierced

Practice C
We had our porch and living room renovated last month. Dad's architect friend, James, was invited to redesign the area. James is said to be both innovative and bold in his ideas. He was asked by Dad to create an informal setting for the living room. He did that by merging the porch and the living room using high French doors. These days, Dad has often been seen sitting inside the living room, enjoying the garden right at our doorstep.

Practice D
1 Bernard is thought to be capable of running his father's factory.
2 The girls were asked by Sue to help her get all the invitations ready.
3 The air-conditioners in the bedrooms will have to be cleaned as they are very dusty.
4 We were told by the airline officials to wait for news of the flight from London.
5 A new security system has had to be installed to protect the office from break-ins.

5.1 DIRECT AND INDIRECT SPEECH
Practice A
1   3   5   8   9

Practice B
1 their	5 bought	8 leave
2 your	6 are baking	9 our
3 to be	7 had to tell	10 not to put
4 my		

Practice C
1 The nurse told me to call back later because Dr Sim was not in.
2 Peter said to us, "Don't be late for rehearsals tomorrow."
3 The captain said that his team intended to win the challenge trophy for their school.
4 My science lecturer told me to pour the solution carefully into a beaker.
5 The instructor told Louis to pay attention while he was driving.

Practice D
1 Jenny said, "These flowers are from Holland."

2 The officer said to Jill, "Do not park in the no-parking zone."
3 Ann said to the sales assistant, "Please help me carry the purchases to my car."
4 Helen said, "I promise to bring your birthday cake later this evening.
5 Mr Francis said to his secretary, "I don't want any interruptions during the meeting."

Practice E
1 Jack said that the weather was really bad.
2 Wendy said that it was raining very hard.
3 Jack said that he was very worried about Lucy. She had to drive home in the rain.
4 Wendy asked Jack to give Lucy a call and tell her to wait until the rain subsided.

5.2 DIRECT AND INDIRECT SPEECH
Practice A
1 Do, want
2 was going, the following
3 don't, wear
4 was, him
5 would, prefer

Practice B
1 Ben asked if my dog usually went into my neighbour's garden.
2 The tour guide asked who didn't want to go on the roller-coaster ride.
3 Fiona asked Helen if she was interested in joining their sewing class.
4 Jack asked his dry cleaner how he removed the grease marks from his shirt.
5 Kellie asked what I didn't like about their plan.

Practice C
1 "Why don't they want to go with us?" Sue asked.
2 "Does your father always come home late?" Joan said to me.
3 David said to his grandfather, "Is Grandma going to take more golf lessons?"
4 "Are you taking part in the contest?" Miss Smith said.
5 Tom said, "What subject does she teach in college?"

Practice D
1 The lady asked Steve how far into the city the commuter train went.
2 Timmy asked me why I had taken his bag.
3 The kennel owner asked Mr Gopal if the dogs had been well-behaved at the show.
4 The doctor said, "Are you waiting to see me?"
5 The interviewer said, "Do you have any experience of writing radio plays?"

Practice E
2 The officer said to / asked Stan, "Did you drink any alcohol at the function?"
3 The officer said to / asked Stan, "What time did you leave the club?"
4 The officer said to / asked Stan, "Were you speeding?"
5 The officer said to / asked Stan, "Did you see the other car coming from the opposite direction?"
6 The officer said to / asked Stan, "Why didn't you swerve to avoid the other car?"

6.1 MODALS
Practice A
1 2 5 7 9

Practice B
1 sent	5 make	8 be
2 have	6 attending	9 carry
3 be	7 been	10 cooperate
4 compete		

Practice C
1 must	7 will be undergoing
2 should	8 must have hit
3 may have left	9 had better start
4 could have fallen	10 will be delivering
5 need to lodge	
6 should have been passed on	

Practice D
2 Maggie and her sister could be sitting in the front row.
3 The plot might have been exposed by a dissatisfied member.
4 They ought to join the team-building activity tomorrow morning.
5 The magazine would have selected the winners of the competition by now.
6 Mr Adams should be given a thorough medical examination at once.

6.2 MODALS
Practice A
1 can not	6 shan't telling
2 shouldn't expected	7 may not look
3 might have not heard	8 mustn't have taken
4 wouldn't working	9 couldn't understood
5 ought not to parking	10 needn't to leave

Practice B
1 shouldn't	5 must	8 could
2 wouldn't	6 ought not to	9 will
3 can't	7 shan't	10 should
4 need to		

Practice C
2 These reference books cannot be removed from the library.
3 The tourists ought not to have been taken to that factory by the tourist guide.
4 David may not be included in the lineup against The Trojans by our football club.
5 Sufficient evidence against the murder suspect might not be produced by the prosecution.
6 Your staircase couldn't have been damaged by my workmen.

Practice D
2 wouldn't surprised → wouldn't be surprised
3 shouldn't had let → shouldn't have let
4 needn't to be stocked → needn't be stocked
5 shouldn't have catering → shouldn't be catering
6 might not succeeded → might not succeed

6.3 MODALS
Practice A
3 4 5 6 9

Practice B

1 A, B   2 B, C   3 A, C   4 B, C   5 A, B

Practice C

1 refer
2 download
3 be delayed
4 be setting
5 have assisted
6 have supported
7 be
8 be postponed
9 have bought
10 enjoying

Practice D

3 Shouldn't the rally participants have driven slowly on the wet road?
4 Won't Sheila be dismayed by the lack of response to her survey?
5 Couldn't Harry replace Jim in the second half of the game?
6 Might I make a simple suggestion at this point?

7.1 PREPOSITIONS

Practice A

1   4   7   8   10

Practice B

1 with, in   2 about, of   3 for, to
4 of, from   5 for, of

Practice C

1 A, B   2 A, C   3 A, C   4 B, C   5 B, C

Practice D

Anna : Lee, what are you doing ~~at~~ here?

Rashid : The same reason ~~for~~ why you're here, I think. Are you attending ~~to~~ the briefing for the youth expedition to Chile ?

Anna : Yes. Oh, isn't it great ~~because of~~ that we're both on the same expedition! It'll be an adventure, don't you think? It'll be ~~about~~ fun to work with young people from different parts of the world who will be part of the expedition too.

Rashid : It's a challenge I wouldn't want to miss ~~out~~. We'd be working ~~on~~ with communities in the interior of Chile.

Anna : This weekend training will be very useful for us, I think.

Rashid : The organisers are supposed to familiarise us with everything ~~for~~ we need to know about the expedition.

Anna : It says in the programme here that we'll be told ~~on~~ the rules we have to abide by during the whole expedition.

Rashid : Oh! This should interest ~~to~~ all of us. According to the programme, the Chilean Ambassador is going to talk on the customs and traditions of his people.

Anna : Wow! I hope he wears his national costume or he sings ~~with~~ the national anthem of his country.

Rashid : You do say the funniest things, Anna.

Practice E

1 of
2 at
3 in
4 about
5 for
6 to / towards
7 in
8 into / inside
9 with
10 with

7.2 PREPOSITIONS

Practice A

1 A, B   2 A, C   3 B, C   4 B, C   5 A, B

Practice B

	B
2	their neighbours' lack of civic-consciousness.
5	who this written message is.
6	reminding us to clear up the mess in the garage.
1	hitching a ride from a friend.
3	the failure of the negotiations.
4	the proposal to increase our club's subscription fees.

2 He managed to get to the airport by hitching a ride from a friend.
3 The ambassador expressed deep sorrow over the failure of the negotiations.
4 We disagreed with the proposal to increase our club's subscription fees.
5 I don't know who this written message is from.
6 The landlord is tired of reminding us to clear up the mess in the garage.

Practice C

3 I am annoyed at your taking your good health for granted.
4 Charles was upset about our not enjoying the film he had recommended.
5 The staff assured their new manager of their support and loyalty.
6 The family was pleased with my attempts to find a job.
7 The woman complained of her neighbour's difficult personality.

Practice D

because I faced stiff competition ∧ the others.	**4**	from
Well, when I think back ∧ what I wrote earlier,	**10**	to
thing. This latest song is ∧ never giving up hope.	**13**	about
Yes. I was on drugs once. I was conscious ∧ what	**15**	of
I know you're watching this. This is ∧ you."	**22**	for

8 SUBJECT AND PREDICATE

Practice A

1 Don't play
2 We
3 Speak
4 me to carry
5 Don't climb
6 some food for us
7 the shopping to her husband
8 Be
9 The director is
10 Have

Practice B

1 B   2 A   3 A, B, C   4 C   5 B   6 A, C   7 B

Practice C

1 Don't be late or we'll miss the opening number of the show.
2 Colin presented Joanne with a beautiful cashmere jacket.
3 Those magnificent pine trees are part of the Alpine forests.
4 She passed me copies of the annual report.
5 Speak louder because I can't hear what you're saying.
6 Make sure that you don't upset the whole tray of cakes.
7 Take a deep breath please, so that I can check your lungs.
8 All afternoon, we were helping out at the charity bazaar.
9 The fishermen cleaned their catch for the day and dried it in the sun.
10 Those colourfully-dressed young men are members of the state's basketball team.

Practice D

1 /Have to watch . . .   <u>subject</u>

2 . . . letter box. It must be still /.   <u>adverbial</u>

3 We gave the reply cards / so she . . .   <u>indirect</u>

4 The girls looked for Katy in / but there . . .   <u>adverbial</u>

5 All night long, Bill / to hear . . .   <u>verb</u>

6 Post / for me . . .   <u>direct object</u>

7 She / very unreasonable . . .   <u>verb</u>

8 /Have to get . . .   <u>subject</u>

9 Its Caesar's salad is /.   <u>complement</u>

10 . . . and cash for /.   <u>indirect object</u>

Practice E

1 Follow that car! We mustn't lose sight of it.

2 Glen made several efforts to get in touch with us yesterday.

4 You have got to show more understanding towards Peter. You know he has to deal with many problems.

5 Don't thank us for these gifts. We think you deserve every one of them.

9.1 RELATIVE CLAUSES

Practice A

1 ~~were~~	5 ~~which~~	8 ~~which~~
2 , which	6 , ~~that~~ I	9 , which we
3 , ~~that~~	7 , ~~who~~	10 ~~which~~
4 ~~had~~		

Practice B

1 B	2 A	3 B	4 A	5 B
6 B	7 A	8 A	9 B	10 B

Practice C

1 B, C	2 A	3 A, B, C	4 B, C	5 A, C

Practice D

1 who	5 which puzzle	8 he
2 which	6 , who	9 who
3 that	7 that	10 the
4 that		

Practice E

2 The sports committee congratulated the athletes who had won gold and silver medals.

3 The doctor prescribed a new tranquiliser that did not agree with me.

4 We must find a guide who has been there many times.

5 Mr Thomas is a teacher who can hold us spellbound with his stories.

6 She poured tea into the little cups which were made of fine porcelain.

9.2 RELATIVE CLAUSES

Practice A

1   4   5   7   10

Practice B

1 B, C	2 A, B	3 A, C	4 A, B, C	5 A

Practice C

2 We have bungled the experiment whose success is vital to our future.

3 Lisa entered the Horizon Hotel, whose lobby was crowded with cameramen.

4 She talked to a reporter, whose face she recognised.

5 He thanked the lawyer whose brilliance had saved his case.

6 They stood by the Red Sea, whose history they knew so well.

Practice D

1   2   4   7   9

Practice E

1 I am lucky to be a student whose parents have a realistic outlook on success at school.

2 They are people whose expectations I can meet without stress.

3 I am also fortunate to be in my school, whose policy is to help every student progress at his or her own pace.

4 Free from tension, I find myself discovering abilities whose existence I never realised.

5 I hope to become a person whose development is balanced.

6 This will enable me to face a world whose challenges get harder each day.

Practice F

1 , whose	5 whose	8 whose
2 whose	6 that	9 , whose
3 who	7 whose range	10 which
4 whose		

9.3 RELATIVE CLAUSES

Practice A

2 The vacation (which) I took made me feel better.

5 The reporters (who) the principal briefed want more information.

8 The principles (which) we hold help us make sensible decisions.

10 Friends (that) you can trust fully are valuable.

11 The clown (who) the children love will perform again tonight.

Practice B

1 that beat	6 who wanted
2 which were once green look parched now	7 which
3 , is	8 which
4 who	9 that
5 that they hatched	10 who are

Practice C

2   4   5   8   10

Practice D

2 The Statuesque, which is a five-star hotel, offers special rates for senior citizens.

3 One of the parties that signed the contract has been arrested.

4 Their leader, who they all revere, is seriously ill.

5 Youngsters who feel neglected are likely to get into trouble.

6 Your departure, which nobody expected, saddened us all.

Practice E

2 The article is about my grandmother, who spoke up for women's rights.

3 You are merely talking about tolerance, which you should practise.

4 The baby who / that my cousins have adopted looks increasingly like me.

5 Africa, whose mysteries I long to explore, draws me irresistibly.

6 Countries whose populations are multi-ethnic need this programme.

Practice F

2 My mother put me on a study schedule from the first day of each year, who was a strict disciplinarian. → My mother, who was a strict disciplinarian, put me on a study schedule from the first day of each year.

3 However, the promises, which I made to my mother, were undermined by my passion for fantasy novels. → However, the promises which I made to my mother were undermined by my passion for fantasy novels.

4 My favourite stories whose authors wove wonderful dreams enticed me away from my textbooks. → My favourite stories, whose authors wove wonderful dreams, enticed me away from my textbooks.

5 The crazy cramming which I did just before examinations was somehow sufficient to get me through lower secondary school. → The crazy cramming, which I did just before examinations, was somehow sufficient to get me through lower secondary school.

6 The disaster cured me of 11th-hour marathons came at upper secondary level. → The disaster which / that cured me of 11th-hour marathons came at upper secondary level.

10.1 ADVERBIAL CLAUSES

Practice A

2 Because he help us once, we must support him now.

3 Since you are a good speaker, you should join the debating society.

4 Laughter is therapeutic because it helps us to relax.

5 As the instructions are clear, you shouldn't make a mistake.

6 They decided to sell their car since they needed the money.

7 Because the harvest was splendid, they held a special thanksgiving feast.

8 As Sally is rather extravagant, she does not have much money saved.

9 The captain was annoyed because a boy had stowed away on the ship.

10 Since exercise promotes health, everyone should do it regularly.

11 I can't join you as I've promised to babysit tonight.

Practice B

1 so you	5 it's because	8 enjoyed
2 because of	6 always	9 won't
3 beneficial	7 so he	10 dislike
4 so I		

Practice C

1 because	5 never	8 smart
2 tough	6 he	9 delight
3 I'll	7 common	10 supported
4 because		

Practice D

1 The dessert was a disaster because I forgot the sugar.

2 She is often misunderstood since she has a gruff manner of speaking.

3 I felt embarrassed because they praised me too highly.

4 You must act fast as time is running out.

5 You will need your cardigan because the night is very cold.

Practice E

2 Since their kitchen was dirty, they received a complaint.

3 As those ornaments are fragile, I daren't even touch them.

4 Smoking should be avoided since it is harmful.

5 Because her father had delicate health, she was protective of him.

6 She spent a lot of time in the room as it was comfortable.

Practice F

You have no idea how boring it can be since you haven't been to my 'sunny paradise'. The climate depresses me as the only change is from hot and dry to hot and wet. I prefer your temperate climate because the four seasons give variety to life. I can make a fair comparison as I've lived in both countries. I even enjoyed your worst winters since they made the prospect of spring doubly delightful.

10.2 ADVERBIAL CLAUSES

Practice A

1 Although Adam is only two, he enjoys spicy curries.

2 She enjoyed the movie though I found it boring.

3 He is still planting rubber even though other trees are more lucrative.

4 Though he turned 80 yesterday, he is still formidable at chess.

5 Even though our new car has power steering, I still have problems parking it.

6 I consider myself lucky although I've had a few setbacks during my life.

7 While this satin dress is too shiny for daytime, it is perfect for evenings.

8 Although ginseng can boost energy, too much of it has the opposite effect.

9 A firm bed is good for your back although a soft one feels more luxurious.

10 While he is a good manager, he is sometimes overzealous in trying to improve the quality of work.

Practice B

1 but she	4 shy	7 since	9 realistic
2 can	5 is	8 known	10 less
3 seldom	6 but all		

Practice C

2 While he is a martial arts expert, he has a scholarly air.

3 Even though she acts well, she prefers writing scripts.

4 The necklace is exquisite although it was designed in a hurry.

5 Although long hair looks glamorous, this short cut is more practical.

6 Many of us don't drink enough water even though it is essential for health.

Practice D

1 A, C   2 A, B   3 B, C   4 A, B   5 A, C

Practice E

2 While it is a double room, it isn't bigger than the single rooms in other hotels.

3 Although she's wearing high-heeled shoes, she's walking steadily.

4 Though the sun was scorching, we went outdoors unprotected.

5 Even though you are the president's son, you must obey the rules.

6 Although I was very late, they accepted my apology.

Practice F

Many women manage well though they have to juggle career and family responsibilities. While some newspaper articles have attributed juvenile problems to working mothers, this allegation is unfair. According to surveys, teenagers can be troubled even though their mothers are always at home. A close relationship can be maintained between a mother and her teenage children although she is at work for part of the day. Though she can't be with them for hours on end, she can give them quality time every day.

10.3 ADVERBIAL CLAUSES
Practice A

1 Since he installed his new telephone, he has received many crank calls.

2 The boss glared at me when my mobile phone rang during the meeting.

3 The boy was fidgeting while his mother was gossiping with their neighbour.

4 As she hugged her brother, she pinched him playfully.

5 They have not been sleeping well since the accident occurred.

6 While the reporter interviewed us, the photographer took some pictures of our school.

7 He smiled at the little girl as she curtsied to him.

8 When the singer stepped out of the limousine, his fans mobbed him.

9 Since she arrived in Hollywood, she has been making a name for herself as a talented newcomer.

10 The boy chuckled when the pony nuzzled him.

Practice B

1 A	2 A	3 B	4 B	5 A
6 A	7 A	8 B	9 A	10 B

Practice C

1 The police tailed the fans while they stalked the film star.

2 As they greeted the new manager, they sized him up fast.

3 The people have been assembling at the village square since the curfew was lifted.

4 When she bought the machine, her life became easier.

5 Since its ancient splendour was restored, tourists have flocked to the castle.

Practice D

1   4   6   7   10

Practice E

2 Anna was listening to music while she was waiting for her friends to arrive. / Anna listened to music while she waited for her friends to arrive.

3 The two armed men jumped off the train as it entered the railway station. / The two armed men jumped off the train as it was entering the railway station.

4 Since the stock market recovered, his financial situation has improved.

5 The children rushed into the house when their mother called them to have dinner.

6 For a moment Jim slipped as he was climbing up the ladder but he managed to steady himself. / For a moment Jim slipped as he climbed up the ladder but he managed to steady himself.

Practice F

1 Since Kate graduated, her friends have been urging her to dress better. Right through university, she wore baggy T-shirts and faded jeans 2 while her fellow-students experimented with fashionable clothes. Now, 3 while Kate is reading up for her first job interview, her helpful friends are putting together an outfit to impress her interviewers. Kate thanks them 4 as she poses in the smart suit with matching accessories. She quietly decides to wear a simple dress 5 when she goes for the interview.

10.4 ADVERBIAL CLAUSES
Practice A

3 In order that Jim can find his way easily, we sent him a detailed map to our house.

6 I wish to see him alone so that I can speak frankly.

7 The movie stars issued a press statement in order that the rumours might stop.

9 In order that they could meet more often, he moved to her city.

11 We are taking precautions so that the disease won't spread further.

Practice B

1 that	5 will	8 would
2 might	6 that	9 that
3 is	7 acted	10 am
4 plugged		

Practice C

2   4   5   7   8

Practice D

1 will	5 so	8 might
2 so that	6 could	9 so that
3 so cunning	7 can launch	10 so
4 in order that		

Practice E

2 The weather forecast was so alarming that I postponed the trip.

3 You must build up her confidence so that she won't be afraid to speak in public.

4 In order that the plants might flourish, they used special fertilisers.

5 You have arranged the flowers so expertly that everyone is amazed.

6 He is seeing to every detail personally in order that nothing may go wrong.

Practice F

Some people start to learn a foreign language in order that they may experience something new. Others think about learning another language so they can have a more interesting time when travelling abroad. They keep studying and listening to CDs, so that they soon can communicate simple ideas. Often they become so interested that they join a club where they can practice the language in a social setting. In order to become fluent, it is necessary to be with native speakers but all practice is useful.

10.5 ADVERBIAL CLAUSES

Practice A

2   5   7   8   10

Practice B

1 Should	5 you've	8 would
2 doesn't	6 feel	9 have given
3 cared	7 had had	10 if
4 might		

Practice C

1 is	5 if	8 raining
2 should	6 give	9 cooked
3 be	7 works	10 were
4 will continue		

Practice D

2 If you were committed to the idea, you would not behave in this way.

3 We could have imported more cars if we had anticipated the demand.

4 Should she have any problem, I'd be happy to help.

5 If he had been put in charge, the venture would have failed.

6 You'll find the beach deserted if you go there tomorrow.

Practice E

1 could	5 had	8 had been
2 tell	6 is	9 be
3 Should	7 would	10 remain
4 say		

Practice F

1 had	5 have	8 can / may
2 Should	6 has	9 have
3 if	7 be	10 could
4 were		

10.6 ADVERBIAL CLAUSES

Practice A

1 would	5 like	8 the way
2 as	6 as	9 were
3 the way	7 as though	10 like
4 could		

Practice B

1 as	5 like	8 was
2 had	6 do	9 could
3 the way	7 as if	10 did
4 were		

Practice C

2   4   5   7   8

Practice D

2 They are living thoughtlessly as if there were no tomorrow.

3 She plays the violin like / as/ the way her grandmother did.

4 It is raining as if / as though it would never stop.

5 We'll make this old building look splendid the way it used to do.

6 Dad treats strangers as though he had known them for years.

Practice E

1 done	5 as what	8 like what
2 be	6 is	9 the way
3 the way how	7 like how	10 burst
4 have		

Practice F

2 The machine is not functioning as it should be.

3 Our top sprinter runs as though his feet had wings.

4 They want to go on protecting her as they have always done.

5 I've learnt not to be thoughtless the way I was in my youth.

6 You act as if you knew the answers to all these political problems.

11.1 REPORTED CLAUSES

Practice A

1 A, B, C   **2** B, C   **3** A, C   **4** B, C   **5** A

Practice B

1 resign	6 had
2 are	7 be
3 if	8 whether
4 we may	9 he would
5 feel	10 those diamonds are

Practice C

1 I told my neighbour that he had always been considerate.

2 I haven't decided if the proposal has any merit.

3 The speaker pointed out that every human being has weaknesses.

4 He vowed he would restore his family's future.

5 She can sense whether or not someone is happy.

Practice D

2 All his friends reminded him that the future is unpredictable.

3 I suggest that your sister take / should take a long holiday.

4 You must find out whether or not you've been immunised. / You must find out if / whether you've been immunised.

5 The millionaire agrees that riches don't guarantee happiness.

6 We enquired if we could fly direct to Atlanta.

Practice E

2 You've even suggested that I carried photos to help me remember my friends! → You've even suggested that I carry photos to help me remember my friends!

3 I ran after him, complaining loudly that he has been neglecting me. → I ran after him, complaining loudly that he had been neglecting me.

4 A smiling stranger turned round and asked I would forgive him. → A smiling stranger turned round and asked if / whether I would forgive him.

5 Still apologetic about not contacting me all these years, he insisted that I joined him for coffee so that we could catch up on old times. → Still apologetic about not contacting me all these years, he insisted that I join him for coffee so that we could catch up on old times.

6 To my delight I realised that I am finding someone even more absent-minded than me. → To my delight I realised that I had found someone even more absent-minded than me.

11.2 REPORTED CLAUSES

Practice A

2 The engineer has estimated when the dam will be completed. (time)

3 I want to learn how a computer programme is written. (manner)

4 We are planning where we should spend the next holidays. (place)

5 He's wondering who he can approach for help to solve his problem. (person)

6 I can't understand why you want to see that movie again. (reason)

Practice B

1 have you   5 which strategy   8 what
2 what   6 did he see   9 whose
3 who's   7 whose one   10 did the old man cope
4 how

Practice C

1   3   4   8   9

Practice D

1 what   5 how   8 which one
2 why   6 which   9 the hamper was
3 whose   7 we are   10 whose
4 he will

Practice E

1 how   4 I should   7 where   9 what
2 I will   5 whose is   8 what   10 I can
3 which   6 why

Practice F

2 He likes to mention who he knows in high places.
3 She tried to explain what she meant by those words.
4 They can predict who's going to win the championship at this stage.
5 I understand why you feel sad.
6 We can demonstrate to you which method is the better of the two.

11.3 REPORTED CLAUSES

Practice A

1   4   6   7   9

Practice B

1 subscribe   5 to stop   8 to return
2 to extend   6 spend   9 be
3 would survive   7 respect   10 should abide
4 do

Practice C

1 A, C   2 B, C   3 A, B, C   4 A   5 B, C

Practice D

2 Matthew recommended that Katy apply for a scholarship since her exam results are outstanding.
3 The police commissioner commanded that his policemen arrest all those breaking the curfew.
4 The speaker said it is vital that we understand what drug addiction can lead to.
5 Larry asked that Steven assist him in the project.
6 Katy suggested that they hold the wedding reception by the poolside.

11.4 REPORTED CLAUSES AND CONDITIONAL CLAUSES

Practice A

1 be read out   5 be separated   8 not ignore
2 be   6 not delay   9 be treated
3 not neglect   7 not consider   10 not be let off
4 be protected

Practice B

1 be   6 not make
2 were   7 were
3 not be scheduled   8 not dump
4 should   9 be highlighted
5 be given   10 would

Practice C

1 built → build
3 obeyed → be obeyed
5 not be prevail → not prevail
9 was → were
10 not adjourned → not be adjourned

Practice D

2 John requested that we not tell Betty about the present he had bought for her.
3 Our neighbours suggested that we pay half the cost of the wall between our houses.
4 It is important that the fine print in legal documents be read carefully.
5 I wish Mr Lee were our neighbour because he is so understanding.
6 Jessie begged that she not be required to give a speech before the large audience.

12.1 ADJECTIVAL PHRASES

Practice A

1 She is staring at the photo on her table again.
2 We finally saw the light at the end of the tunnel.
3 He was honoured for his contribution towards peace.
4 Her dispute with the company is still unresolved.
5 The fingerprints on the glass belong to the murder suspect.
6 Her house is full of junk from various sales.
7 The close bond between the twins is something I wish I had with my sister.
8 Our new employee is the man with the cheerful grin.
9 Hazel's hard work behind the scenes helped a lot.
10 I like the sense of satisfaction after finishing a task.

Practice B

1 A stroll along the beach will relax you.
2 He is a supporter of women's rights.

3 The resort is two hundred metres above sea-level.
4 Nobody in his right mind would do that.
5 Now we see the person behind the mask.

Practice C
1   4   5   6   9

Practice D
1 This famous magician has performed feats /.   Ⓑ

2 The difficulties / before her final triumph.   Ⓑ

    The difficulties before her final triumph /.

3 Killing / is not murder.   Ⓐ

4 Letters of complaint without the writers' names
    or addresses /.   Ⓑ

5 Viewers / enjoyed the programme.   Ⓐ

Practice E
1 is	**5** in	**8** for
2 from	**6** with	**9** to
3 without	**7** between	**10** by
4 on		

Practice F
2 If the ambassador and his wife come, there must be perfect behaviour in their presence.
3 Hit songs from old musicals are becoming popular again.
4 This movie is not recommended for viewers below 18.
5 The enormous lady in front of me blocked my view.
6 She realised the kindness behnd his gruff manner.

12.2 ADJECTIVAL PHRASES
1 The workers <u>evacuating the flood victims</u> are volunteers from the community.
2 The visitors <u>taken to see the sights</u> were unimpressed.
3 I felt grief <u>mixed with exhaustion.</u>
4 He beckoned to the boy <u>hesitating in the doorway.</u>
5 The bells <u>chiming so merrily</u> brought back her childhood.
6 A chair <u>flung out of a window</u> hit a passer-by.
7 You have a son <u>blessed with a happy nature.</u>
8 I love to hear these voices <u>harmonising so well.</u>
9 The lawyer <u>cross-examining the witness</u> is formidable.
10 He strikes me as a man <u>disillusioned with his profession.</u>

Practice B
2   5   7   8   10

Practice C
1 Children forced to study music may detest it.
2 He loves steaks grilled to perfection.
3 A girl wearing a kimono greeted me.
4 The money set aside for our trip to France is insufficient.
5 I remember her climbing trees in our backyard as a child.

Practice D
1 hiring	**5** sworn	**8** overprotected
2 rated	**6** glistening	**9** sinking
3 have	**7** don't	**10** who's done
4 shaken		

Practice E
2 She looked disdainfully at the youth approaching her.
3 Overseas students yearning for home need help to deal with the loneliness.
4 The person chosen for the post is very experienced.

5 They came in carrying cameras slung on their shoulders.
6 The Master of Ceremonies gave a speech filled with anecdotes.

Practice F
1 appearing	**5** becoming	**8** known
2 offer	**6** deemed	**9** is
3 buried	**7** recommending	**10** keeping
4 spent		

12.3 ADJECTIVAL PHRASES
Practice A
1 The boys found themselves staring at a farmer's face <u>red with anger.</u>

2 A child <u>forlorn in a corner</u> caught my eye.

3 Rice fields <u>golden in the sun</u> make me think of home.

4 She has skin <u>allergic to nylon.</u>

5 We were a group of students <u>ready for adventure.</u>

6 A policy <u>brilliant in conception</u> will fail if poorly implemented.

7 Her smile hid a heart <u>heavy with anxiety.</u>

8 A guest <u>reluctant to depart</u> was straining our patience.

9 The racing car was watched by boys <u>green with envy.</u>

10 Children <u>eager to learn</u> are a delight to teach.

Practice B
1 They have a future bright with promise.
2 We saw faces alive with interest.
3 Managers adept at motivating people are needed.
4 We'll choose a place close to you.
5 Students keen to join our jungle expedition must register by tomorrow.

Practice C
1 A, C	**2** A, B	**3** B, C	**4** A, B, C	**5** C

Practice D
1 proud	**4** beautiful	**7** eyes	**9** sickness
2 is	**5** easy	**8** requires	**10** painful
3 need	**6** are		

Practice E
2 She touched a forehead clammy with cold sweat.
3 We entered rooms bare of furniture.
4 A boy thoughtless during childhood may become a fine man.
5 A pet sure of its master's love is full of energy.
6 I watched a tailor busy at work.

Practice F
1 eager	**5** was	**8** dependent
2 responsible	**6** free	**9** certain
3 different	**7** is	**10** were
4 full		

13.1 ADVERBIAL PHRASES
Practice A
1 Our report was commended <u>for its accuracy.</u>

2 <u>For their persistence in upholding justice,</u> they will always be remembered.

3 <u>Because of the elegance of its furnishings,</u> this hotel is our first choice.

4 He almost ruined his fishing rod <u>because of a momentary carelessness.</u>

5 <u>For your generosity when we were in serious trouble,</u> you've earned our gratitude.

6 A curfew has been imposed <u>because of the riots.</u>

7 <u>Because of his sad experiences in childhood,</u> he is very compassionate.

8 Children love her <u>for her affectionate nature.</u>

9 <u>For the incisive humour of his lectures,</u> Professor Lee is much admired.

10 That building has been restored and preserved <u>because of its historical value.</u>

Practice B
1 2 5 6 10

Practice C
1	because of	**5**	poor	**8**	failure
2	his courtesy	**6**	the good	**9**	their
3	his	**7**	behaviour	**10**	terror
4	its				

Practice D
2 He is disliked by some for his refusal to conform.

3 The universe is beyond our grasp because of its awesome vastness.

4 For the beauty of its lyrics, the song stayed at the top of the charts for 10 weeks.

5 Because of a silly misunderstanding, we lost contact for years.

6 The entire platoon was punished for its slowness to obey orders.

Practice E
1 A, B   **2** A, C   **3** B, C   **4** A, B   **5** B, C

Practice F
2 <u>Because of her performed outstandingly in sports, Asha won the title 'College Sports Star'.</u> → Because of her outstanding performance in sports, Asha won the title 'College Sports Star'.

3 <u>The 'Best Speaker' title went to Fara for a brilliance of her debating.</u> → The 'Best Speaker' title went to Fara for the brilliance of her debating.

4 <u>For their excellent in the science subjects, Andy and Sheila shared a prize.</u> → For their excellence in the science subjects, Andy and Sheila shared a prize.

5 <u>It was awarded to Lisa for her kind to other students.</u> → It was awarded to Lisa for her kindness to other students.

6 <u>This unexpected appreciate almost made Lisa cry.</u> → This unexpected appreciation almost made Lisa cry.

13.2 ADVERBIAL PHRASES
Practice A
1 <u>To heighten environmental awareness,</u> the minister suggested launching a publicity campaign.

2 My uncle is saving as much money as he can <u>in order to retire in comfort.</u>

3 She chose her words carefully <u>so as not to offend her client.</u>

4 <u>In order to increase your chances of a promotion,</u> you should work extra hard.

5 I'm practising conscientiously <u>so as to become a good violinist.</u>

6 We'll work extra hours <u>to make sure the goods are ready on time.</u>

7 <u>In order to earn the respect of your team members,</u> you must be a firm and fair leader.

8 She lets her children share in the housework <u>so as to teach them useful skills.</u>

9 They quickly settled the issue out of court <u>in order not to attract media attention.</u>

10 The computer system will be improved <u>so as to protect it against hackers.</u>

Practice B
1 In order not to go bankrupt, they're cutting costs drastically.

2 He'll try to persuade everybody to vote for him in the 'Most Popular Resident' contest.

3 We'd better tell the truth so as not to prolong the suspense.

4 To develop a child's self-esteem, parents should not be afraid to provide challenges.

5 He keeps quiet most of the time in order to avoid arguing with his roommate.

Practice C
1 3 4 6 9

Practice D
1	put	**5**	get	**8**	not to
2	galvanise	**6**	ensure	**9**	run
3	to seem	**7**	help	**10**	so as not
4	not to				

Practice E
2 You are saying these things to humour me.

3 In order not to be outdone, she's attempting the highest peak when we go mountain-climbing.

4 To let Susan know when I'll be back, I left a note on the refrigerator door.

5 Ben stood still, hardly daring to breathe in order not to awaken the sleeping tiger.

6 So as not to forget important dates, Nancy always carries a notebook with her.

Practice F
One involved imagining the people she was shy of in their pyjamas so as to lose her awe of them. Unfortunately, this made her even more nervous and she hastily reclothed them in proper clothes to restore her composure. Another technique was rather more successful. In order not to be tongue-tied, she asked people questions about themselves, their families, schools or jobs, hobbies, favourite colours and so on. The people responded happily but she had to keep on asking them questions so as not to give them a chance to question her back. To cope with this need, Diana compiled a list of questions long enough to qualify for the Guinness Book of World Records.

13.3 ADVERBIAL PHRASES

Practice A

1 The demonstrators refused to disperse, <u>leaving the police no choice but to arrest them.</u>

2 The lecture had been well-advertised, <u>drawing a large crowd.</u>

3 A fresh breeze blew, <u>tempering the heat of noon.</u>

4 Two friends joined us, <u>making up a four-some for a game.</u>

5 The speaker kept contradicting himself, <u>bewildering the audience.</u>

6 Someone yawned, <u>causing the rest of us to do the same.</u>

7 He acted swiftly and wisely, <u>preventing a crisis.</u>

8 We left the building unlocked last night, <u>exposing it to vandals.</u>

9 Finally the rains came, <u>enabling the farmers to plough their lands.</u>

10 Her grandchildren arrived, <u>making her much more cheerful.</u>

Practice B

1 A, B   2 B, C   3 A, C   4 A, B   5 A, C

Practice C

2   3   6   9   10

Practice D

1 toppled   5 break   8 upsets
2 hence causing   6 worked   9 eaten
3 make   7 poverty   10 meets
4 therefore resulting

Practice E

2 Their attempts at covering up were useless, resulting in ugly paintwork.

3 Those opal earrings suit her, enhancing her delicate beauty.

4 The idea of the trip was suggested last night, delighting the youngsters,.

5 He kept losing at cards, ending up with nothing.

6 This morning's exertion was too much for him, triggering a bad headache.

Practice F

Driving a car can change a person, making a monster out of a man or woman. It exposes you to spicy language, widening your vocabulary greatly. Soon you are an expert at exchanging insults, shocking family and friends travelling with you. You cannot bear to be overtaken, often breaking the speed limit to even the score. After some time, you may realise the lunacy of it all, reverting to your sane self. You start to drive sensibly, learning to return rudeness with courtesy.

13.4 ADVERBIAL PHRASES

Practice A

1 <u>While travelling in Africa</u>, we took some splendid pictures.

2 She let me down badly <u>after promising to help me.</u>

3 He showed no fear <u>when threatened by the robber.</u>

4 <u>Before accepting the offer</u>, you should consider it carefully.

5 <u>When bargaining at a bazaar</u>, some people are very successful.

6 We had a brief problem <u>before landing safely in Madrid.</u>

7 <u>After graduating from college</u>, he set up a business.

8 I was day-dreaming <u>while watching the documentary.</u>

9 <u>When given a free hand</u>, you did a good job.

10 Ada looks chic <u>after having her hair styled.</u>

Practice B

1 being gored   5 mastering   8 committing
2 loitering   6 handling   9 hurried
3 complimented   7 keying   10 sending
4 catching

Practice C

2   3   5   8   9

Practice D

2 When used as an excuse, a headache sometimes becomes real.

3 After analysing all our tactical errors, we made a new plan.

4 He worked seven days a week while being prepared for the top job.

5 We are giving him a last chance before taking legal action .

6 While investigating the disappearance of the millionaire, the inspector himself vanished.

Practice E

2 The princess was smiling and waving while passing by in her chauffeured limousine.

3 After pursuing his dream for years, he suddenly lost interest.

4 She wanted to see her son before going on a long journey.

5 While exploring the cave, they found a strange object.

6 I plan to hitchhike around the world after graduating from college.

Practice F

She said: 'While acting, I portray emotions through my eyes and not my facial muscles.' She added this piece of advice: 'In everyday life too, you must think before allowing yourself to smile. The loveliest woman will look a wreck after smiling recklessly over the years. When smiling into the camera or at anyone, I never let my eyes crinkle up at the corners.' After reading this, are you prepared to give up 'smiling recklessly' to avoid wrinkles?

14.1 NOUN PHRASES

Practice A

2 They forgot <u>to tell me about it.</u>

3 This doesn't entitle you <u>to speak at meetings.</u>

4 She no longer avoids <u>singing in public.</u>

5 He expects <u>to be served immediately.</u>

8 I don't intend <u>to get myself poisoned by this food.</u>

Practice B

2 She did not fancy sunbathing on such a crowded beach.

3 I beg you to give this plan a second chance.

4 He must not let this shatter his confidence in his ability.

5 We saw the barrels rolling downhill that day.

6 The boy wants to be tutored by that particular teacher.

Practice C

1 to go	5 worrying	8 face
2 make	6 be	9 to blind
3 teaching	7 following	10 dressing
4 to control		

Practice D

1   3   4   7   8

Practice E

2 We saw him flinching at the sight of the letter.
3 Some people won't even try to understand how to use the Internet.
4 The neighbours often hear her talk to her plants.
5 At his birth, his parents started saving for his education.
6 I don't want you to sacrifice your free time for this project.

Practice F

She asked to speak to the chief administrator and began to explain she was willing to work as a volunteer to gain experience. He listened for a while and then told her the hospital had a vacancy for a trainee and she only needed to apply. She felt herself skipping with delight as she ran to tell her friends and she started to write her application letter that afternoon.

14.2 NOUN PHRASES

Practice A

1 Your candidate has proved <u>to be a dedicated party member</u>.
2 He disappointed us after <u>raising our hopes</u>.
3 We congratulated her <u>on her being elected president of the Nature Society</u>.
4 The mysterious visitor turned out <u>to be an old friend</u>.
5 Their business seemed <u>to prosper despite the recession</u>.
6 She is committed <u>to improving the services in this city</u>.
7 They will not succeed <u>in intimidating that girl</u>.
8 I always do <u>a sketch before painting a landscape</u>.
9 The children came <u>to love the trips to the city</u>.
10 Our greatest joy will be <u>to see the garden flourishing</u>.

Practice B

2 Gradually they came to understand the culture of the country.
3 She charmed them into revealing a number of interesting secrets.
4 You don't appear to care about your club's future.
5 He is not above using all his savings on a party.
6 We soon gave up fantasies of being knights in shining armour.

Practice C

1 ~~nursing~~	4 ~~was~~	7 ~~in~~	9 ~~in~~
2 forgotten	5 ~~not~~	8 appear	10 ~~have~~
3 ~~have~~	6 ~~loves~~		

Practice D

2   4   5   7   9

Practice E

2 He won the boys' confidence by treating them as adults.
3 The root of her troubles was having a very bad memory.

4 I can't get over seeing her in such a predicament.
5 Every mannerism of his seems to irritate the audience.
6 They are obsessed with maintaining their old sports car.

Practice F

She always seemed to be worried even when my friends insisted on seeing me safely home after extra science classes. One night, when my family was away at a wedding, the lady next door saw what must have appeared to be thieves hiding in my backyard. She hurried over to check. She looked rather disappointed when the burglary turned out to be three schoolgirls organising 'Operation Catch Toads' for the next day's biology class.

14.3 NOUN PHRASES

Practice A

1 <u>Rushing around</u> makes me feel dizzy.
2 <u>To organise all these books</u> won't be easy.
4 <u>Talking about the past</u> can be fascinating.
6 <u>To avoid bankruptcy</u> seemed impossible.
9 <u>Confronting him</u> would probably be best.

Practice B

2 To promote global peace is their mission.
3 To lose this fight would upset him.
4 Rehabilitating stroke victims needs special skills.
5 To leave the country was his own decision.
6 Indulging in petty jealousies wasted our time.

Practice C

1 A, B	2 B, C	3 A, C	4 A, B	5 A, C

Practice D

1 helps	4 will be	7 seems	9 bores
2 is not	5 remains	8 may be	10 was
3 has	6 was a		

Practice E

2 Collecting Asian proverbs was my late uncle's pastime.
3 To make money was once his reason for living.
4 Facing their disapproval doesn't frighten her in the least.
5 To help the community develop has been / had been our concern all these years.
6 To go on doing this is / will be sheer waste of time.

Practice F

1 been	4 had	7 bring	9 hugging
2 turned	5 prepared	8 was	10 kissing
3 Growing	6 see		

15.1 SENTENCE STRUCTURE

Practice A

2 (1, 2)	3 (2, 1)	4 (1, 2)	5 (1, 2)	6 (1, 2)

Practice B

1 The sunrise didn't interest them and neither did the sunset.
2 You either stop wasting time or go straight home.
3 The dress may neither fit her nor suit her.
4 That grandfather clock either stops or goes really fast.
5 Our parent company has not made any profit this year and neither have our subsidiaries.

Practice C

1 This piece of news will either make you pleased or (make you) angry.
2 I wouldn't deceive anyone and neither would you (deceive anyone).

4 The roses haven't bloomed and the chrysanthemums haven't (bloomed) either.

7 Age has not dimmed the castle's splendour and neither has neglect (dimmed the castle's splendour).

10 We can either go to the book fair with our friends or (go to the book fair) with our parents.

Practice D

2 Either he works reasonable hours or his health suffers. / He either works reasonable hours or his health suffers.

3 They aren't prepared and I'm not either.

4 We shouldn't be difficult and they shouldn't be either.

5 My parents don't like my music and neither do I enjoy their old tunes.

6 Either the hotel manager didn't understand my instructions or the receptionist is forgetful.

Practice E

1	plunge	4	nor	7	would	9	bother
2	did	5	either	8	either	10	nor
3	join	6	neither				

Practice F

2 B : Either a fireman or a neighbour rescued the baby.

3 B : The dialogue is not / isn't convincing and neither is the acting.

4 B : Your son will either do well or perhaps perform brilliantly.

5 B : The soldiers did not / didn't know anything about the terrain and the officers didn't either.

6 B : Your friends shouldn't waste time and you shouldn't either.

15.2 SENTENCE STRUCTURE

Practice A

1	A, D	2	B, D	3	B, C	4	A, B	5	C, D

Practice B

2   3   7   8   9

Practice C

1	As a result	5	Besides	8	Besides
2	Besides	6	As a result	9	Moreover
3	As a result	7	Moreover	10	As a result
4	Moreover				

Practice D

2	1, 3	3	2, 1	4	2, 1	5	1, 3	6	3, 1

Practice E

1 The room was crowded. Besides, the air-conditioning was not working. As a result, we were very uncomfortable.

2 Some picknickers litter the beaches. As a result, the beaches are dirty and unattractive. Moreover, our country gets a bad name.

3 This airline has a good safety record. Besides, it offers excellent service. As a result, it is very popular.

4 The neighbourhood is very noisy. As a result, the residents' hearing may be affected. Moreover, they become nervous and irritable.

5 I did not join them for the movie. Besides, I had read the book. Moreover, the reviews were no good.

Practice F

1 Some more she was from another country and she was a shy girl. → Moreover, she was from another country and she was a shy girl.

2 As the result, she was very unhappy. → As a result, she was very unhappy.

3 Beside, she liked Nita although she hardly talked. → Besides, she liked Nita although she hardly talked.

4 Beside, Nita was really a nice girl. → Besides, Nita was really a nice girl.

5 As the result, she became quite popular. → As a result, she became quite popular.

15.3 SENTENCE STRUCTURE

Practice A

1	At last	4	Thirdly	7	Next,	9	After
2	Firstly	5	At first	8	Firstly,	10	At last
3	After	6	Lastly				

Practice B

1	A, B	2	B, C	3	A, C	4	A, C	5	B	6	B

Practice C

1	At last	5	At last	8	Third,
2	After that,	6	Then,	9	After that,
3	Secondly,	7	At first	10	At last
4	Firstly,				

Practice D

1	Firstly,	5	Then	8	Then
2	Secondly,	6	Lastly	9	After that,
3	Firstly,	7	At first	10	At last
4	Next,				

Practice E

1 To make banana fritters, you need to buy some fresh bananas. Then, you peel the bananas. Next, coat them with flour. Finally, fry them.

2 At first, he ordered mushroom soup. After that, he changed his mind and said he wanted tomato soup. Finally, he settled for chicken soup.

3 First, shampoo your hair. Then, rinse it. After that, dry it. Lastly, comb it.

4 First, wash the towels. Then, hang them up to dry. Finally, fold them.

5 First, Jack looks at the cartoons in the newspaper. Then, / After that, he reads the sports pages. Lastly, he scans the front page news.

Practice F

2 Firstly, read the passage. After that, jot down the important points Lastly, use the points to write a summary of the passage.

3 At first I kept failing my driving test. Then, I passed it on my fourth attempt. At last I could drive around town.

4 First, Dad had the flu. Then, Mum caught it from him. Finally, the whole family was ill.

5 First, switch off the electricity. Then, change the bulb. Lastly, switch on the electricity to check the new bulb

6 Firstly, I cleaned the cut on my finger. After that, I applied some ointment on it. Lastly, I put a plaster over it.

16 CHANGING WORD ORDER

Practice A

1   3   6   9   10

Practice B

2 Seldom is an author's first novel accepted by this publisher.

3 If this strategy should fail, we'd have to give up.

4 Generally, I would be reluctant to make a decision so soon.

5 Had you listened to my advice, you would have done brilliantly.

6 She had barely caught her breath when she rushed off again.

Practice C

1 would I	5 they expect	8 Had
2 Should	6 Were	9 she were
3 had she	7 get	10 he be
4 does he open		

Practice D

2 3 5 8 9

Practice E

2 Were it just a question of courage, you'd win.

3 If I had controlled my temper, I would have won the match.

4 A woman rarely reaches the top rung of the corporate ladder.

5 Never would they be able to go sailing again.

6 Should he find the treasure, he'd definitely tell the police.

Practice F

2 (a) No sooner did I step / No sooner had I stepped
  (b) I no sooner stepped

3 (a) Had I known   (b) If I had known

4 (a) Seldom did I get   (b) I seldom got

5 (a) Were I   (b) If I were

6 (a) rarely does a day pass (b) a day rarely passes

17 REDUNDANCY

Practice A

2 We walked all the way there ~~on foot~~.

3 You are behaving like a ~~crazy~~ lunatic.

4 The pearl diver plunged ~~down~~ into the sea.

5 She ~~gently~~ coaxed her little son to finish his porridge.

6 A car hurtled down the road ~~at great speed~~.

7 Your sister will grow up to be a ~~gorgeous~~ beauty.

8 Soon Yoshiko will be returning ~~back~~ to Japan.

9 The fire razed the planetarium ~~completely~~.

10 The prices of goods are soaring ~~up~~.

11 I've finished my assignment but I may have to redo it ~~again~~.

Practice B

1 entered	5 corpses	8 surrendered
2 went	6 man	9 delayed
3 dived	7 Speaking in a rage	10 troops
4 young		

Practice C

1 talk	5 go	8 agreed
2 tire	6 child	9 plummeted
3 lost	7 genius	10 pass
4 out		

Practice D

2 5 6 8 10

Practice E

2 The bullets could not penetrate these walls.

3 Without shedding a tear, she walked through the departure gate. / She walked dry-eyed through the departure gate.

4 The rich old man is known to be a miser.

5 Feeling miserable, I lay staring at the ceiling. / I lay staring unhappily at the ceiling.

6 Carl was overjoyed to hear of your success.

Practice F

1 made	6 childishly chubby
2 teenager	7 noticed joyfully
3 fortunate and lucky	8 totally transformed
4 participants	9 added extra
5 secret worry	10 unfortunately hated

Practice G

1 Lady : Don't look now, but the woman in dark glasses alone at that table is a celebrity.

2 Friend : Actually, I spotted her when she entered the restaurant. / I spotted her when she entered the restaurant, in fact.

3 Lady : Why did you keep quiet? / Why didn't you say anything?

4 Friend : I always feel sorry for stars trying to escape from their fans.

5 Lady : Okay, we'll leave her alone to enjoy her meal. / Okay, we'll let her enjoy her meal undisturbed.

18 REFERENCE

Practice A

1 they	4 They	7 us	9 them
2 it	5 their	8 those	10 its
3 these	6 those		

Practice B

1 it → an education fair

2 that thriller → *House of Wax*

3 it → the site of an old disused mining pool

4 This → he (John) was not coming to work

5 they → Members of the public

6 those → a facial wash, a toner and a moisturiser

7 This → Jennifer is going to marry Steve in a month's time.

8 It → the problem had disappeared

9 she → our neighbour

10 these things → I am studying for an exam so you need to lower the volume of your music. When you don't do your chores properly, Mum gets me to finish your work. That's not fair.

Practice C

1 A	2 A	3 B	4 A	5 B

Practice D

2 them → the many outstanding speakers

3 That speaker → a law lecturer

4 this → "If your father committed a murder and he confessed the crime to you, what would you do?"

5 that → the very difficult question

6 these → I would listen to him. I would hold his hand. I would put my arms around him. I would even cry with him.

7 him → the lawyer's father

8 the crime → the murder

9 it → His answer

TEST 1

A

1 remember	7 need
2 didn't take note	10 to retrace
4 must find	12 located
5 wearing	13 noticed
6 has been watching	14 taken

B

1 seems	6 are willing
2 is	7 are
3 has been building up	8 was written
4 inspires	9 receive
5 was	10 focuses

C

2 had declined	13 ached
3 had already made up	14 was parched
4 used to often go	15 wouldn't have been
5 did not foresee	16 indicated
6 will be	17 was heading
7 had been trudging	18 was jammed / had
8 had not been	jammed
9 was drenched	19 didn't I see
10 squinted	20 were waving
11 was slowly moving	21 had decided
12 haven't taken	

D

1 The dog is usually taken out in the evening for a long walk by one of us.
2 The group's rowdy behaviour thoroughly shocked us.
3 Traditional methods of weaving and dyeing have been practised by the women of that community for hundreds of years.
4 The renovations to the house will have been completed by Wilson just before Christmas. / The renovations to the house will have been completed just before Christmas by Wilson.
5 The red van was being tailed all the way from the airport by a police car and a helicopter.

TEST 2

A

1 ought not to be divulging
2 be sewn
3 might resort
4 Could they be waiting
5 should have been raised

B

1 She is a person who everyone finds easy to confide ⁁. | in |

3 The president listened to all the complaints that the club members brought ⁁ regarding the sports facilities. | up |

5 Maisie doesn't care that she is always late ⁁ appointments. | for |

8 The preliminary investigations ⁁ the disappearance of the well-known businessman did not provide any leads. | into |

10 She is filled ⁁ remorse because she had seriously misjudged somebody. | with |

C

1 The prime minister advised the people to stand together in unity and strength so that no one could divide them.
2 The senior manager told Jennifer that he was caught in a traffic jam so he would be a little late for the meeting.
3 Sean asked me whether I found the book fascinating.
4 Jean said to Mary, "Is Bill performing at the musical concert on Saturday?"
5 Mrs Reed said to Jean and Diana, "Concentrate on your work and not on the fashion news."

D

1 Don't let Adam remove the reports from the table.
2 Sarah is the youngest chemical engineer in that company.
3 The envoy presented his credentials to the king.
4 My grandfather was a man of strong convictions.
5 Let's help those elderly women in wheelchairs.

E

1 B	2 A	3 B	4 A	5 B

F

1 I don't know whether that is a Portuguese, Spanish or Italian song.
2 It is imperative that every passenger be screened before being allowed to enter the departure lounge.
3 I fail to see why this is so important to you.
4 If I were Marie, I would ask about the warranty period before buying the electric mixer.
5 His secret wish was that he would make it to the top of his profession.

TEST 3

A

1 Sam has charisma and he's very helpful. ⁁ He is very popular in school.

2 Can we take a cab there? The bus ride is terribly bumpy. ⁁ I feel a little unwell.

3 Firstly, it's not right to tell a lie. ⁁ You may be forced to tell another lie to cover up the first lie.

4 ⁁ I was unable to balance myself on the ice-skates. Later, I found I was able to move without holding on to the side of the rink.

5 They ⁁ post their entry forms to our office or hand them in personally.

B

1 to strike	5 deprived	8 To leave
2 Winning	6 on	9 teeming
3 is	7 being made	10 to relinquish
4 causing		

C

1 A	2 B	3 A	4 C	5 B
6 A	7 B	8 C	9 B	10 C

D

1 Often wished he	4 Had
2 A riot had	5 Will never
3 we do	

E

1 A	2 C	3 B	4 A	5 C

1 they → John and Janice
2 that → the ability to be discerning.
3 this → You dislike Monica yet you spend a lot of time with her.
4 those → cheese tartlets
5 it → *Rising Roar*

TEST 4

A

1 from
2 importance
3 I
4 their
5 college
6 when
7 live / lead / have
8 to
9 am
10 that

B

1	B	5	C	9	B	13	C	17	A
2	A	6	B	10	A	14	A	18	B
3	A	7	A	11	C	15	C	19	C
4	A	8	B	12	B	16	B	20	A

C

1 The motivation course which they attended has proved to be effective.
2 His fingers trembled as he signed the contract.
3 When our project will be completed is the big question.
4 I can't imagine where you got that silly idea from.
5 Should he lose everything tomorrow, he would start afresh cheerfully.

D

1 Dealing with criminals has affected you.
2 He is discovering facts forgotten by the people.
3 While they are happy with our work, they still have to make us redundant.
4 His speech seems to have galvanised them into action.
5 The tears glistening in her eyes belie her cheerful smile.

TEST 5

A

1 to
2 early
3 for
4 should
5 watching
6 were
7 I
8 this
9 about
10 be

B

1	B	5	A	9	C	13	A	17	B
2	A	6	C	10	B	14	C	18	A
3	B	7	B	11	B	15	B	19	C
4	C	8	A	12	C	16	C	20	A

C

Yesterday, I looked at some photographs in a very old album. Seeing my parents as college students was a revela-

tion. Though serious and staid today, they were once teenagers. I took out the best picture showing them in comical costumes. They burst out laughing on catching sight of the funny old photograph.

D

1 A few weeks ago, a friend who was in that choir asked me I was interested in a reunion. → A few weeks ago, a friend who was in that choir asked me if / whether I was interested in a reunion.
2 The next day, I decided to have copies made of the photograph because of they would be good to give as presents at the reunion. → The next day, I decided to have copies made of the photograph because they would be good to give as presents at the reunion.
3 I went to the storeroom but the photograph was no longer with the posters neither it was anywhere in the room. → I went to the storeroom but the photograph was no longer with the posters neither was it anywhere in the room.
4 Somebody in the family had done this that I would have a lovely centrepiece for the party. → Somebody in the family had done this so that I would have a lovely centrepiece for the party.
5 I asked as who had done it. → I asked who had done it.

TEST 6

A

1 book/novel
2 is
3 in
4 of
5 to
6 reaches
7 he
8 is
9 and
10 in

B

1	C	5	A	9	C	13	A	17	A
2	A	6	A	10	B	14	B	18	B
3	C	7	C	11	A	15	C	19	B
4	B	8	A	12	C	16	A	20	B

C

1 is beyond her means
2 am forced to accompany her to expensive shopping centres
3 is able to afford the most fabulously expensive dress
4 are eager to let her try on numerous outfits
5 she is charming

D

1 . . . enjoying my first camping trip . . .
2 . . . pack the van properly . . .
3 . . . cooking a meal . . .
4 . . . for suggesting one night in a hotel . . .
5 . . . by my idea, . . .